DANGEROUS COMMERCE

Dangerous Commerce

Insurance and the Management of International Risk

Virginia Haufler

CORNELL UNIVERSITY PRESS

ITHACA AND LONDON

First published 1997 by Cornell University Press.

Printed in the United States of America

Library of Congress Cataloging-in-Publication Data

Haufler, Virginia, 1957–
Dangerous commerce : insurance and the management of international risk / Virginia Haufler.
p. cm.
Includes bibliographical references and index.
ISBN 0-8014-3231-6 (alk. paper)
1. Risk (Insurance)—History. 2. International trade—History.
I. Title.
HG8054.5.H38 1997
368—dc21 96-53653

Cornell University Press strives to utilize environmentally responsible suppliers and materials to the fullest extent possible in the publishing of its books. Such materials include vegetable-based, low-VOC inks and acid-free papers that are also either recycled, totally chlorine free, or partly composed of nonwood fibers.

Cloth printing 10 9 8 7 6 5 4 3 2 1

for my parents

Herbert E. and Joan F. Haufler

Contents

Preface

In December 1957 the nationalistic Indonesian government seized forty Dutch ships to protest continued Dutch control of the territory of Western New Guinea. To the government leaders, the ships represented the hated colonial power, even though they were privately owned and served as the main source of transportation among the Indonesian islands. This ship seizure did not simply threaten large losses for a Dutch shipping concern, however; it could also have ruinous consequences for a major British institution—Lloyd's of London. Most of the Dutch ships were insured at Lloyd's under policies that forced them to be declared a total and complete loss if they were held longer than four months. This could wipe out a number of Lloyd's underwriters and potentially undermine the financial capacity of the insurance market as a whole. Given the central position of Lloyd's in the international insurance market, a weakened Lloyd's of London would leave many international risks, especially for shipping, uninsured. Without that insurance many commercial transactions simply would not be concluded—in Indonesia and potentially everywhere else. Thus, the direct and indirect consequences of this one political gesture could ripple throughout the world.

What happened next? The Dutch government could do little, and the British government was unwilling to intervene. Instead, a group of Lloyd's representatives took diplomacy into their own hands and traveled to Indonesia to try to convince the government that this poke in the eye of the Dutch would slice into the heart of the British. With the clock ticking on the four-month deadline, the men from Lloyd's waited and hoped to avert disaster. Almost at the last moment the Indonesian government finally released the ships, largely because of the good relations between key Indonesian officials and the Lloyd's delegation.

This story illustrates some key relationships between the risks of foreign commerce and the ways in which commercial and political systems respond to risk. In this case, the shipowners decided to continue their business in Indonesia despite the deteriorating political environment. Some of their risk would be covered by insurance. But there also existed the possibility that the extent of the risk, which was difficult to calculate in any case, would overwhelm the resources of the insurers. Underlying the concerns of both the shippers and the insurers was a profound uncertainty about what the three relevant governments would—or should—do. Governments can both generate and mitigate economic losses, but their ability and willingness to do so interacts with the ability and willingness of the private sector to act on its own behalf, either through developing techniques and institutions to mediate risk or by acting more directly through private diplomacy. Should governments intervene, or do they bear no responsibility when their citizens encounter political risks in commercial ventures abroad? When governments do not intervene, what alternatives exist? How have perceptions about risk shaped both the public and private sector institutions we see around us today? And what happens to economic growth and development when the institutions that reduce or redistribute the risks of commerce break down?

Our current era has been characterized by Anthony Giddens as a "risk culture," symbolized by the eager participation of "ordinary" people in the sometimes wild gyrations of increasingly globalized financial markets. People today can bet the family nest egg on economic opportunities in unknown countries halfway around the world. The entrepreneur conquering new markets, at home and abroad, is held up as the hero of our times, as someone willing and able to overlook the possibility of disaster in the search for new sources of profit, stimulating growth and progress for all. Such "heroes" have always existed, but what is striking today is the degree to which they, and the free markets they exemplify, are glorified in almost every corner of the globe.

This research began with the realization that this model of the heroic risk taker does not actually appeal to most people, especially those in the business community. The best deal, in the eyes of many, is one with a great deal of certainty about future positive returns. We can see this in the lengthy history of cartelization, the antithesis of a risk-taking strategy. In transactions that take place in foreign territory involving people from unfamiliar cultures, certainty about outcomes tends to be distinctly less than in home markets. Thus, individuals search for ways to reduce or eliminate the downside risks of their activities, especially when they go abroad. When they cannot do so, they may not pursue a particular opportunity. Unmitigated risk can lead to the danger that productive investments will not be made, new technologies will not be discovered, and trade and commerce will not expand. The history of economic development shows us that institutions and techniques created to deal with uncertainty and risk, such as insurance, proved crucial to the expansion of markets. Surprisingly, very little has been written on the important role of insurance in the development of a modern economy.

What interested me particularly was the relationship between international risk and the development of alternatives to government intervention or protection of commerce. What role has insurance played in the expansion of the global economy? How did insurers deal with the political risks peculiar to foreign economic affairs? What was the relationship between the public and private sectors in the development of insurance? The answers to these questions should appeal to two audiences—first, to those intrigued by the insurance industry itself, perhaps from personal involvement, perhaps from interest in business history or finance in general, or perhaps from the tidbits of scandal about insurers we sometimes see in the news today; and second, to those who want to understand the role of institutions, including both the state and the firm, in the globalization of markets and the distribution of power and resources.

When I started this project, the reaction among my colleagues could not be called universally enthusiastic. Their concerns centered on whether the insurance industry made a suitable subject for a political scientist to explore; some declared insurance dreadfully dull. Certainly, few had bothered to explore this area previously. When I began my interviews, I discovered many insurers who honestly did not see any political significance in what they did. The challenge to me was to demonstrate to readers in both the scholarly and business communities that the historical development of insurance reveals something broader about political-economic development and the changing relationship between the public and private sectors. I hope I have succeeded.

A book such as this one is not produced without the help, support, and participation of many people. I spent hours interviewing insurance industry representatives and government officials and poring over archival documents and clippings files in London, Geneva, New York, and Washington, D.C. This research would not have been possible without the generous financial support and encouragement provided by the FERIS Foundation/Gallatin Fellowship, the Cornell University Center for International Studies/MacArthur Fellowship, and the University of Maryland General Research Board and Office of International Studies. I bear a debt of gratitude to those in the insurance industry who were willing to spend their time with me and let me use their library resources, including Orio Giarini, director of the Geneva Association; Antony Baker, of the Association of British Insurance Underwriters; representatives of the United Nations Conference on Trade and Development; officials of the U.S. Department of Commerce, Overseas Private Investment Corporation, and Export-Import Bank; as well as insurers, reinsurers, brokers, and lawyers in London and New York. The last category includes my father, Herbert E. Haufler, former vice-president of an insurance company, who introduced me to some of my interview subjects. This research also relied on documents from the Chartered Insurance Institute of London, the Geneva Association library, the library of the League of Nations/United Nations in Geneva, the Guildhall Library in London, the Public Record Office of Great Britain, the British Library, the Library of Congress, and the National Archives of the United States.

Many people contributed their time, advice, and support to help me in this endeavor. They challenged me intellectually in ways that forced me to grow and change in how I viewed both this project and my profession more generally. I am deeply indebted to them. First and foremost, Richard Rosecrance, then at Cornell University, gave me the initial idea for this project and provided an enthusiastic source of intellectual stimulation and support as it developed. He asked the big questions that helped me link the minutiae of insurance with the issues and ideas of a political scientist. Susan Strange egged me on with her eagerness to see someone fill that gap where analysis of the role of the insurance industry in contemporary affairs should have been but wasn't. Many people read and commented on portions of the book, and their questions often forced me to rethink my argument. Thanks go especially to Philip Cerny, Claire Cutler, Francine D'Amico, H. Richard Friman, Lori Gronich, John Kroll, David Lake, Jeannette Money, M. J. Peterson,

Tony Porter, Simon Reich, Volker Rittberger, and Geoffrey Underhill. I also would like to recognize the contributions made by the anonymous reviewers of the manuscript, whose suggestions helped me significantly improve the coherence of my argument and the presentation of the material.

Of course, this book would not have been possible without a supportive editor. I am deeply thankful for the encouragement and criticism of Roger Haydon at Cornell University Press; his patience surpasses understanding. I also would like to thank Kay Scheuer and Kristina Kelsey at the Press, and Kim Vivier for copyediting.

My friends and family have kept me going throughout the entire process of research, writing, and publishing. Deserving special mention are my good friends Linda Jarschauer Johnson and Jack Moran, who fed and entertained me, and Julie Hoffman, who literally yelled at me to "finish that book!" My sisters, Marge and Carol, looked impressed at what I was undertaking but certainly kept me from taking myself too seriously. My brother, Michael, and his lovely family took my mind off work and made me play. And I especially thank my mother and father, who always—always—assumed I knew what I was doing, despite regular evidence to the contrary.

VIRGINIA HAUFLER

College Park, Maryland

DANGEROUS COMMERCE

1/ *The Search for a Sure Thing: Risk and International Political Economy*

In 1984, in the throes of the global debt crisis, CIGNA insurance company sold Citibank a $900 million policy on the bank's portfolio of developing country loans.[1] If one of the bank's borrowing states officially delayed payment on its loans, CIGNA would reimburse Citibank for its losses. The bank wanted to diversify liability for default risk, and the insurer wanted to develop a market for a potentially profitable new insurance product. Financial analysts and policymakers alike expressed surprise at the idea of private insurance acting as a vehicle to redistribute risks on foreign loans. After all, governments had been actively negotiating these liability issues in the multilateral debt reschedulings that were becoming common. But why is it that some risks are assumed to be the responsibility of political authorities, and others are considered to belong in the realm of private exchange? Why is this particularly true for international risks? How and why have the private and public institutions that redistribute foreign risk developed historically, and how have they changed over time? Who is or should be liable for losses to international business when the source of loss is a foreign political entity?

The decision to spread risk through insurance raises important questions about the impact of political risk on commerce and the locus of liability for risk in all types of international transactions. Should the firm that participates in foreign trade, investment, or lending bear all risk—even when that risk is political in nature? Should the risk bearer be that firm's home government, which has some obligation to its citizens and their welfare even when they are abroad? Or should it be some third party, such as an insurer? In the case of the debt crisis, national and international agencies took the lead in apportioning liability among debtors and creditors, both public and private. The insurance policy held by Citibank was allowed to expire in six months, since the bank estimated the cost of the policy outweighed its benefits and the insurers were reined in by their less adventurous reinsurers. This path toward resolution of the debt crisis was not inevitable, however, and the outcome might have varied given a different time period or a different type of transaction.

Given the existence of risk, what are the alternative ways to respond? As one economist has commented, "the principal effort to deal with risk in social systems, as with hang gliding, is to try to influence the probabilities."[2] Theoretically, under a liberal regime the responsibility for trying to influence those probabilities and also for bearing any losses should rest with the private sector, with little or no liability incurred by the government. The defining feature of the international system, however, is that there is a constant threat of disruption of business, since there is no central government to enforce and maintain order.[3] Throughout history those involved in transporting and exchanging goods abroad, making investments in foreign countries, and lending to foreign firms and governments have sought to protect themselves from foreign risks, and often this meant turning to their own governments to demand political or military intervention. But just as often political leaders have been unable or unwilling to intervene directly, and so entrepreneurs had to develop their own techniques and institutions to overcome this "political market failure." In the twentieth century those techniques and institutions have been used increasingly by political authorities themselves as an instrument of foreign policy. One such set of techniques and institutions can be found in the insurance sector.

We can trace variations in the participation of private and public actors in insurance activity by focusing on the dominant insurance centers in Britain and the United States. Three periods in the institutional development of insurance for international risks can be discerned. First, by the end of the nineteenth century the private market centered in the City of London had developed the institutions of a private international insurance regime, with little regulation, intervention, or competition from government. Second, in the first half of the twentieth century the state began to develop programs to reduce risks on foreign trade and investment by providing specialized forms of political risks insurance, such as trade credit insurance and foreign investment guarantees. Government agencies operated within the constraints of preexisting legal and customary rules and practices developed by the private insurance industry and explicitly avoided direct competition with them. Third, by the final decades of this century the responsibility for protecting private commerce from political risk shifted increasingly toward governments and international organizations, despite a continuing expansion in private activity, as the norms and practices of insurers changed. In essence, the private sector created an international insurance regime which regulated the behavior of all market participants, whether insurance firms or government agencies, but in which the locus of authority began to change hands by the end of the century.[4]

Three factors have driven changes in the relationship between state and market actors in the insurance regime: increases and decreases in the demand for protection from political risk by those involved in international exchange, transformation of the norms and practices of the insurers themselves as the character of risks changed, and changes in the resources available to public and private sector actors. The forces of supply and demand, as in most markets, have the largest effect on the level of international risks insurance. We would expect the overall level of demand for insurance against political events to be strongly related to the stability of the international political system. When there is peace among the most powerful states and a relatively open system for commerce, the demand for political risks insurance should be relatively low, except in peripheral areas, and thus the level of insurance supplied should be minimal.[5] When the system is breaking down, one would expect a high level of demand for political risks insurance would provide incentives for expansion of the amount and types of insurance.

The relationship between systemic level demand and the level and character of supply is not so simple, however. It tells us nothing about the division of labor between private and public sector actors, why one or the other has dominated at different historical periods, and how their interaction within a regime for international risks insurance has evolved. Nor does it explain why the demand for insurance against foreign risks has rarely been met by a sufficient supply. A more complete explanation lies in the development of norms for judging the insurability of foreign risks and how to manage them and in the variability of financial resources available to the different actors. The private sector took the lead in developing the norms and institutions that govern the character and supply of international insurance, but its resources cannot match those of the public sector.

Risks of all types pose a significant barrier to trade, lending, and investment, and the attempt to reduce or redistribute such risks imposes major costs on participants in global commerce. Political risks on foreign commerce are particularly intractable, since it is not clear whether states should automatically intervene on behalf of their citizens, despite regular pressure to do so. Anything that reduces such risks, whether accomplished through the state or through the market, provides benefits not just to the particular actors involved but also to the wider society, since it facilitates market activity that benefits everyone. There are "spillovers" to risk reduction that make it a public good to some degree.[6]

Surprisingly little attention has been paid by international relations scholars to the complex responses by states and firms to the potentially severe effects that excessive risk has on international commerce. The theoretical contributions of the dominant perspectives in international relations theory only partially explain the dynamics of this issue area. They dismiss or downplay the influential role of nonstate actors, which have been crucial in developing a set of techniques and institutions that can ameliorate the risks of foreign commerce. Traditional resources of states, such as military force, are often inappropriate or unusable for resolving threats to international economic activity.[7] The evolution of institutions for international risks insurance is a response, initially by financial entrepreneurs and later by political authorities, to meet the demands of economic actors oriented toward a global economy when force is not an option.

The Nature of Risk

The concept of risk is central to any discussion of international risks insurance. Risk is not the same as uncertainty. Technically, *uncertainty* refers to situations where one cannot determine the likelihood that an event will occur or even, for that matter, what is the universe of possible events. *Risk,* in contrast, is simply the possibility of suffering harm or loss. Economists distinguish between uncertainty and risk by the degree to which one can determine the probability that an event will occur. Risk characterizes situations where one can make some judgment about the likelihood, or probability, of an event and therefore can take reasonable precautions against it.[8] In other words, pursuing an action fraught with uncertainty implies taking a gamble; acting in the face of risk implies a more calculated move. Insurers profess to deal with risk, not uncertainty.[9]

Risk is not inherently bad for commerce. An investor can expect to receive above-average returns for taking on particularly risky ventures.[10] Risk can be a source of potential profit—there is often as much a probability that good things will happen as bad. This is the essence of entrepreneurial activity. For instance, when a corporation launches a new product, it risks pouring money and time into something consumers may not buy. If company management has gauged the market correctly, however, that product may fill a niche in the market and earn the company millions of dollars.

In a capitalist economy, we expect entrepreneurs to take these kinds of market risks in the search for profits, thereby increasing the efficiency and wealth of the economy as a whole through the mechanism of the "invisible hand." Unfortunately, the line between uncertainty and calculable risk often can be hard to define, for both entrepreneurs and insurers. Estimating risk can be a creative exercise that may have little to do with actual statistical probabilities; the outcome of effort may turn out to be a gamble pure and simple. And not every participant in exchange is comfortable taking risks; many individuals are risk averse, preferring a "sure thing" to a risky prospect.[11]

Within the broader category of risk most business analysts distinguish between commercial and political risks; the latter can be subdivided further into sovereign and nonsovereign risks.[12] If a loss occurs due to commercial risk, it is considered a normal though unwelcome aspect of doing business, such as in the failure of a new product introduction. In any case, a firm should be able to judge the likelihood of a commercial loss and hedge against it through conservative business planning, diversification of products and markets, and insurance. Political risk, in contrast, as David Jodice notes, refers to "changes in the operating conditions of foreign enterprises that arise out of the political process, either directly through war, insurrection or political violence, or through changes in government policies that affect the ownership and behavior of the firm."[13] In other words, political risks are the impact on commerce of actions or inactions by governments and political groups; they are risks whose sources are the workings of political systems, not the workings of the market.[14]

Risks can be further categorized as those created by entities that can be sued versus those that cannot, that is, risks created by those subject to law versus those that make law through legislative powers—sovereign risk.[15] Sovereign risk derives from the actions and inactions of political authorities, including their ability to change the legal framework within which exchange occurs. Sovereign risk can be a particular problem for foreign enterprises, which stand in a different position vis-à-vis the local governing authorities than do citizens and thus are particularly vulnerable. For instance, many newly independent states in the 1950s and 1960s targeted foreign property for expropriation, treating the property rights of foreigners differently from those of citizens.

The distinctions among different types of risk can be analytically confusing, especially given the difference between common usage and more theoretical understandings. Sovereign and nonsovereign political risks are typically combined by insurers as risks of political origin, despite the fact that they involve very different entities. Historically, the lines drawn by insurers between commercial and political risks, and between risk and uncertainty, have shifted. In fact, part of the story of international risks insurance concerns how their understanding and treatment of political risk has changed. For instance, the outbreak of war clearly is a political risk of the sovereign type. Today many corporations also label as political the risk that their international operations will suffer losses when local governments pass regulatory legislation that affects their markets.

The aspects of political risk most relevant to this book are the ways it affects international transactions. International risks are unique because the transactions that are involved are deliberately separated into national components.[16] The sources of political risk spring from activities at a number of levels: global developments in war and peace, regional and local conflicts and wars, domestic regulatory policies, and relations among partners in a business transaction who are of different national origin or who represent different private or public interests. Note that these factors are not all purely international risks, since many stem from domestic political developments, but they all can disrupt opportunities to pursue global exchange.[17]

Alternative Strategies in Risky Environments

Given all these potential risks, what strategies can entrepreneurs pursue? What choices do those firms engaged in trading, shipping, lending, and investing abroad have when they discover they need to manage their international risks? Basically, there are two broad alternatives: self-help and intermediation.[18]

Diversification and Internalization of Risk

In response to political and commercial risk, corporate executives can use self-help methods, which they formulate and implement on their own, or they can turn to an intermediary, or third party, to reduce or redistribute the costs of managing risk. The historical development of insurance reveals the degree to which businesses have gone through different phases in self-help versus intermediary risk management.[19]

Self-help includes the obvious and common method of simply diversifying activities. For instance, one can plan to shift transactions into the future in order to reduce the concentration of risk in the present, though this tactic may lead to increased risks over time as the environment changes. One can spread investments geographically in order to reduce a concentration of risk in one place, although this policy may be limited by the locations of profitable opportunities.[20] It is only common sense to distribute economic activity widely, so as to reduce the probability that one single event will affect all projects equally and lead to disastrous losses. In making decisions concerning factory location, sources of raw materials, export markets, and financing alternatives, a smart business strategy would be to distribute these carefully among geographic areas, diverse supplier firms, and expected time frames.[21] If a major corporation obtains inputs from more than source, finances projects in more than one way, and markets its products in many countries, one would expect to see only a low probability that natural disasters, bankruptcies, wars, and economic recessions would affect all areas at once.

Some important risks, however, are global in nature and almost unavoidable. For instance, global recession in the early 1980s and the impact of the commodity price collapse limited the ability of individuals and firms in almost every region of the world to repay their bank debt, nullifying any diversification strategy a bank may have had. Creditors involved in sovereign lending in the late 1970s who thought that a combination of loans to various Latin American nations plus some Soviet bloc states would be sufficient diversification were caught by surprise when first Poland and then Mexico threatened default, followed soon after by a parade of other indebted nations. Other risks that are difficult to manage effectively through diversification include projects that require a large commitment of time, money, and expertise in one place and are therefore somewhat "lumpy" in nature, or "asset-specific."[22] For instance, an offshore oil drilling platform in the North Sea is a highly profitable multibillion dollar investment located in an unusually hazardous physical environment and suffering from an occasionally volatile political context, given the politics of oil production.[23]

Another form of self-help involves reorganizing the structure of production and the contractual nature of the firm. Large integrated corporations expand their direct authority over business processes in order to circumvent the price system, one of the major sources of commercial risk.[24] Through vertical and horizontal integration, corporations can reduce the number of outside contracts for supplies and services, lessening vulnerability to price swings, supply disruptions, and the costs of contracting in general.[25] In other words, firms internalize their risks. The literature on industrial organization, particularly the transactions cost approach of Ronald Coase and Oliver Williamson, highlights the extent to which changes in organizational form reduce the uncertainty and risks of the economic system by decreasing the effect of the external environment and increasing the scope of internal authority.[26]

Such business integration generates costs and risks of its own, however—some of it more political than commercial in nature. Subsidiaries abroad that were established as part of an integration strategy may be targeted deliberately for expropriation or nationalization by foreign governments.[27] Large conglomerates that become unwieldy and inefficient may attract corporate raiders, as demonstrated by the mergers and acquisitions frenzy of the 1980s. In an attempt to decrease the risks of an integration strategy, investors in the 1980s and 1990s have tended to use looser forms of contract, such as joint ventures and licensing agreements.[28] Not all sources of risk can be internalized and organized away by a corporation, nor is it desirable to do so, since the costs of internalization in specific cases ultimately may outweigh the benefits.[29]

Self-help methods can be a useful but sometimes limited means of managing international risks. They should be only one tool among a larger set of risk-minimization strategies. Other than self-help, businesses can follow the strategy of persuading an intermediary institution to bear some of the risks of commerce. These institutions can be other businesses or they can be governments, both domestic and foreign. It is here that we come to the crucial intersection of private and public interests in supporting trade and investment abroad.

Sharing Risk through Intermediary Institutions

A firm confronted by high levels of risk in a desirable transaction can arrange to shift some of its liability to a third party. These intermediaries in economic transactions include such institutions as stock and futures markets, banks and insurance firms, and even the somewhat vaguely defined "information industries."[30] For instance, investment markets allow individuals to hold a diversified portfolio, hedge investments against future changes in prices, and widen the financial backing of a corporation. Banks and insurance companies also act as intermediaries between a firm and those with whom the firm contracts business. Insurance has become today simply the most obvious form of sharing risk, in which one individual or firm contracts with an insurer to share specified amounts of the losses if a specific event occurs.

In the absence of alternatives, a firm also may opt to lobby the government either to prevent the loss itself or to redistribute losses by taking a share of them in order to facilitate economic activity. From a public goods standpoint, the government would be intervening in imperfect markets to correct a potential market failure.[31] From another perspective, however, such intervention could be viewed as a method of using public agencies for private gain. For example, Anne Krueger and other economists see it as "rent-seeking" behavior and argue that interest groups seek profit through the political system by asking the government to guarantee them a portion of some market, thereby reducing their risks nearly to zero.[32] In either case, a wide array of government activities, from agricultural subsidies to defense contracting, can be viewed as forms of risk intermediation that interpose the government between a business venture and its potential losses.[33]

A third perspective views the particular types of government intervention common today as facilitating the functioning of the market, as a response to global competition for capital and market share. Phil Cerny calls the modern state a "competition state."[34] For instance, business scholar John Dunning has highlighted the extent to which governments and corporations in the 1990s cooperate more than they compete with each other, as a result of the globalization of the world economy. He maintains that the effective boundary lines of a country have softened, as have those of the firm, with governments playing a market facilitating role.[35] Similarly, Cerny has persuasively argued that globalization has forced a change in the role of the state. Following a wave of deregulation in the 1980s designed to increase the competitiveness of national firms, governments began to reregulate and intervene in markets in ways that promoted competition, often by reducing risks.[36]

Some of the tools governments can use to act as an economic intermediary are tariffs or quotas, tax favors, subsidies, loans, insurance, and favorable regulatory changes. In the case of international transactions, the government may turn to its more traditional role as political (as opposed to economic) intermediary and use its diplomatic or even military power to respond to corporate demands for protection. As political intermediaries, government policymakers often act to prevent events that cause loss to business; as economic intermediaries, the aim is to redistribute the burden of paying for such losses.

Douglass North argues that one of the most important innovations of the Western world, and of economic development in general, was the transformation of uncertainty into risk. Diversification, insurance, and hierarchical business organization all provided a means for the institutionalization of risk, which increased the efficiency and productivity of markets.[37] But the demand for insurance as a specific response to risk depends on the relative efficacy and availability of alternative self-help and intermediary strategies for managing risk.

International Business and International Relations Theory

If, as North argues, the institutions that transform uncertainty into risk were crucial to national economic development, then we should view the institutions that do so at the international level as a significant advancement in the development of the world economy. A large part of this institutionalization has occurred through the efforts of private sector actors, and not through the efforts of states. Traditionally, the discussions among scholars about the degree of institutionalization in the international system have focused solely on interstate organizations, and international relations theorizing has only sporadically paid attention to nonstate actors in its theoretical models. Dominated by realist and neorealist approaches, in which states and their foreign policy decisions are considered the heart of the field of international relations, scholars generally have slighted the historical role and political influence of nonstate actors.[38] Even liberal and radical perspectives tend to take the state as the central international actor, although firms, interest groups, and classes may be given a prominent place in the analysis.

International relations theorists thus can present a unified perspective on world affairs, but by doing so they miss some of the important transformations that have occurred. As said in a different context but applicable here, "First, it will be necessary to clear away certain conceptions that commonly have been associated with our subject matter, but point in misleading directions. These can be located within . . . what might be called hyper-history, that is, powerful organizers of political and social experience that, by overexplanation, distort important dimensions."[39] In order to capture those important dimensions without distortion, we must clear away the conception of states as the only powerful organizers of political and social life in international affairs. We need to conceptualize how nonstate actors influence the character and direction of international developments.

Historically, even as states strengthened their authority over society, entrepreneurial actors began to expand their activities. For instance, during the early stages of the imperialist era, which generally is studied as the work of increasingly powerful European states, much of the initial colonial exploration and settlement was in the hands of firms such as the Hudson Bay Company and the British East India Company. It may be difficult to think of these companies as entirely private actors, since they often had financial and even military support from the state. But in a sense, that is the point—the definitive line drawn between private and public entities is a relatively new development.[40]

Although mainstream international relations theory has slighted the importance of nonstate actors, the study of corporations as powerful actors in world affairs has garnered great attention and certainly is not a new endeavor. Firms have been viewed as important objects of government action in the literature on issue area bargaining, regimes, and trade policy, with special attention paid to the power of banks and the financial community in general. But as the globalization of production increasingly characterized modern capitalism, symbolized most potently by the transnational corporation, there has been a corresponding increase in interest in corporations as independent sources of power and authority. This has become particularly marked in the current era, in which political officials have deliberately shifted power away from the state and into the hands of the private sector, not just in the domestic sphere but in the international realm as well.

Susan Strange has argued that "trade between countries in goods and services will be, and is being, sustained by a complex network or web of transnational bilateral bargains—bargains between corporations and other corporations, between corporations and governments, and between governments."[41] In other words, focusing on agreements between states when analyzing the shape of the modern world economy is insufficient for capturing the multiple places in which negotiation occurs. Although a free trade agreement between, for instance, Israel and the United States may have an effect on the level of trade between the two countries, so does an agreement between an American investor and the Israeli government or an agreement among a group of American companies concerning whether or not to market a product in Israel. All these interactions have an impact on the level and character of trade and investment, which in turn have some influence on American-Israeli political relations. Note, however, that this example concerns bilateral relations. Susan Strange correctly emphasizes the importance of corporate "diplomacy" and the degree to which interactions among firms and states may involve the participation of many different actors in building a broader multilateral institution or network.

Private ordering and private contracts constitute a large proportion of the framework or institutional context within which international exchange takes place. As North has noted, when it is costly to transact, then institutions matter. But "throughout most of history, the contracting parties themselves devised their own enforcement mechanisms—which were supplemented sometimes by the state."[42] The flip side is that the lack of a central political authority in world affairs means that instability and uncertainty characterize interstate affairs, often leaving the private sector with no recourse at all.

Under what conditions do firms have recourse to the state, and under what conditions do they provide their own "governance without government?"[43] Beth and Robert Yarbrough have argued that the extent to which such private contracting and private institutions are effective and efficient determines the degree to which actors need recourse to the state.[44] But the state itself may not have devised effective or efficient institutions, leaving all participants no choice but to rely on the private sector. In the realm of international risks insurance, the commercial insurers have developed over time a private regime that governs their behavior and, in many cases, the behavior of states. The existence of such a regime represents the ability of private actors to create global institutions and mold the decision environment for others. Changes in the relationships among major private actors within such a regime and the entrance of new ones can lead to new negotiated outcomes within the framework of interfirm cooperation and affect government policies.[45]

The Sources of Change in Institutional Structure

This book analyzes three crisis-ridden periods in the development of an international regime in insurance: 1870–1914, when British hegemony began to decline and instability increased; 1917–39, when no state dominated world affairs and political risk became an obvious and pressing issue; and 1979–89, when U.S. political leadership came under attack and the political and financial systems were disrupted by repeated external shocks. In those periods changes in three factors—the level and character of the demand for protection from international risks, the norms and practices of the insurance industry, and the resources available to insurers, both public and private—affected the institutional structure of the insurance regime by changing the degree and character of public and private participation.

The Demand for Protection from Political Risk

The market for international risks insurance obviously has been influenced by the level and character of demand. One of the fundamental reasons that a firm seeks insurance is nonpolitical: when the assets at risk are extremely large, a firm will try to protect itself through both self-help and intermediary institutions. The size, technological complexity, and value of transactions have grown tremendously over the past few hundred years. When what is at stake outstrips the ability of a firm to use its own resources to make good on losses, then the demand for insurance will be high.

The sheer size of commercial transactions is only one element in explaining the actual demand for insurance, however. It is also determined by the firm's assessment of the probability that the loss will occur, which in some cases is directly related to the political environment. As the probability of political disruption of economic exchange increases, we can expect the demand for insurance to grow. The probability of such disruption increases as political relations deteriorate, both in the system as a whole and in specific bilateral relationships between states and between governments and specific firms. In states with extensive global economic relations, we can expect a high level of demand for protection.

Perceptions of the degree of stability in the system are strongly influenced by the activities of the most powerful states, which have the ability to extend direct political and military protection abroad. As the literature on hegemony and regimes demonstrates, the existence of a powerful leading state may bring generalized stability in political and economic contracts, precluding the need for active military enforcement.[46] When necessary, a powerful state can modify the probabilities of political risk by preventing foreign threats to commerce, particularly when they occur in weaker, peripheral areas of the world. For instance, the United States has a notorious history of sending in the Marines when Latin American governments either could not maintain order, endangering the economic activity of American businesses, or threatened to default on loans. Order was restored and contracts honored through coercion.

Business analysts tend to distinguish between risks at the system level, state level, region level, and transaction level. Systemic risk grabs attention, because it involves the breakdown of relations among the most powerful states and perhaps the onset of great-power war. As a powerful state loses its ability to enforce order in the world, political risk may increase as conflicts among countries multiply and negotiated cooperation subsides. But even during periods of stability the most powerful states do not control every corner of the world where economic exchange takes place. Many of the real political risks facing business are only partially derived from systemic conditions. Nevertheless, the overall environment influences the perceptions of business decision makers, who may equate weakness in major powers with a higher probability of risk in foreign transactions. Calculating systemic stability and instability cannot account for the entire demand for protection from the effects of political events, although it is one contributory factor.

Further elements affecting the demand for insurance are the political relationship between the home and host countries of the business involved in a transaction, the political relationship between a foreign business and its host country government, and the political stability of the country itself.[47] As the bilateral interstate relationship deteriorates, we would expect the perception of risk to increase. Similarly, as the relationship between a firm and the host government deteriorates, we would expect an increased perception of risk. Finally, changes in the broader domestic political environment may affect the degree to which contracts with foreigners are upheld or broken. At the extreme, each of these factors may tempt traders, investors, and lenders to withdraw from foreign markets as the perception of risk overwhelms any expectation of profit.

The probability of political risk in almost all times and places will be greater than zero. Firms that conduct business with foreign entities will always search for the correct strategy to prevent a loss from political events. The question is the degree to which perceptions of increased risk translate into increased demand for insurance—or for some other strategy. This demand varies to the degree other strategies besides insurance are available and effective for the kinds of transactions the business community undertakes abroad.

The particular way in which international commerce has developed has an impact on the extent to which insurance against political risks is perceived to be the appropriate strategy. The expansion of the multinational corporation in the twentieth century increased investor exposure to foreign risk, especially in extractive industries, which are highly asset-specific and require long-term contracting. At the same time, the structure of the corporation itself provided more opportunities for self-help strategies to modify risk, for example, by increasing the ability to diversify sources of raw materials internationally. Global production promotes diversification of markets and internalization of transactions and aids in the management of foreign risks. The development of increasingly sophisticated financial techniques also allows large corporations to manipulate their financial assets and to set aside financial reserves, hedging themselves against possible losses. Thus, there is no direct and simple correlation between the demand for protection from risk and the demand for insurance, nor is it obvious whether that demand will be directed toward firms or states.

Insurance Norms and Practices

As demand for international risks insurance increases, one would expect to see an increase in insurance supply, but in fact, the supply of insurance does not completely meet demand. Insurance is an imperfect market, since not all kinds of insurance are offered at all times and since the sellers (insurers) do not just sell a product or service but also attempt to influence the behavior of their customers.[48] The issue here is why the privately constructed international risks insurance regime cannot completely meet the demand for insurance, why and how governments began to participate in insuring the foreign commercial activities of their citizens, and how the relationship between private and public sector insurance evolved over time.

The most important influences on both the public and private supply of political risks insurance are the norms and practices of the insurance industry.[49] The relevant norms and practices concern both the treatment of customers and the ways insurers, reinsurers, and ancillary businesses cooperate among themselves. Insurers have developed standard business practices to rein in the possibility of strategic or opportunistic behavior on the part of customers (discussed in more detail below). These norms and practices also were designed to support the market by regulating the competitive behavior of insurers themselves, in order not to undermine the viability of the industry. Moral and ethical norms reduce the costs of enforcing collective rules and regulations; since private insurers have few means of enforcement, such norms take on even more significance.

The ability and willingness of insurance firms to participate in the political risks market rely to a large degree on the commitment of participants to the norms and practices of the industry, which establishes appropriate behavior toward customers and others involved in this business. Private insurers had firmly established the institutional context within which the insurance industry as a whole operated by the late nineteenth century. Most participated in a range of formal and informal institutions that regulated their behavior in predictable ways. As the business of insurance expanded and different market niches developed, the specialization and interdependence of the market itself deepened. Because of the nature of the risks facing insurers, especially when they entered new markets or developed new products, they had to establish mutually agreeable standards of behavior to facilitate interactions among themselves.

The development of an international risks insurance regime can be traced in large part in the evolution of norms regarding which risks are insurable and which are not, which ones are the responsibility of the private sector and which belong in the public realm. Insurance underwriting experience, backed by more and more sophisticated information-gathering techniques and analytical skills produced an increasingly refined standard insurance contract. These contracts define the exact relationship between the insurer and the customer and attempt to determine all possible contingencies. They contain the exclusions and limitations that protect both the insurer and the insured by establishing incentives designed to modify the potential for opportunistic behavior by either one. By placing some kinds of risk out of the normal range of insurance underwriting, the industry puts the onus on business customers to pursue other strategies in addition to private insurance, including government intermediation.

The private sector can enforce these norms and practices to a degree because of two characteristics of the business. The first is the central role played by the London market in the late nineteenth century and continuing throughout most of the twentieth. In international risks insurance, the insurance underwriters of Lloyd's of London have particular influence. The London insurers dominated foreign markets and thereby acted as the industry leaders in setting the framework of rules under which underwriters around the globe operated. In the arena of political risks insurance in particular, the London underwriters could be termed "hegemonic" in their position, especially the Lloyd's underwriters, who dominate both the political risks insurance and reinsurance markets. As the locus of financial power shifted away from London in the late twentieth century, and as Lloyd's became mired in managerial difficulties, the centralization of the private sector broke down along with the effectiveness of earlier underwriting norms and practices.

The second element that gave force to informal prescriptions and prohibitions on behavior was the importance of reputation to the success of the insurance business.[50] The buyer of insurance must have confidence that the money paid in premiums will in fact be used to pay claims for losses, since the customer is paying money up-front for a service that may be provided some time in the future. In other words, insurance is based on contractual relationships, and not purely exchange relationships.[51] If an insurer develops a reputation for unreliability, it will lose business, as customers will not have complete faith in the insurance contract they sign. The incentives to develop a positive reputation operate even more strongly within the insurance community itself. The interlocking business of underwriters, brokers, reinsurers, and others has created great interdependence within the industry. Formal and informal contracts coexist among the participants, undergirded by a strong sense of appropriate behavior and reinforced by the fact that this is not a market characterized by arm's-length transactions.

The norms and practices of the industry that have evolved over time ultimately determine a large part of the relationship between the private and public sector. In the early part of this century private insurance firms developed an extensive regime governing what kinds of risks they would cover as "insurable," the terms under which they would do so, and the ways insurers would relate to one another and to their customers. This regime included the institutionalization of interfirm associations and self-governing organizations within the industry. The dominant perception of the role of the state was that governments were ill-equipped to provide insurance, and any transaction not considered insurable by the insurers themselves simply should not be insured, period. This belief weighed particularly heavily on the market for political risks, which often were labeled uninsurable.

The influence of insurance norms on state practice has been consistently strong but has also been entwined with societal conceptions of the appropriate role of the state in foreign economic activity. Rulers throughout history have been concerned with protecting and maintaining the reach of their merchants abroad, typically relying on their military forces to do so. Britain, for instance, maintained military convoys for the merchant fleet for decades to ensure the safe continuation of the trade that was vital to the power and wealth of the nation. The use of nonmilitary, or financial, support for trade has not always been as widely accepted, however. The course of the nineteenth and twentieth centuries has been marked by changing norms with regard to state intervention in the market, fluctuating from liberalism to mercantilism and Keynesianism to monetarism. These norms regarding acceptable government behavior have not always coincided with the norms generated by insurers regarding insurable risk and the role of government in insurance, nor do dominant norms always predict whether the political regime will support or oppose government insurance as foreign economic policy.

The Resources of Insurers

The private and public sectors draw on different resources to conduct their business, based on profitability for the former and budget constraints for the latter. Insurers cover political risks only when it is profitable to do so; their customers request insurance only when political risks threaten their profits; and governments take on this responsibility only when the threat to the national economy from competition outweighs the costs to the treasury.

Despite their differing resource bases, both private and public agencies have experienced fluctuations in their finances owing to two elements that have changed dramatically over the course of the twentieth century. First, they both must manage their costs of doing business by calculating risks correctly, a task that is complicated by the possibility of opportunistic behavior by their customers. Second, both have been profoundly affected by changes in the overall financial system. The financial boom of the 1980s had the unanticipated side effect of undermining long-held practices that had previously kept losses in check. The ability of customers to self-insure has also grown, as the size and resources of global corporations has increased. Finally, the collapse of the monetary order, the increasing mobility of capital, and the heightening of economic competition overall undermined the budgets of governments at the same time as they were under pressure to increase the competitiveness of national firms.

The costs of selling insurance against international risks may become prohibitive at times, as insurers go bankrupt or simply stop writing certain kinds of contracts. The insurance industry as a whole suffers from a regular business cycle, called the "underwriting cycle." When the industry is expanding and demand is high, insurers raise their prices and make a nice profit on their insurance business. High profits attract new competitors, especially given the low barriers to entry in this industry, and the market quickly becomes saturated. Increased competition forces underwriters to lower their prices, sometimes to the point where they actually lose money on their insurance business. Insurers then begin to retrench, limiting the risks they will cover and eventually raising prices again as weaker firms go out of business. At the low point of this cycle, firms cannot satisfy completely the demand for insurance; in extreme cases, the market for specialized insurance such as that on international risks may collapse altogether. The high transactions costs involved in drawing up contracts, gathering information about political events, and monitoring customer behavior can discourage underwriters from offering this kind of policy.

For insurers, the problems of information asymmetry raise the costs of doing business, because incentives must be designed into their contracts that discourage opportunistic behavior. If they are not successful, the insurers will suffer continuing losses and potentially go out of business. If full protection is provided against a loss, the incentives for the individual thus protected are changed in a way that might encourage risky behavior. For example, the savings and loan crisis in the United States can be traced to the ability of bank managers to escape the consequences of their reckless management since all bank deposits were insured by the government. Or if homeowners have fire insurance policies that cover the full value of any losses, they may not be as careful about preventing a fire as they would otherwise. Completely shifting the burden of losses to a third party may make an individual indifferent to the outcome of his or her behavior.[52] This is the problem of moral hazard, and it produces two types of outcome. On the one hand, it can lead to market failure, as potential suppliers perceive their own risks to be higher than their overall profits, and the costs of monitoring are too high. On the other hand, potential suppliers may attempt to transform their own risks by influencing the behavior of their customers and by investing in some means of monitoring the transaction.[53] Contract law for insurance differs from other kinds of contract law in response to this information problem. Insurance contracts are based on the principle of the "utmost good faith" (*uberrima fides*) of the customer in supplying all relevant information about the risk to be insured, as opposed to the more typical principle of "let the buyer beware" (*caveat emptor*).

The problem of adverse selection can aggravate the disincentives on the supply side. Potential customers run the gamut from those that are extremely cautious and unlikely ever to cause a loss, to those that behave recklessly or engage in activities with high exposure to risk. In many cases, the lower risks choose to forgo insurance entirely and essentially "self-insure," paying for the few losses from internal resources. The remaining pool of customers is much more likely to suffer losses, is more likely to desire insurance, and thus worsens the average quality of the insurers' portfolio of risks. The response of insurers often is to raise the price of their products to cover their increased payments for claims—thus further driving away the better, low-risk customers.

Both moral hazard and adverse selection directly affect the resources available to insurers and other providers of protection by increasing the costs of doing business. These problems thus influence the availability of insurance in general and the extent to which a firm is willing to supply the "quasi–public good" of financial protection.[54] If private firms can supply protection in a way that minimizes these problems, then they will be more likely to participate in the market and government intervention will be unnecessary. If the costs of managing both the risk of loss plus the risk of opportunistic behavior become too high, then the private sector will choose to exit the market. In such a case, those in need of protection may turn instead to the government, which may be better able to police the behavior of customers and limit the problems of moral hazard and adverse selection.[55]

Government insurers also face problems of information asymmetry and must design incentives similar to those used by the private sector in order to restrain their losses. In general, however, governments are not as sensitive to losses as are the commercial insurers. The objectives of most government insurance programs are not profit-oriented but related to national goals such as pursuing particular foreign policy aims or providing general support to national firms. Therefore, the resources available to the public sector insurers are affected primarily by budget constraints and political commitments. If the political leadership is committed to subsidizing foreign economic activity through insurance and guarantees, the budget constraint may be very weak. In other cases, the debate over government spending levels may overwhelm any perceived benefits to be gained by such a program.

Insurance and International Political Risks

Despite the ubiquitous presence of insurance in our lives, most people do not fully understand either the product or the industry. Insurance is a product designed specifically to indemnify against loss. It is based on the principle of pooling together a series of monetary contributions over time from many individuals. The participants contractually agree that when a specified event occurs to one member of the group, that person can draw on the pool of money to cover the loss. Each individual thus avoids disaster and bankruptcy by contributing relatively small amounts at periodic intervals into a pool, with the right to draw out large amounts in an emergency.[56] The actual amount contributed (the premium) is determined by the probability and size of potential losses. The more money there is in the pool, the more and larger the risks that can be covered.

The earliest development of insurance can be dated to the time of the Greek city-states. The owners of shipping vessels would band together in a group to set up a mutual insurance fund to cover their losses on sea voyages. The market for insurance, especially for such marine risks, has a long and varied history, marked by increasing specialization as it became an established industry.[57] Although mutual insurance companies, in which insurers and customers are the same people, continue to operate, the majority of insurance today is sold in arms-length transactions between corporations and customers.

The technical intricacy of insurance contracts has expanded along with the growth in size and complexity of modern corporations. Many firms today use insurance as part of an overall financial strategy, and not simply as a response to a particular risk. For instance, one analysis of the functions of modern insurance argues that insurance contracts can (1) allocate risk among a firm's claimholders to those best able to bear that risk, (2) lower the costs the firm may face in case of bankruptcy, (3) provide an efficient means of administering claims, (4) perform monitoring on other contracts, and (5) bind decisions regarding real investments.[58] Insurers act as a buffer between a firm and those persons or events that can affect the value of its assets. North has noted, speaking in more general terms, that the more easily someone can affect the income from someone else's assets, the lower is the value of that asset; therefore, possession of an insurance contract can help stabilize asset values.[59]

By transferring and managing the risks to commerce, insurance increases economic efficiency and allows many transactions to be completed that would not have been otherwise. But potential customers have been surprisingly resistant to using insurance to manage their risks. As Adam Smith himself noted:

> The chance of loss is frequently undervalued, and scarce ever valued more than it is worth, we may learn from the very moderate profits of insurers. In order to make insurance, either from fire or sea-risk, a trade at all, the common premium must be sufficient to compensate the common loss, to pay the expense of management, and to afford such profit as might have been drawn from an equal capital employed in any common trade. . . . Moderate, however, as the premium of insurance commonly is, many people despise the risk too much to care to pay it.[60]

The services provided by the insurance industry change the liability for risk, shifting it from the one who suffers loss to a third party—the insurance pool (or, today, the insurance corporation).[61] The insurance contract lays out for the participants the division of losses between the direct sufferer of harm and any other parties to the contract. In other words, it assigns liability to different persons or groups for the costs that result from a harmful event. Insurance permits the expansion of economic activity by relieving individuals of the full costs of disaster and decreasing any uncertainty about who pays. The actual uncertainty surrounding the transaction itself does not decline, but the uncertainty about financial losses following disaster does. Thus, we can say that uncertainty is transformed into risk through the institutions of insurance.[62]

Although the insurance industry tends to have a staid image, the business of insurance itself can be a relatively risky proposition, especially for specialty insurance such as that for political risks. Insurers can be successful and profitable only when they are able to develop detailed knowledge of the probabilities for the risks they cover. It is this need for information by insurers that stimulated the development of the science of statistics and probability, especially by life insurers.[63] Unfortunately, commercial risks on trade, lending, and investment are not as amenable to statistical insight as mortality, and political risks even less so. Information on overseas conditions is much more difficult to collect and interpret than is information on local conditions. Even today, with all the publicity about the globalization of stock market trading, most investors still prefer to invest in their home markets, where they have greater access to reliable information about specific industries and firms and about the economy in general.

Surprisingly little attention has been paid to insurance in the field of political science and even less to its role in international affairs.[64] The existing literature tends to fall into four categories: histories, especially of specific companies and overwhelmingly about Lloyd's of London;[65] business studies, which describe the character of the market, often with a managerial/industrial organization perspective;[66] economic analyses of insurance that regard it as a solution to imperfect markets or discuss it in the context of uncertainty and information;[67] and a few analyses of the barriers to trade in insurance, as part of a general interest in services trade.[68] The majority of this literature disregards the international dimension and focuses on the role of insurance and the insurance industry within domestic society.[69] Given the extremely large size of the modern life and auto insurance industries, which tend not to be international, this emphasis is somewhat to be expected. Nevertheless, the lack of attention to international insurance is surprising, given that the origins of insurance itself lie in an explicitly international form of it—the marine insurance sector.

This book concentrates on highly specialized types of insurance that target political risk in international transactions. The definition of what constitutes a political risk will be based on the perspective of insurers, who have defined it differently at different times. International transactions refer to cross-border transportation and exchange of products, short-term credit, and long-term investments. The types of relevant insurance include political risks insurance, marine insurance, export credit insurance, and investment guarantees. All these kinds of insurance address the problem of political risk, but each has developed in its own way, with political risks often combined in one contract with other commercial risks.[70]

Political risks insurance is the most straightforward for our purposes. It is provided by the private sector and covers losses due to actions or inactions by governments or other political entities, including, at various times, the risk of loss due to war, civil war, expropriation and nationalization, terrorism and kidnapping, inconvertibility of funds, contract repudiation, embargoes, and the calling of financial guarantees.[71] It grew out of the marine insurance business, and the exact list of covered events has changed over time, expanding and contracting in response to customer demand, insurance practice and profitability, and the availability of information for estimating the probability of loss. Marine insurance contracts themselves cover ships and ship cargoes against both natural and man-made disasters; though not specifically oriented toward political risk, the early forms of marine insurance contained clauses insuring against war and piracy, and it is still possible to combine marine and political risks in one contract.

Export credit insurance covers loan defaults and payment delays for loans that are extended by a seller to foreign buyers to assist them in buying the goods and services.[72] Export credit insurance is offered by both private and public agencies, often in conjunction with the underlying credit. Not all export credit insurance includes liability for political events, but most of it does, particularly export credit insurance extended by governments. Finally, investment guarantees are a special category of political risks insurance that insures foreign direct investments against nationalization and expropriation, war risk, and foreign exchange risk. Investment guarantees are usually provided by governments, and the list of risks covered tends to be fairly narrow.

One further category, not well understood by the public but of vital importance to the industry, is that of reinsurance. Reinsurers provide insurance to other insurers (the "direct" insurers). They can insure the direct insurers' portfolio of risks or only a specific risk or category of risks; they either take a percentage of the business or agree to make payments on claims when they exceed a set amount. They thus allow the direct insurer to sell more insurance than their financial reserves, from which losses are paid, might normally allow. As the value of the underlying goods and services has grown, individual insurers have found it increasingly difficult financially to bear the cost of major losses. In order to expand the insurance market itself, insurers must enlarge their sources of capital and also diversify their risk. Reinsurers are thus crucial to the successful development of new markets, especially those with the potential for massive loss. In the case of political risks, reinsurers have varied in their willingness to provide coverage, thus affecting the availability of political risks insurance in commercial markets.

International Risks Insurance and Private Authority

International political risks insurance is embedded in a broad network of insurance business, most of which is not international in character at all—for instance, life and auto insurance. But institutions of insurance have been a vital element in the construction of a modern capitalist economy and have become a characteristic aspect of the most advanced economies. The expansion of the variety of techniques and institutions designed to modify or redistribute the risks of commerce is a crucial factor in the globalization of the world economy. The risks of foreign commerce often are significant barriers to the consummation of international transactions. As such, they also can be a source of conflict between states and between states and firms. Just as insurance was a critical part of the establishment of modern national economies, insurance and other methods of manipulating the risks of foreign commerce will play an increasingly vital role in the development of a truly global economy.

The results of the research presented here need to be taken with some caution because of certain problems with the data. The insurance industry generates hundreds and thousands of pages annually on its operations, but little is relevant to political questions. That goes doubly true for political risks insurance, for which exact data on premiums and volume of business remain hazy.[73] The private insurers maintain a deep secrecy about their activities and look with suspicion on anyone asking questions. In large part, this is because of the sensitivity surrounding their estimates of a particular government's stability or power as implied by the sale and price of political risks insurance. Finally, remarkably few academics have asked questions about insurance, except for some British historians researching insurance as a whole. Only recently have insurance archives been made available to the research community, and their value in determining trends in economic history should be clear.[74] The information in this book comes primarily from libraries and archives, specialist journals, and interviews.

The following chapters detail the way in which demand, norms, and resources interacted in producing a particular division of roles between the public and private sector in the international insurance regime. In all three periods studied here—1870–1914, 1917–39, and 1979–89—the demand for international risks insurance was high and rising, particularly in the two periods preceding the outbreak of World Wars I and II.

The basic principles and norms of the regime, which varied across the three periods, stem from the common understanding that insurers have about their business, what risks are insurable, and how insurance contracts might be structured to increase the incentives for customers to behave in ways that reduce loss. In the period from 1870 to 1914 natural disasters, war, and piracy were viewed as the main types of insurable loss, and most others were simply not seen as manageable by insurance. At that time insurance contracts for shipping encouraged captains to pull into port at the first sign of danger in order to reduce the probability of loss. Over the course of the next half-century the insurance contract itself became much more complex and self-conscious in establishing a legal framework for liability, in which the behavior of the customer explicitly entered into the determination of what the insurance would cover. The norms of insurance changed to encompass a much wider number of risks, including such things as expropriation risk and contract frustration. In addition, the definition of what is an insurable risk began to take account of the fact that governments, with their "deep pockets," have become active in insuring international risks; the larger, long-term risks that entail significant problems in controlling customer behavior now can be covered by government agencies and international organizations, although somewhat selectively.

In each period the resources of public and private agencies had a significant impact on the character of the regime. In the earlier period the commercial insurers alone dealt with international risks but had limited resources; governments did not participate in insurance at all until World War I. Between the two world wars the private insurers expanded their capacity to cover foreign risks, but government also stepped in with its seemingly limitless resources. After World War II, the resources of both public and private sector agencies initially expanded, but a breakdown in financial discipline in the private sector eventually sapped its strength, and recession and budget crises put strict limits on government activity.

The first period is one of British decline as an imperial power; it is also the era in which the British insurance industry, especially marine insurance, dominated international markets and established the norms and institutions that guided the industry for decades. In the second period the British government tried unsuccessfully to reestablish its political and financial dominance in the world. It turned to indirect means of supporting its commercial position, setting up the first government programs of trade credit and insurance and investment guarantees, which included coverage for foreign political risks. The third period witnessed the shift of global financial power to the United States, although the perception was that U.S. power had waned. At the same time, the private market expanded its underwriting of political risk contracts but also weakened its norms and practices and eventually its resource base.

The analysis of the relationship between public and private agencies in supplying a form of protection against political risk indicates that some common conceptions about the development of the world political economy need to be rethought. Private firms can and do construct regimes in areas of social, political, and economic importance without the prior participation of state authority and have a significant impact on the structure of the system. Furthermore, our image of the past few hundred years of international relations history as being essentially state-centered misses important evolutionary developments that reflect the extent to which the division of authority between the public and private sectors, even in foreign affairs, has been contested.[75] The strength of the private sector in the late nineteenth and early twentieth centuries runs counter to this image. The diffusion of sources and instruments for reducing political risk in the 1980s may indicate that today's interdependence is affecting states and firms equally, perhaps demonstrating a loss of control by both sides. Finally, the increase in institutionalization of political risks insurance may be caused in part by the diffusion of control over economic affairs among international organizations, regional organizations, states, and firms. The international risks insurance regime, originally established by private firms and later modified by individual governments, may be incorporated into a larger multilateral regime that will undergird the transition to some new structure of the world political economy.

2/ *Creating an International Risks Insurance Regime, 1870–1914*

The techniques of insurance date back to the long-distance trade of the Greek city-states, when something that was a cross between a loan and an insurance contract among shippers allowed them to share the risk of loss on dangerous sea voyages.[1] Thus the very earliest form of insurance covered marine risks on shipping, which included what we now think of as political risks such as war and piracy. Over time the techniques and practices of insurers evolved in sophistication, complexity and institutionalization. They grew especially rapidly during the commercial revolution of the eleventh to fourteenth centuries, when the financial industry as a whole made tremendous progress. Insurance centers sprang up in those cities and states with extensive trading networks and financial resources, such as Venice and Genoa for the Mediterranean trade and eventually, as the center of commerce shifted northward, Antwerp, Amsterdam, and London for the North Sea, Baltic, and Atlantic trades.

From the fourteenth to the nineteenth centuries the techniques and organization of insurance became increasingly specialized. That process of specialization depended in large part on the development of common rules and practices that would be both institutionalized among the insurers themselves and given legal standing by the political authorities. Eventually, as I argue here, the relations among industry participants took on the characteristics of a negotiated regime that acquired increasing importance with the internationalization of economic activity. Powerful states such as Great Britain and the United States were unwilling or unable to intervene militarily on behalf of merchants abroad in every case, so such a private regime for managing international risks became an important supplement or alternative. As noted below, the regime encompassing international risks was founded as an extension of the marine insurance industry in the late nineteenth century. The zenith and decline of British power, from 1870 to 1914, coincides with the institutionalization of insurance practice. We would expect the demand for protection from offshore risks to rise and fall in tandem with British hegemony, but such a systemic perspective does not provide a sufficient explanation for the establishment of an international risks management regime based on the preferences and activities of the private sector.

The Concept of a Private Sector-Driven International Regime

International regimes can be negotiated and maintained by private sector actors alone and not just by interstate negotiation or hegemonic coercion and persuasion, contrary to the perspective taken by most regime literature. The norms, rules, practices, and decision-making procedures of a regime can evolve from the activities and decisions taken by those involved in an industry, such as occurred in insurance. Furthermore, the decline in power of the leading state, such as Britain at the turn of the nineteenth century, does not necessarily undermine a private regime; instead, it may grow in importance and utility in the presence of what may be termed an international political market failure. The existence of a privately based international risks insurance regime provides part of the explanation for the expansion of international commerce in the face of intense and often discouraging political risks. Moreover, it indicates the extent to which authority over international economic relations resides not just in the hands of states or interstate organizations but also in the hands of firms and interfirm organizations.

Regime theory, which up to now has been firmly state-centric, has not addressed directly the manner in which nonstate actors, especially firms, participate in regimes.[2] This omission is due in large part to the influential hypothesis that the creation of regimes rests on the capability and willingness of a hegemonic state to support the costs of establishing them, thus emphasizing the role of states. The debate over hegemony that began in the early 1980s, however, has since evolved into a more sophisticated analysis of functional regimes and the possibility that small groups of states may continue supporting a regime even after the hegemon declines in power, drawing attention to a broader focus on cooperation.[3] This development can be tied to a more concentrated focus on the importance of mutual interests among states in regime formation.[4] More recent research further extends the analysis of regimes by hypothesizing a role for nongovernmental organizations in the development of regime norms and practices. Oran Young, Ernst Haas, Peter Haas, and Martha Finnemore have all examined the ability of private voluntary organizations, formal international organizations, and informal scientific communities to act as catalysts for change within regimes.[5] Scholars also have become more careful terminologically, positing analytical differences among organizations, regimes, and institutions.[6]

Surprisingly, after more than a decade of research and debate over the concept of regimes and their role in world affairs, little attention has been paid to the activities of the corporate community in regime creation and maintenance. And yet it is hard to see how to gain a deeper understanding of the relationship between political authority and the increasingly global markets in which transnational corporations wield great power without understanding the relations among firms. As the work of growing numbers of scholars reflects, corporations often create cooperative institutions or networks to guide or govern their behavior. For instance, Debora Spar maintains that international cartels can be analyzed as instances of corporate cooperation, which can be modeled in the same manner as interstate cooperation.[7] John Stopford and Susan Strange have convincingly argued that modern diplomacy is a three-sided affair, encompassing state-to-state, state-to-firm, and even firm-to-firm negotiations.[8] These works present the view that international economic structures are not made up of state power or organization alone.

The commonly accepted definition of regimes is the one drawn from Stephen Krasner's edited volume: "Regimes can be defined as sets of implicit or explicit principles, norms, rules, and decision-making procedures around which actors' expectations converge in a given area of international relations."[9] Volker Rittberger and Michael Zürn add that some minimal level of effectiveness and durability is essential for a useful definition of regimes.[10] In their terms, a regime is a form of regulated conflict management (among states) that is resilient in the face of deteriorating relationships among the participants.[11]

For a regime dominated by private sector participants, we would need to see evidence that the participants are wholly or primarily firms and that they have cooperatively developed a set of principles, norms, rules, and procedures which provide a template to guide their behavior in areas of common interest. The ultimate test of the effectiveness of such a private regime would be if the participants acted on the basis of their own norms and rules despite opposition from other firms or, especially, from states. States can press their claims on the private sector by changing the legal framework or, in extreme cases, through the coercive use of police powers. The insurance industry at its height indeed withstood such a test, as discussed in the following chapter. But just as important, by regulating its own behavior and establishing the framework within which all insurers acted, the relevant firms shaped the kinds of choices available to others, including governments.

There are three ways we can conceive of the relationship between firms and states within a regime. The most common perspective is the dominant one in mainstream political science—that states construct regimes, which may include firms either as the targets of regulatory action or as subordinate participants. In fact, certain regimes depend for their effective implementation on the ability and willingness of corporations to abide by their mandates, such as environmental regimes in which the activities of firms and not states are regulated. The implementation of the Montreal Protocol to protect the ozone layer of the atmosphere, for example, depends on the ability and willingness of firms to develop and utilize chemicals that are not damaging.

Another way to conceive of the relationship between firms and states within regimes is to view the private sector as generating particular norms, rules, and even informal law that is then sanctioned by state authority. The majority of commercial law governing both domestic and international transactions evolved in this manner.[12] Both these perspectives allot relatively little importance to the initiative and influence of the private sector, although they give it more weight than traditional realist models of world politics and international institution building.

The cooperation evident among firms in associations, networks, and perhaps cartels may actually constitute a different kind of international regime—a private regime.[13] Logically, there seems no reason to exclude initiatives by nonstate actors from the definition and description of regimes, and in fact, the initial discussion of regimes was not exclusively state-centric. But that raises the question whether there is a distinction between a private regime and an oligopoly or cartel, and whether that distinction matters.[14]

An oligopoly exists when supply is dominated by only a few firms, competition among them is restrained, and there are high barriers to entry by new firms. Oligopolists agree either formally or informally, publicly or secretly, to establish uniform prices for their products; the largest corporations often act as "price leaders" through indirect signaling of their intentions.[15] Cartels, in contrast, are explicit, formal organizations among producers (rarely among consumers) in which the participants agree to cooperate over price, production levels, and market share and attempt to monopolize the market as a group.[16] A cartel agreement typically operates through self-enforcement, although external enforcement by states has often occurred.[17]

In oligopolies and cartels each firm pursues partly shared and partly conflicting goals. As a group, firms use their leverage to obtain monopoly rents through their market power. In an oligopolistic industry all firms might charge similar prices for competing products so that each maintains the status quo in market share, keeps prices and profits high and stable, and discourages the entry of new firms. In a cartel the participants negotiate an explicit formula for dividing the market and establish a set of procedures to implement their goals. Individually, however, they compete among themselves for larger shares of the benefits of their market domination.

Neither an oligopoly nor a cartel completely fits the definition of a regime, and the characteristics they leave out are an important element of what gives intercorporate cooperation a degree of authority and even legitimacy in international affairs. A private regime exists when firms cooperate over issues beyond price, supply, and market share alone. Although these matters are obviously important goals for any firm that wants to remain in business, the distinctive element in a private regime is the degree to which the regime governs a wide range of behavior among those who created it and among many actors outside it. Regimes regulate appropriate industry behavior, establish jurisdictional competencies both inside and outside the regime, and establish a framework for members to negotiate agreements among themselves and form mutual associations.[18] The member firms in a regime may be highly competitive with one another, as they are in the insurance industry, and industry concentration and barriers to entry may be quite low, unlike the case in an oligopoly or cartel. A private regime is about more than simply market structure or money. Regimes include principles and norms, not just rules and decision-making procedures, and thus require the participants to reflect on their behavior in a way that goes beyond straightforward market competition or collusion. In a private regime the participants converge in their expectations about correct behavior regarding both market issues and broader social and political ones.

A number of elements distinguish the relationships among insurers as a regime and not an oligopoly or cartel. First, and most obvious, the insurance industry as a whole is not oligopolistic in structure, particularly given the relatively low barriers to entry.[19] The industry is highly competitive, fragmented, and multitudinous, although there clearly are market leaders in particular lines of insurance and despite a series of recent takeovers that has increased the degree of concentration in some areas. Second, unlike an oligopoly or cartel, the insurers at times have promoted policies that actually restricted their profits, put markets out of reach, and limited or regulated a wide range of behaviors unrelated to price and production. This behavior clearly goes against the prime motivation behind oligopolies and cartels—the capture of superprofits. Third, industry participants developed and enforced their own principles and norms through establishing cooperative institutions linking underwriters, brokers, and related service activities. Thus, the level of institutional complexity is much greater than what is found in an oligopoly or cartel.

Does it matter whether or not we define a private regime to include oligopolies and cartels? We would expect the behavior of participants in a private regime to be different from the behavior of simple oligopolists or cartel members. We should see them cooperate in areas besides price and market share. More important, in developing norms and principles within a regime framework, we would expect them to seek and attain a degree of legitimacy and accepted authority for their rule within the larger society. Oligopolies and cartels are considered illegitimate and in most countries are illegal under antitrust laws or competition policy. Private regimes, in contrast, may come to be viewed as an acceptable form of informal governance.

The insurance industry provides an excellent case for analyzing the development and evolution of a private international regime and the changing balance of private and public power in managing international risks. Insurers have responded to changing levels of demand for protection from overseas risks, at the same time protecting themselves from the possibility of overwhelming financial loss by constructing an elaborate structure of norms and practices governing what risks would be covered. From 1870 to 1914, as British power declined and European war drew near, British insurers established common norms, practices, and institutions among themselves.

Great Britain and the World Political Economy, 1870–1914

Great Britain in the late nineteenth century became the center of finance, shipping, and trade throughout most of the world, backed by the protection of the British navy. Nevertheless, political risks remained a constant companion to British entrepreneurs in foreign territories, particularly in the most distant colonial lands. The success of Britain's commerce can be laid in part to the strength of its shipping interests, and the development of an effective and efficient marine insurance industry was vital to its growth.[20]

The British government provided protection to commerce in the traditional manner—by defending open sea lanes with its naval power. The end of the Napoleonic Wars had left Europe fragmented, with Britain in the position of maintaining the balance of power among competing states and shifting alliances. The British navy, superior to all others, protected access to foreign markets in Europe and elsewhere, and British imperialism extended the island nation's commitments around the globe. The most important foreign colony, in the view of many political leaders, was the Indian subcontinent, and British strategic policies in the late 1800s concentrated on safeguarding the sea routes to India. Military protection of the Suez Canal and political ties in Egypt also were viewed as vital to the national interest.

Britain had become integral to a growing world economy in the mid-1800s when it threw open its borders to free trade. British economic ties to other markets deepened as its exports expanded and vast sums of capital were invested overseas.[21] London became the world center for transportation and finance, and British politics were dominated by financial and trading interests rather than by industrial ones.[22] Phyllis Deane and W. A. Cole observe, "By the end of the nineteenth century the British economy was heavily dependent on world markets, and the rate and pattern of British economic growth was largely conditioned by the responses of producers and consumers in the rest of the world."[23] Throughout this period the position of London as the key to global liquidity made it particularly vulnerable to external shocks.[24] Under the gold standard, however, international confidence remained high and the risk of losses due to inconvertibility or exchange rate changes was low in Europe, though peripheral regions suffered numerous currency crises.[25]

The height of British political-economic power is generally considered to be around 1870, after which it fitfully declined up to the

Table 2.1. British balance of payments, 1870–1913 (in millions of pounds)

Year	Merchandise Trade	Investment Earnings	Invisibles Trade	Bullion Specie	Balance on Current Account
1870	−57.5	+35.3	+76.8	−10.5	+44.1
1875	−90.5	+57.8	+89.6	−5.6	+51.3
1880	−121.1	+57.7	+96.4	+2.6	+35.6
1885	−98.5	+70.3	+90.7	−0.2	+62.3
1890	−86.3	+94.0	+99.6	−8.8	+98.5
1895	−126.5	+93.6	+87.8	−14.9	+40.0
1900	−167.0	+103.6	+109.1	−7.5	+37.9
1905	−155.9	+123.5	+120.1	−6.2	+81.5
1910	−154.2	+158.0	+138.3	−6.5	+135.6
1913	−131.6	+199.6	+168.2	−11.9	+224.3

Source: Brian R. Mitchell and Phyllis Deane, *Abstract of British Historical Statistics* (Cambridge: Cambridge University Press, 1971), pp. 333–35.

outbreak of World War I.[26] The export success of British industry grew weaker, and the merchandise trade balance consistently remained in deficit at the turn of the century. At the same time, both investment returns and "invisibles" or services trade, including insurance, generated larger and larger positive balances. The current account surplus depended on economic returns from British overseas investments and on the competitiveness of its services industries. Insurance income, though increasingly dwarfed by the rest of the financial industry in size, contributed a significant amount to the current account, remaining at relatively stable levels for most of this period and then growing dramatically from 1900 on (see Tables 2.1 and 2.2).

By the end of the century Germany, the United States, and France challenged British supremacy in political and economic affairs. They had been industrializing rapidly, stimulated in part by overseas investments from London, and Germany and the United States had overcome their domestic divisions to establish stronger and more effective state institutions. British policymakers at the turn of the century talked openly about their expectation that great-power war was inevitable, but it was not clear with whom they might be fighting. In fact, France and the United States seemed more threatening to Great Britain than Germany in the early years of the new century.

As part of its expansion abroad, the British upheld certain minimum principles concerning protection of property located in foreign jurisdic-

Table 2.2. Five-year average on trade, shipping, interest and dividends, and insurance/brokerage, 1870–1913 (in millions of pounds)

Years	Merchandise Trade	Shipping Credits	Interest/ Dividends	Insurance/ Brokerage
1866–70	–58.12	+44.50	+30.20	+13.20
1871–75	–62.50	+50.40	+49.98	+16.44
1876–80	–124.56	+54.16	+56.34	+15.68
1881–85	–104.28	+60.32	+64.76	+15.64
1886–90	–91.10	+57.12	+84.16	+15.48
1891–95	–130.30	+57.28	+93.98	+14.84
1896–00	–160.60	+62.44	+100.20	+15.76
1901–05	–174.58	+71.24	+112.94	+18.20
1906–10	–142.10	+88.78	+151.42	+22.36
1911–13	–134.30	+100.33	+187.93	+26.57

Source: Albert Imlah, *Economic Elements of the Pax Britannica: Studies in British Foreign Trade in the Nineteenth Century* (Cambridge: Harvard University Press, 1958), pp. 72–75. Copyright © by the President and Fellows of Harvard College. Reprinted by permission of Harvard University Press.

tions. European states had set the standard that there should be no confiscation of assets, extending it internationally as they colonized Asia, Africa, and Latin America. Devised initially to protect merchants and long-distance trade, these rules—imposed through colonial annexation, capitulation treaties, treaty ports, political intervention, and even coercion—later provided an effective framework for the international expansion of industrial and financial capital.[27] British preferences tended toward domination with as little direct military or political coercion as possible.[28] The British Foreign Office defined very narrowly the risks to foreign economic transactions which the government would actively defend, relying on the fact that strong British private financial interests could generally defend themselves well enough.[29]

The Development of London Insurance Markets

The period of British hegemony and decline, from the mid-nineteenth century to World War I, coincided with the elaboration of insurance practice and innovations in insurance organization in response to the explosion of overseas commerce. As the British Empire expanded and the City of London bankrolled the world, British overseas financial institutions developed new administrative systems and new products to cope with increased trade and investment in unknown and underdeveloped markets. The modern marine insurance industry, crucial to the development of London as a center of transportation and finance, was well established by this time, and many of the institutions we still know today were in existence.[30]

As Britain rapidly industrialized, the City of London became the center of international insurance, partly because of the congregation of global trade, finance, and shipping interests there. These are the very interests that were the primary customers of the insurers. Its role as a major insurance center also rested on the early development of its insurance industry, which had the expertise, information, and institutions to bolster its reputation and efficacy and help it compete successfully for new markets. The large amount of British capital available for investment could also be cycled through the insurance industry, supporting its expansion; the fifty years before the First World War saw the greatest outpouring of capital ever invested abroad by one nation.[31]

The institutions of the insurance industry evolved in tandem with the centralization of political authority in the state; both could be seen as newly developing institutions of protection, with insurance essentially supplementing the still incomplete power of the state and vice versa. Long-distance trade expanded tremendously even before the establishment of the modern state, and therefore other mechanisms and institutions were needed to enhance the security of property and contracts.[32] As one early-twentieth-century observer noted, marine insurance "bears to commerce the relation of body-guard rather than of mere servile attendant . . . of the active forces which influence, control, or forbid the employment of shipping, none have greater effect than the marine insurance power."[33] Insurers enhanced this effect by developing private law, methods for adjudication of claims, and more sophisticated contracts as one response to the demands of growing commercial activity, along with innovations in organizational design.

Early in the eighteenth century, after the disastrous financial crisis caused by the South Sea Bubble and when the notion of a limited liability joint stock company was still new, the British government banned all such companies in insurance except two royally chartered monopolies, the Royal Exchange Assurance and the London Assurance Company.[34] A loophole allowed individuals to continue underwriting insurance, however, a practice that eventually thrived at a local coffeehouse called Lloyd's. Lloyd's of London became a loosely organized "market" for insurance. Members underwrote insurance contracts as individuals with unlimited liability; their contracts were guaranteed only by a deposit placed with the Committee of Lloyd's. According to one account, a nineteenth-century Lloyd's underwriter described it to a lady visitor this way: "Individually, madam, we are underwriters. Collectively, we are Lloyd's."[35] With limited domestic competition and a thriving customer base in London, Lloyd's underwriters prospered and came to dominate marine insurance markets in Britain and the world.

Throughout the nineteenth century the British insurance industry created cooperative institutions for salvage and claims processing, established professional associations, and used the latest technology in compiling information on the state of the world to calculate the probability of loss. In building foreign business, the insurance companies made growing use of the idea and practice of reinsurance in order to increase their financial resources and to spread their risks. They also maintained geographical diversification of the risks they covered. All these advances in insurance organization and practice helped the underwriters maintain a balance between expanding their business in response to growing demand and controlling their own losses.

The insurance industry became quite centralized in London, especially the foreign risks side of the business. Lloyd's of London was particularly influential, exercising a degree of hegemony over the industry both at home and abroad. Lloyd's power should not be exaggerated, however, given the venerable presence of the Royal Exchange Assurance and London Assurance Company. In 1849 the royal monopolies had been withdrawn and competition in the British industry expanded, although many of the new companies quickly failed. Despite this competition, the London underwriters at the companies and at Lloyd's generally agreed on what constituted an insurable risk and what did not, and the latter category included most political risks. This lack of political risks insurance throughout the market raised some concerns among government ministers, but they rejected the idea of having the government provide any kind of insurance that the private sector refused to supply. Once the royal monopolies had been revoked, the British government remained relatively uninvolved in insurance regulation, largely because of industry lobbying. As one insurer argued extravagantly, "All laws are an abomination to the natural man."[36] Only after the turn of the century did the government once again intervene.

The British insurance industry thrived on the constant conflicts of the day. After years of only reluctantly insuring themselves against war risks, most merchants finally came to accept the value of financially protecting their assets; standard marine insurance policies included coverage against a number of named violent and political risks.[37] Before 1840, the two royal monopoly insurance companies put some limits on these policies. They were unwilling to sell marine insurance on trade between two foreign ports (called "cross-risks"), owing to the difficulty of obtaining sufficient information on conditions there, although they willingly covered trade between a British and a foreign port. At Lloyd's of London, however, underwriters insured cross-risks, because at Lloyd's, as Barry Supple notes, "the enormous variety of underwriting skill and knowledge meant that there was always *some* group of underwriters willing and able to accept risks which (to a single company) might appear hazardous because their context and details were unknown."[38] Overall, there was a significant increase in insurance business from 1859 to the turn of the century.[39] Shipping interests also were more willing to participate in marine insurance markets themselves (generally through shippers' mutual clubs) in what one analyst evaluated as representing a cooperative effort on their part to reduce their international risks.[40]

London attracted increasing numbers of customers for marine risk insurance during the revolutionary uprisings of 1848, the Crimean War (1854–56), and the American Civil War (1861–65). These conflicts brought further foreign business to London underwriters, including merchants from other European nations who felt they could not rely on the financial stability of their domestic insurers.[41] Almost all American business was insured in London.[42] One particularly difficult risk for insurers to calculate probabilities for was privateering, or government-sanctioned piracy. To the relief of insurers, the signatories to the Treaty of Paris of 1856 finally agreed to eliminate privateering.[43] British policy leaders at the time expressed a certain amount of confidence that international law would restrain belligerents from attacking commerce even if war broke out, as a government report later recounted.[44]

During these European upheavals the choices for potential customers concerning where or from whom to buy insurance became quite complicated. Insurance prices immediately and dramatically responded to the location and participants in military conflicts. Customers and insurers both had to factor in political considerations of nationality and government restrictions on commerce with the enemy. As so gracefully put by one historian, "and so the business of marine insurance, under the rising pressure of belligerence, found itself driven from the consortium of the market into the arena of both domestic and international politics."[45]

The development and establishment of an international risks insurance regime can be tied to the growing prominence of Lloyd's of London as a leader within the insurance community, particularly in marine insurance. By the middle of the 1800s Lloyd's underwriters actively worked to develop industry norms, practices, and cooperative institutions: "The story of the development of Lloyd's as an institution is the story of ever greater protection for the commercial public; it is also the story of how the rules of a private club have been gradually given the sanction of law by the authority of Parliament."[46] In the Lloyd's Act of 1871 the constitution of Lloyd's was sanctioned by Parliament with respect to marine insurance, and the small administrative staff (formerly the waiters at the original coffeehouse) incorporated as the Committee of Lloyd's. In the 1911 Lloyd's Act legal acceptance was extended to its expanding non-marine insurance business.

One key to the success of Lloyd's was its advantage in gathering and analyzing the most current information on shipping and political conditions abroad. It maintained an extensive network of agents in foreign cities who reported regularly about local events and also carried out duties with respect to settling claims. It was an honor to become an agent of Lloyd's, reporting to the home office the arrival and departure of ships, news of wrecks, and any item relevant to the shipping business. Once a loss occurred, the interests of the vessel owner, the cargo owner, and the underwriter became intertwined, and the agent on the spot had to mediate conflicts among them. The agent is not supposed to defend any specific insurance contract but represents the interests of good underwriting in general, guarding against fraud, negligence, and mismanagement. The agent also communicated information on cases of salvage, in order to monitor the behavior of salvers and to control costs.[47] These agents shared their shipping and political intelligence with the British Foreign Office, which often depended on Lloyd's agents for the most reliable information about international events. Lloyd's also published daily shipping news, which recorded details such as the movements of ships, and information on the condition of specific vessels.

One aspect of Lloyd's that attracted customers was its reliable reputation.[48] The underwriters demonstrated their financial security by their capability and willingness to pay claims promptly. Furthermore, Lloyd's underwriters are supervised by other Lloyd's members and by a central organ, the Committee of Lloyd's. In order to be a Lloyd's member, one must pledge a large amount as a deposit against future claims and agree to unlimited liability.[49] Lloyd's calls itself a market for individual underwriting and broking, and it is explicitly not a company, although it has established certain minimal central administrative institutions. These institutions conduct regular audits, manage a separate trust fund for premiums, require extra deposits for particularly risky types of business, and maintain deposits held as guarantees against nonpayment of claims.[50] All these practices enhanced the group's reputation, which became its most prized asset in attracting customers.

Lloyd's also developed a reputation for being willing to insure any risk that could be imagined, a reputation that clings to it even today. A creative and entrepreneurial underwriter named Cuthbert Heath began in the 1880s to insure nonmarine risks, literally inventing whole new fields of insurance in the process, such as theft and auto insurance. In 1901, as Harold Brown notes, the first Lloyd's policy on motor insurance "was written in the marine market, and the car was treated as a ship navigating on dry land."[51]

Early indicators of a private regime can be seen in the development of organizations and laws for salvage on shipping, which is a crucial area of potential loss to marine insurers. As firms selling marine insurance grew in number over the course of the nineteenth century, they perceived a need to cooperate and harmonize practice with regard to the salvaging of ships run aground or otherwise damaged. They wanted to ensure that ships would indeed be salvaged and not scuttled by the ship's owner or ransacked by others.[52] Shipowners could be tempted to sink the ship deliberately or limit how much of the cargo was recovered in order to get their hands on the insurance payment. The problem of moral hazard in this case is clear. Therefore it was in the interest of insurers to design a system that would encourage owners and salvers to preserve the ship and its cargo to the greatest extent possible. Shipowners' clubs, marine insurance companies, and Lloyd's of London negotiated industry rules for dealing with, for instance, the regular occurrence of ship strandings in the Black Sea and the Dardanelles.[53]

Lloyd's acted as the leader among London insurers in establishing the Salvage Association in 1856 and became the main executor of its policies. Its members consisted of Lloyd's of London, the London Assurance, the Royal Exchange Assurance, the Alliance, and the Indemnity Mutual Companies, along with some smaller marine insurance firms, and the Royal Mail Steam packet company.[54] These were primarily well-established firms, and their longevity probably made them more willing to collaborate with Lloyd's than some of the newer companies. In the 1870s the insurance community debated the close relationship between Lloyd's and the Salvage Association, with talk of whether they should be combined or separated and even some discussion of removing from Lloyd's control its foreign agents, intelligence-gathering operations, and newspapers.[55] Although some degree of separation was supported by the Committee of Lloyd's itself, implementation required an act of Parliament to revise the 1871 Lloyd's Act. Political debate led to revisions that were unacceptable to Lloyd's, and the bill never passed.

Lloyd's dominated the marine insurance business throughout this era, although increasing competition from insurance companies whittled away its lead in other lines of insurance. One limit on its capacity to remain competitive was that it could write insurance only up to the limits of what an individual underwriter held in reserves. Unlimited liability did not mean unlimited capacity to underwrite risks. In order to overcome this capacity restriction, in a move that probably saved Lloyd's as a whole, the members agreed to pool the resources of more than one individual by forming "syndicates" of underwriters.[56] They would remain independent, individual insurance underwriters, but they would be able to share risks up to their combined limits.

For their part, the insurance companies sought to compete with Lloyd's, in salvage and in other areas, through their own cooperative activities. In 1884 they agreed to share their information and experience concerning risks and to this end created the Institute of London Underwriters. The institute promotes uniform policies and pricing strategies among its members.[57] Lloyd's led the market in many areas of business until the creation of the institute, and even afterward most of the London market continued to cooperate closely with Lloyd's agents even as they competed for business.[58] Furthermore, many Lloyd's underwriters developed a specialization in reinsurance, which insures the risks of other insurers, thus linking the business fate of the companies with the individual underwriters at Lloyd's.

In the 1890s Lloyd's, the Salvage Association, the Liverpool Salvage Association, and the marine insurance companies negotiated among themselves to combine into a single association. This particular effort failed, but Lloyd's went on to promote successfully its own contract form for salvage (the Form of Salvage Agreement). The members of Lloyd's had developed what they considered an effective contract between shippers and potential salvers, one that also protected the interests of insurers. This form is almost universally accepted even today.[59] It established incentives for preserving a damaged ship and its cargo, which would reduce the amount the insurers paid in claims or allow them to recover some of what they paid. It also binds shipper and salver to settle salvage costs and rewards by arbitration in London. Lloyd's "open form" of salvage agreement can even be "signed" over the radio as a ship is sinking.[60]

Another area of cooperation in the London market is in the processing of insurance claims. The methods for settling claims on losses suffered while abroad goes back to practices instituted in 1885. Some Lloyd's underwriters settle their own claims but most use a centralized claims office. The London companies are invited to weekly meetings of the claims adjusters of Lloyd's to discuss current problems and decide on cooperative action, especially when a particular claim involves many different individuals and firms, as is common for very large risks. Today the Average Department, as it is called, handles claims and settlements on salvage, and its services are used by both Lloyd's underwriters and the marine insurance companies.[61]

Keeping Foreign Competitors at Bay

The London insurers, especially in marine risks, controlled the largest amount of premium income and insurance contracts in the world, although their position did not go unchallenged. Insurers in continental Europe and the United States repeatedly attempted to establish a foothold in the business. As the case of the United States demonstrates, however, the London insurers undermined, often deliberately, the ability of foreign competitors to succeed. That was particularly true for marine insurance and the new and growing reinsurance business, the two forms of international risks insurance then in existence.

Insurance did not become well established in the United States until the latter half of the twentieth century, which is surprising considering the eventual importance of New York as a center for global insurance. Americans had begun buying insurance from British underwriters before the War of Independence, establishing a pattern that would continue for more than a century. The first American insurance company was organized in 1794, when the Insurance Company of North America was chartered by the General Assembly of Pennsylvania, in part to avoid the outflow of American money to European insurers. Insurance entrepreneurs then set up other firms, many of which were ruined during the Napoleonic Wars by heavy losses to American shipping from blockades, counterblockades, and the capture and detention of American ships. Many claims for losses generated by this conflict eventually had to be decided, or "adjusted," by international negotiation.[62]

The War of 1812 was an absolute disaster for U.S. marine insurance. American shipping was driven from the seas, and American insurance declined from an already low point for approximately thirty years thereafter. Foreigners simply did not buy from American companies, and neither did Americans. When U.S. shipping weakened, as it did during the war, so did marine insurance. Fraudulent claims for losses in the West Indies and Gulf of Mexico from 1828 to 1844, a turbulent period when attempts to unify Latin America collapsed, further hurt the industry, reflecting the weak norms and limited resources of American insurers. In competing for business, they did not apply effective controls on opportunism among their customers and did not have the expertise to calculate risks accurately.[63] One contemporary observer noted:

> Some of our [U.S.] leading marine companies, it is true, do possess a large mass of experience which is used as a basis in computing rates. Yet it is also true that . . . there is no other branch of insurance in which success is so largely dependent upon the native sagacity, the keenness for observation, and the general specialized ability of the individual underwriter to know not only men, but the effect of climate, seasons, geographical localities and numerous other considerations upon any of a large number of risks, as in marine insurance.[64]

American marine insurance had a brief period of success during the era of the clipper ship, which captured a large share of international shipping from about 1840 to 1860. Long voyages to the Far East confronted numerous natural and political risks, and marine insurance was considered a vital accompaniment to these ventures. This business—both the clipper ships and American marine insurance—declined again in the succeeding decades when British shipping lines introduced the modern steamship. At the same time, the American Civil War disrupted trade between Europe and America and led to devastating losses for insurers. The decline of the American merchant marine at the turn of the century explains much of the weakness of the U.S. marine insurance business.[65]

The position of market dominance held by London insurers, especially Lloyd's, also severely hampered the development of U.S. business.

Insurers competed fiercely for business as trade expanded throughout the nineteenth century and insurance became recognized as an important facilitator of overseas commerce. The London insurance market was quick to take advantage of the U.S. government's willingness in 1871 to let foreign insurers operate in the United States.[66] There also existed clear biases against American marine insurers and shipping interests within important business institutions. For instance, Lloyd's had established a ship rating service that evaluated the seaworthiness of vessels. This service was used by almost all marine insurers and their customers to establish the potential risk of loss for a voyage and therefore the appropriate insurance premiums. U.S. insurers accused Lloyd's of consistently underrating ships built in the United States, thereby requiring higher insurance rates that made the U.S. mercantile fleet uncompetitive.[67] Since the U.S. insurers found most of their business among U.S. merchants, any decline in U.S. shipping or increased reluctance by shipowners to buy expensive insurance meant a concomitant decline for U.S. insurers.

The U.S. insurance industry eventually established a solid base in the domestic market, in life and property/casualty insurance. The demand for these kinds of insurance depends on highly developed industrial markets and a high standard of living, so the American insurance industry expanded with the rest of the U.S. economy. Only after World War II did U.S. insurance corporations tentatively enter foreign markets and begin to challenge the dominance of London underwriters, especially in nondomestic insurance lines.

Prelude to the Great War, 1890–1914

By the turn of the century many British leaders anticipated an eventual war in Europe. The alliances among the great powers were becoming increasingly inflexible, and relations between countries were deteriorating. The British still supported the largest navy in the world, but France and the United States came hard on its heels, and eventually Germany joined as a challenger to British naval supremacy. Competition and conflict increased among the major powers, as particularly reflected in imperialistic rivalries in Africa and Asia.

Throughout most of the nineteenth century marine insurers had been perfectly happy to insure war risks just as they did any other type of risk. Special policies to cover political risk finally began to be offered on a regular basis by the end of the century but not by the regular insurers. Mutual associations and clubs of shippers, and not the major companies or Lloyd's, began to sell special war risks insurance policies against losses on shipping from military conflict (traditionally labeled "King's Enemy Risks"[68]). The mutual associations and clubs could control losses and build up financial capacity for such unpredictable risks better than the traditional underwriters could, since the insurer and the insured were the same people and thus unlikely to pose any danger of opportunistic behavior. Associations such as the North of England Protecting and Indemnity Association, the London-based group of War Risks Associations, and the London and Liverpool War Risks Insurance Association covered shipping against the damages of war if the United Kingdom remained neutral; otherwise, coverage was extremely limited.[69] If the United Kingdom became embroiled in war, then the losses to shipping would be tremendous and the financial resources of the mutual insurers would be glaringly inadequate. It was these shipowners' associations that pressed the government most closely to establish some sort of government war risks insurance scheme as a service to shippers and to British trade in general.[70]

In the 1890s the British government faced crises on several fronts that threatened to make war risks turn to war realities. The United States and Great Britain became embroiled in a boundary conflict between Venezuela and British Guiana in 1895 when the United States challenged British authority in the Western Hemisphere; the crisis came close to war, but the British eventually backed down. Three years later the Fashoda crisis in Sudan nearly ended in war between Britain and France. Both Germany and Russia began to upgrade their naval forces to compete threateningly with the British navy, beginning the naval arms race that would heighten fears of conflict throughout Europe.

Insurers began to rethink their commitment to including war risks coverage in their marine insurance policies. In 1896, the London Assurance Company even suggested in a letter to the Committee of Lloyd's that war risks should be specifically excluded from marine insurance policies. Lloyd's did not go along with this suggestion, largely because of competition between Lloyd's and the companies in marine insurance. But more doubts arose among insurers as there were, in the words of D. E. W. Gibb, "signs of some uneasiness about what the next war at sea would be like and searching of hearts as to how far the ordinary machinery of insurance would stand the strain of modern war."[71] Two years later the Committee of Lloyd's would change its mind as to the wisdom of insuring war risks.

During the Fashoda crisis of 1898 the rates on British shipping through the Suez Canal rose dramatically, and merchants tried to avoid using that shipping route. Insurers profited greatly from this business, however, not just because of the increase in rates they charged but because no war actually broke out and therefore no claims for losses had to be paid. In contrast, both the Spanish-American War in the same year and the Boer War the next caused extensive damage to insured property, particularly when insured gold was commandeered by President Paul Kruger in South Africa. Many underwriters had not expected the outbreak of conflict, despite high tension levels, and covered these risks at low peacetime rates.[72]

In response to repeated crises and challenges to British authority, in June 1898 the members of Lloyd's of London reversed their stance and declared that henceforth all marine insurance policies should exclude war risks unless a separate agreement to include them was signed. From that point on, marine and cargo insurance policies included the clause, "Warranted nevertheless free of capture, seizure, and detention, and the consequences thereof, or of any attempted threat, piracy excepted, and also from all consequences of hostilities or warlike operations, whether before or after declaration of war" (referred to as the F.C. and S. clause).[73]

It was during this period that insurers, using their growing experience and information, began to develop more sophisticated contract terms in order to manage their international risks. The policy terms were constructed in such a way as to increase the incentives for ship captains to avoid running high risks during a British conflict; under the terms of the insurance contract, the outbreak of war meant that all ships had to put in to the nearest protected harbor and stay there until the conflict ended. In addition, the payment of war claims depended on the ability of shippers and underwriters to ascertain the exact time war broke out and among whom, in order to determine when the exclusion clause became operative. War risks insurance associations also maintained active institutions for controlling the settlement of claims and the valuation of losses.[74] Through more specific contract terms and supporting institutions the insurers became more willing to develop specialized policies separate from regular marine insurance to cover the risks of war.

Despite these safeguards and the existence of war risks associations, many shippers and cargo owners found it nearly impossible to buy insurance against war risks on the open market at the turn of the century.[75] Even those willing to sell war risks insurance simply did not have the financial resources to cover fully numerous ships and cargoes in time of war, especially as their size and value had grown. The technology of both shipbuilding and warmaking had become much more sophisticated, complex, and expensive, and therefore the risks became more difficult to calculate. For instance, the French in 1893 launched the first submarine, opening a whole new area of war risks that had never before been considered and that clearly would pose a threat to shipping in time of war.[76]

British policymakers feared that these new and strictly defined war risks insurance contracts meant that all British ships would be sitting in safe harbors at the outbreak of any war. The Admiralty pondered the question, If the Straits of Dover and entrance to the Thames were closed at night during war, what would be the effect on the Port of London? The ships would remain in "any place of safety in which they might be, or which they could reach, until they could proceed under protection of adequate insurance, or until absence of danger was so obvious that such protection was unnecessary."[77] Furthermore, they anticipated that marine and cargo insurance would experience huge rate increases at the outset of any conflict. Increased insurance costs would strain the ability of shippers and cargo owners to support their business and would tempt them to limit or halt their trade for the duration of the conflict. Political discussions focused primarily on marine insurance and much less on cargo insurance, since marine policies contained clauses covering certain cargo and defining what would be covered under different conditions, whereas cargo policies simply excluded war risks entirely.

As a response to concerns about the links among insurance, shipping, and trade, in 1903 an association was formed to explore the security of the food supply in wartime, and the Balfour administration also appointed an official commission to look into the matter. The Royal Commission on Supply of Food and Raw Material in Time of War confirmed the dependence of Britain on overseas trade for vital food supplies and raw materials. In evidence before the House of Commons in 1903 a representative of one of the major insurance companies, the Commercial Union Assurance Co., stated unequivocally that rates on shipping would climb at the outbreak of war, reinforcing the fears of the politicians that shipping would be limited.[78] The company representative estimated that in a war between the United Kingdom and a European power, rates would probably climb to about 10 percent of the value at risk, compared to peacetime rates of around 1/8 percent, for ships going through the Mediterranean Sea and Suez Canal.[79] He admitted that many insurers would stop covering war risks entirely in case of war, however, and that most standard insurance contracts have a clause excluding payment of claims on war losses.[80] Nevertheless, a Lloyd's underwriter declared, "Personally, I fear war risks insurance when war is threatened, but once it happens, fine."[81] The calculation of risk is easy in war and peace but extremely difficult during the period of uncertainty before the outbreak of conflict.

The report of the Royal Commission on Supply of Food and Raw Materials in Time of War, published in 1905, further stimulated anxiety over the effects of a crisis in insurance and thus on shipping and suggested that the government establish a war risks program. The report attempted to analyze the supply patterns of the nation, how a naval war would affect those patterns, what effect an increase in prices would have, and what kinds of programs might help maintain supplies at reasonable prices. "However ample may be the sources of supply," the report asserted, "and however anxious the countries of origin may be to sell, it is obvious that the quantities which the United Kingdom will obtain and the prices which will have to be paid, must ultimately depend upon the safety and sufficiency of the transport available."[82] In conclusion, the report recommended building up reserves of grain and instituting national insurance and indemnity plans.[83]

Many political leaders believed the nation should rely for protection on the navy, and not on government insurance or indemnity programs. Balfour, who headed the 1903 commission that favored establishing a national indemnity program, agreed: "We look mainly for our security to the strength of our Navy; but we rely in only a less degree upon the widespread resources of our mercantile fleet."[84] According to this view, if the war were going badly, no amount of government indemnity or private insurance would persuade suppliers to maintain their shipping business.[85] Therefore, government policy needed to be concerned primarily with winning the war, not insuring losses. The commission report also concluded that, although conflict probably would lead to interference or interruption in shipping, there was no risk of the total cessation of shipping of food or raw materials to the British Isles.

In 1904 the Committee of Imperial Defence also began considering whether the government should provide state insurance for war risks on merchant shipping. Various proposals for government insurance schemes began to be floated, and over the course of the next few years three alternatives emerged: (1) that the war risk insurance should be sold by the private sector, but its cost should be reimbursed by His Majesty's Government, (2) that the government should itself provide insurance against war risk, though not on a profit-making basis, and (3) that the government should "make good" to shipowners the losses from the capture of ships in war. The purpose would be to keep the cost of commodities low and to keep British shippers from laying up in port or transferring to neutral flags as required by their insurance policies.[86] The debate also took into account the fact that the wide availability of inexpensive war risks insurance might put less pressure on the Admiralty to provide shippers with the traditional and expensive response to conflict: naval convoys.

In 1905 the navy feared entanglement in the Russo-Japanese War and expressed mounting concern over the war's impact on shipping. The assistant director of naval intelligence helped prepare plans for a scheme for national insurance, just in case a declaration of war materialized.[87] The design of the proposed program, particularly the specific form of its insurance policy, was directly based on Lloyd's "Standard Form of Marine Policy." The government would be prepared to provide insurance cover for what was excluded from this standard policy under the "free of capture and seizure" exclusion clause.

These fears about the Russo-Japanese War proved to be exaggerated or simplistic, and no government program was necessary. Private insurers offered marine insurance on shipping to Japan at relatively low rates, while high rates were charged on shipping to Russia. They expected Japan to win. Ultimately, however, the insurers lost money on this business, because the Japanese navy had applied the new technology of torpedoes as weapons of war and for the first time used the telegraph system to assist the capture of ships.[88] These losses increased the nervousness of insurers, highlighting once again the possibility that war risks were uninsurable. Afterward most war risks could be insured only through mutual clubs among shippers themselves.[89]

In addition to debating the merits of insurance and indemnity schemes, the Admiralty proposed more direct methods of protecting overseas commerce. In a letter to London insurers intended to reassure them, the Admiralty indicated:

> As you will be aware, anxiety is from time to time displayed by the Mercantile community as to the position of British Commerce in the

event of Great Britain becoming engaged in hostilities, involving the risk of capture and destruction of property at sea. The Lords Commissioners of the Admiralty, recognizing the importance of this question, and desiring in concert in time of peace such measures for the safety of British Commerce as would be called for in the event of war, contemplate including in the Naval Manoevres for 1906 a scheme of attack upon and defence of British Commerce.[90]

In 1907 a commission formed under Treasury direction, headed by Austen Chamberlain, to consider once again proposals for government war risks insurance. This commission, unlike earlier ones, did not recommend such a program, owing to the insuperable administrative difficulties it foresaw. Indemnity programs in particular were viewed by many witnesses before the commission as useless for maintaining commerce. For one thing, dishonest shipowners would be tempted to pursue a loss deliberately in order to obtain an indemnity payment; such a program would exacerbate enormously the moral hazard problem.[91]

A year later and in marked contrast to the Chamberlain commission, the *Report of the Committee on a National Guarantee for the War Risks of Shipping* proposed a national scheme in which the public and private sectors would cooperate in a war risks insurance program. The report pointed out that such a scheme would increase public confidence, encourage continued trade, free the Admiralty of pressures for convoy protection, prevent shippers from staying in port or transferring to a neutral flag, stop a run-up in commodity prices, uphold the supremacy of the British merchant marine, and maintain supplies of food and raw materials. Such optimism about the powers of government-sponsored insurance was unprecedented for the time. Unlike earlier reports, this one noted that anyone involved in shipping during war would be likely to reap huge profits and thus would be fully able to bear the increased insurance rates charged by marine insurers; the price of insurance would not be a barrier to continued commerce. But the report noted the possibility, demonstrated by events during the Russo-Japanese War, that shippers would perceive the capture of their vessels as something of a lucrative market and not as a total loss.[92] A government program would need to be structured in such a way as to minimize the problem of moral hazard, which could lead to unnecessarily large payout on claims.

Another option, articulated in a report by the director of naval intelligence, declared that Great Britain needed to have command of the sea and required protection of all kinds of trade, not just of food. In this view, anything else would be dangerously pacifistic; these individuals feared that the proposal for a Peace Organization floated in 1908 reflected the risky interference of politicians and amateur strategists: "There will always be a large number of demagogues, socialists and traitors, who will agitate for peace at any price."[93] They proposed that the resources of Lloyd's of London and of private shipping intelligence be placed officially at the service of the government as a support to foreign policy (although there was some concern that Lloyd's agents might be foreigners and liable to give false information).

The political debate contained a range of positions on what actions the government should take to make certain that shipping, on which this island nation depended, would be maintained in time of war. Political leaders remained concerned that an insurance program would not help them attain their underlying goal—that vital supplies actually arrive in Britain, and not that their loss be made good. Merchant vessels really required direct naval protection. The Committee on a National Guarantee stated, "No scheme of National Guarantee can compensate for the absence of effective provision for the protection of commerce and of carefully prepared plans of commercial defence."[94] Besides, such guarantees would be unfair to nonshipping interests and would constitute a form of rent to shipowners above what the market would provide.

At the same time, the private insurers expressed their doubts about whether the government could or should establish such a program. In general, they believed that government entry into war risks insurance would be extremely difficult, perhaps impossible. They reasoned that there would be acrimonious disputes between private underwriters and government officials over the exact distinction between sea risks (to be covered by regular insurers) and war risks (to be covered by the government), leading to litigation, confusion, and delay. They argued that government agencies probably would be incapable of immediately paying out on any claims, especially during the course of war, when there would be other, more pressing demands on the Treasury. They also predicted a high level of opportunistic behavior on the part of customers, as government bureaucrats would not have the necessary expertise and information to monitor their behavior. Of course, they also feared competition from government insurance. Although all underwriters opposed government insurance of war risks, those from Lloyd's of London seemed to oppose it most vigorously.[95]

The London war risks insurers tried to control their potential losses on war risks business by limiting rate competition within the industry.

Lloyd's and the companies had established a "rate ruling," which was a cooperative understanding that insurance premium rates would not go below a certain point for that particular type of risk. They anticipated that competition for war risks business could lead to the setting of overly low rates, driving some underwriters out of business. Without competition, and with many underwriters reluctant to insure against war risks, the structure of this portion of the market would become oligopolistic and rates would rise.[96] Not only might this situation lead to superprofits, but in case of loss, it could lead to superlosses: the concentration of liability in a small number of hands would make these insurers very vulnerable. It was at this time, in 1909, that Parliament passed the Assurance Companies Act, requiring insurers to deposit twenty-thousand pounds as a demonstration of their stability and commitment.

The Committee of Imperial Defence began investigations in 1911 into the potential financial consequences of an Anglo-German war (instead of war with France or the United States). Lloyd's had insured a large proportion of the German merchant marine, and its underwriters fully expected to fulfill the terms of their contracts, even if war broke out and even if the losses were caused by the British navy. The Admiralty had planned a strategy of deliberately capturing as many German ships as possible, which would lead to a steady stream of payments from Lloyd's to the Germans.[97] In 1912 the chairman of Lloyd's expressed doubt that the private sector could bear the current level of risk, and underwriters became even more unwilling to sell war risks policies than before.[98] In that same year shipowners organized a number of so-called protecting and indemnity mutual associations, which were the main source of insurance against war risks until war broke out. These associations limited their insurance to vessels actually at sea or in enemy port when war began, and coverage lasted only until they arrived at a British or neutral port. The system essentially encouraged ships to avoid all real war risks. In 1913 about two-thirds of British shipping and 10 percent of cargo was insured against war, and in case of a crisis it was likely that a large amount of shipping would be paralyzed and the sudden skyrocketing of demand for insurance would choke the market.[99] This situation reinforced the arguments of those who favored a government insurance program.

The debate over a possible government insurance program considered not only a variety of administrative options but also some principles on which to base such an effort. The Committee of Imperial Defence put forward the following principles: that the shippers and cargo owners must pay some sort of premium but that the government should not make profits; that it should nevertheless be operated so as to avoid excessive losses and protect against fraud; that it should not antagonize shipowners, insurance brokers and underwriters, merchants and bankers; that it should not look like a "gratuitous gift from the State" to one trade; that it should avoid disclosing information to the enemy through its rate-setting decisions; and that administrative difficulties should be kept to a minimum.[100] All these conditions would take heroic efforts to meet; the committee came to a conclusion that essentially reinforced the arguments of the private sector insurers that the government would not be capable of running such a program.

The committee also preferred that the government administer any war risks through the private war risks associations already in existence. The state program would take 80 percent of King's Enemy Risks, and the remaining portion of political risks would be carried by the associations themselves. The Admiralty would directly monitor and control the movements of insured ships, to guard against their taking unnecessary chances, for instance, by attempting to cross enemy lines. Under this structure, the moral hazard problem would be managed through the authority of the state to coerce the insured shippers. The committee further asserted that once war had been openly declared, war risks should be directly insured by the private war risks associations but would be reinsured by the government.[101] Once again, however, no action was taken and no such program was established.

The committee had conferred with leading private underwriters on how to construct such a war risks insurance scheme, and the results of this report confirm the strength and influence of the private insurance industry in government decision making. Any government scheme would operate in such a way as to complement the extant insurance market and would be based on principles and institutions already developed within the private international risks insurance regime. The primary decisions regarding insurability had already been made by the private sector firms; policymakers simply reacted to their perceptions of what the effects of those decisions would be on the level and geographical extent of that lifeblood of the British Isles—shipping.

The Committee of Imperial Defence continued to debate the pros and cons of government war risks insurance right up until 1914. All knew the outbreak of war was imminent, and war risks insurance on shipping had become almost impossible to obtain unless one belonged to a shipowners' indemnity association, with even the more daring Lloyd's underwriters withdrawing from the market. The members of the committee agreed that any government scheme, which would be established only on the outbreak of war, must have the "hearty support and co-operation of the insurance market." The problem of adverse selection might lead all the poorer risks to take part in the program, making it very expensive, but the committee insisted that the object was not to compete with the private insurers.[102]

The Admiralty, which did not believe that British sea trade would be affected seriously by war, criticized the committee's efforts as amateurish and alarmist. "It is impossible to say exactly what view the Mercantile community and Underwriters will take as to the risks of using ports in the North Sea and the Thames, and it is possible they may be disposed to exaggerate them at first, but as their profits depend on their gauging the risks correctly they are not likely to hesitate long when they know that H.M. Ships are moving freely in those waters."[103] In the two years before World War I the stalemate between those favoring and those opposing government war risks insurance continued to produce more committee reports and no action.

In 1913 the government appointed another committee to look into the effects of war risks on shipping one more time. The Huth Jackson Committee, with prominent participation by a leading member of Lloyd's, decided that the mutual war risks clubs could not be relied on. It recommended that if and when war broke out, the government should immediately accept 80 percent of the war risks on shipping, and government and the mutual clubs should act in concert to provide war risks cover. Cargo insurance would be handled through a separate State Insurance Office.[104] The government would offer a uniform rate for all voyages, and Lloyd's and the insurance companies could continue to provide marine insurance and war risks policies of their own.

The cynical expectation of war at this time was matched by a certain strain of idealism that fueled the pacifist movement so feared by military officials. This pacifist sentiment spilled over into some unusual and impractical insurance proposals. A leading American proposed that states insure one another against war through an international insurance organization, thus preventing the initiation of war as against their own interests: "My thesis is that whenever insurance of the nations, by the nations, and for the nations begins, it will henceforth never vanish from the face of the earth, but will begin to make visible to us the holy city of the community of all mankind."[105] The notion that any state would be deterred from declaring war because its opponent would receive a war claim payment seems laughable, but the proposal was put forth in all seriousness.

When war at last broke out, the private market, as predicted, could not handle the scale of protection required by British commerce. As one observer noted, "if commerce had been left in the hands of the market, it would have been embarrassed and checked at every turn."[106] Not only was the insurance market essential for covering marine risks, but the crisis revealed the degree to which the financial security given by insurance encouraged the banks to extend the credit on which voyages were launched. Given the disastrous consequences if trade ceased, the government finally stepped in. From 1914 to 1918 the government operated war risks insurance and indemnity plans for ships, cargo, and even aircraft bombardment.[107] The government initially set rates uniformly across all risks, which led to heavy losses in some areas, such as cargo war risks, and profits in others, such as for bombing losses. The insurance companies and Lloyd's competed vigorously for business on those shipping routes that the government overpriced, and generally profited from the war.

Throughout the conflict the British government intervened directly in the economy in order to support the war effort, as we can see from the decision to establish war risks insurance programs. The underwriters at Lloyd's forcefully expressed their desire that this intervention promptly halt at the cessation of hostilities, though they acknowledged the country would require government aid for reconstruction. Thinking ahead, the London insurers questioned government officials concerning how enemy insurers would be treated after the war, when all insurers would renew their international operations.[108]

A postwar assessment of the government schemes remarked on the success they had in preventing many of the feared reactions to war. Commerce went on despite enemy attack, international credit continued to support British shipping activity, and imports of food and supplies were maintained without prices rising to famine levels. The existence of the schemes, however, may have masked to the general populace the actual cost of war and provided a false sense of security to everyone, including the Admiralty, which had reacted slowly to the dangers of German submarine warfare.[109]

International Commerce and Political Risks

Demand, norms, and resources each played a role in the development of an international risks insurance regime in the late nineteenth century. This regime consisted of commercial insurers—individual underwriters, joint stock companies, and mutual associations—that established cooperative associations among themselves and attempted to negotiate common contract terms for the insurance business. The principles and norms of the regime from 1870 to 1914 established a relatively limited definition of insurability and clearly delineated the boundaries within which the insurers themselves had jurisdictional competence, leaving little or no room for a government role.

The demand for some sort of protection from international risks escalated at the turn of the century. In the late 1800s the commercial sector became more and more uncertain that it could rely for protection abroad on British political and military power. In the early years of the new century war among the great powers seemed inevitable. Shipping interests in particular began to plan for the coming conflict by raising the issue of what would happen to them, and to the nation, if shipping was disrupted by war or the fear of war. Throughout this period their concerns generated an increasing demand for war risks insurance. While the demand for war risks insurance steadily rose, the question of who would be a reliable supplier became a subject of debate.

By the early part of the nineteenth century London had become the most active and well-established insurance market in the world, especially for marine insurance. As Fernand Braudel has argued, leading cities throughout history have had a variety of "weapons of domination," among which he included shipping, trade, industry, credit, political power, violence—and insurance.[110] London seemed to have control in all these areas. Within the British insurance industry Lloyd's of London and the royal monopoly insurance companies, joined later by the company market in general, cooperated in setting up numerous associations and committees through which the industry dealt with common problems such as salvage on shipping. Lloyd's and the major companies established standard guidelines for writing insurance contracts, in which they defined what was insurable and what must be excluded. At the same time as the shipping industry began to expect the outbreak of war, however, the insurers began to expect the outbreak of *modern* war. In order to limit the amount they could lose, the insurers sought to separate traditional marine risks from political ones and developed standard marine insurance clauses that excluded the latter. They declared war risks to be basically uninsurable or insurable only under a special exception, requiring special rates and terms. As political tensions increased and threats to shipping became imminent, war risks could be insured only by membership in a mutual association of shipowners, in which the behavior of the shippers could be closely monitored to restrain them from taking unncessary risks.

The nineteenth-century insurance underwriters grew wealthy in a very profitable industry. Once the royal monopolies ended in the early part of the century, competition in London increased, but Lloyd's retained its position as the leading marine insurer because of its expertise, information sources, and reputation. Its capacity to insure modern risks could have been restricted by two factors: the extent to which it could limit costs by influencing the behavior of customers, and the limits of its reliance on the financial reserves of each individual member. The latter resource constraint was solved ingeniously at the turn of the century with the institutional innovation of allowing syndicates of members to pool their resources. The former depended on the ability of underwriters to develop contracts that both appealed to the customers and limited their risk-proneness. Both Lloyd's and the companies managed this aspect of their business through more sophisticated policy terms and rates, including the decision to separate marine and war risks insurance in order to avoid the dire consequences of modern warfare. In addition, the insurers designed marine policies that directed insured ships to pull into the nearest friendly or neutral port on the outbreak of war, reducing the likelihood they would come under attack. These standard policy terms constituted the norms of the industry regarding what is an insurable risk and legitimate claim.

The British government became increasingly concerned in the early years of the twentieth century with the relationship among shipping, food and raw material supplies, and insurance. Officials established numerous special committees to explore this subject, led by prominent political and military leaders. If the norms of the insurance industry propelled the shipping industry to retreat from its business at the threat or outbreak of war, the political leadership feared the results would be a cessation of British access to food and raw materials at reasonable prices and the potential for severe domestic instability as a result. At the same time, the insurance industry repeatedly stated that war risks generally were uninsurable, and most government officials accepted this proposition. British leaders did not automatically consider the state liable for the risks of its merchants abroad, even though the island nation depended so heavily on its shipping industry. But given an imminent war and British reliance on foreign markets for vital supplies of food and raw materials, political leaders found themselves debating the merits of an insurance program as a way to maintain shipping during war. They were driven to this solution in part by the reluctance of private insurers to provide sufficient levels of war risks coverage to meet demand and by their insistence that shippers adhere to strict rules guiding their behavior on the outbreak of war. The political debate reflected an internalization of private sector beliefs about insurability, with leading participants arguing that the government had no role in insurance; instead, British military power was the ultimate protection for the mercantile fleet.

The years leading up to World War I can be characterized as a slow, deliberately paced, and somewhat unthinking movement toward "political market failure," as states failed to restrain their political and military competition and thus produced new and onerous risks for overseas commerce. Such political failures were followed by an economic market failure, as insurers severely limited the amount and types of insurance they would sell, especially for war risks. Finally, on the outbreak of war, the government stepped in as the "insurer of last resort." Over the course of the twentieth century, as we see in the next two chapters, changes in customer demand and the norms and financial resources of insurers, both public and private, would repeatedly challenge the growing international risks insurance regime. As the relationship between the government and the insurers evolved, in Britain and elsewhere, there gradually occurred a shift in power and resources between them within the regime. Whereas the government had almost no role in the establishment of the regime, it became a steadily more important participant over the course of the next century. The institutionalization of insurance practices defined a line between public and private sector responsibilities in the protection of commerce, a line that became increasingly blurred in the late twentieth century.

3/ *Testing the Limits of Private Protection, 1917–1939*

With hindsight it seems as if every event following the Great War acted as prelude to the next war. The great powers repeatedly attempted to put the pieces of the old order back together again without success. Negotiations over international monetary affairs, naval armaments competition, and the issues of debt and reparations payments produced conflict and not cooperation. By the early 1930s most efforts to promote or even simply maintain foreign trade, credit, and investment relationships met formidable barriers generated by the unsettled political relationships among and within states.

Against this background of international uncertainty, the international risks insurance regime both expanded and changed. Insurers responded to the environment by devising new products to meet demand and by modifying their perception of what was insurable. Governments stepped into this market in peacetime for the first time but attempted to do so in a way that meshed with the norms and institutions previously established by the private sector. London remained at the center of the international risks insurance business well into this period, even as British economic and political power waned in other areas. The inability or unwillingness of governments to provide for the safe conduct of overseas commerce, and the failure of interstate negotiations to resolve outstanding conflicts, led to a "political market failure" as each state pursued its own ends to the detriment of all.

During this waiting period between the wars commercial insurers became adept at creating new forms of insurance and developing the contract terms that would allow them to pursue new markets profitably. The community of British shippers, banks, and insurers maintained a relatively high degree of stability in its international economic activity, even with the political uncertainties of the time. Lipson argues that foreign investment during this period was relatively secure despite British political weakness, because the activities of these private sector actors supported it.[1] Among insurers, political risk no longer was an adjunct to marine risks; specialist underwriters began to cover a wider range of commercial transactions against political misfortune, including exports, export credit, and eventually investments. In their eagerness and initial inexperience, they misjudged their own risks and nearly undermined the entire industry. Their failure to protect themselves against extremely high losses, despite their well-developed system of information gathering and dissemination and a general consensus over insurance norms, depleted their financial resources. The insurance community, prodded by the market leaders at Lloyd's, ultimately redefined specific political risks as uninsurable and created a stronger international regime as a result. The norms promulgated by the private sector determined widely accepted prohibitions on particular practices, leading to complete withdrawal from the market and a real market failure.[2]

After the war only a handful of British insurers covered political risks. It was during this period that underwriters at Lloyd's of London became noted not just for their sterling reputation but also for their willingness to develop new forms of specialized insurance, such as for political risks and reinsurance. Lloyd's dominated this market, spurring innovations in insurance products and establishing the rules and norms of the insurance underwriting business. The major London insurance companies competed with Lloyd's and cooperated among themselves in the Association of British Insurers, but on many common issues they tended to follow the lead of Lloyd's.

The political debate in the 1920s and 1930s over the role of the government in providing political risks insurance echoed the arguments heard before World War I. Many policymakers questioned the need for government intervention, given the existence of a private market and a still powerful British presence abroad. The debate also began to include a growing realization that Britain had to remain competitive in foreign markets and that it was in the national interest for the government to help British firms. Technological innovations had increased the potential size and duration of projects, straining the capacity of the private insurers to insure them. The very strength of the private sector regime in limiting what was considered insurable also opened an area for public provision of political risks insurance.

Britain in the World

Several features of the period from the end of World War I to the decision by Great Britain to rearm in preparation for World War II shaped the debate over the appropriate response to threats to foreign commerce. These features directly affected the level of demand for protection from international risks. First, the relative decline in British power in the world gave government leaders an incentive to promote and support commerce without using military force. Second, the government's financial weakness after World War I limited its policy options, especially in war debt and reparations negotiations, and was one more indicator of Britain's diminished international influence. Third, leading decision makers in the British government perceived the nation to be increasingly vulnerable to German political and economic ambitions, heightening the perception that the environment had become especially uncertain. The British navy could no longer be relied on to protect international commerce, and no alternative powerful state was willing to replace the British by providing similar security.

Until World War I, Great Britain maintained world order through its possession of empire, its naval supremacy, and its actions as a power balancer on the Continent. Its position facilitated the expansion of its economy, which in turn could support the British global role. The British economy had generated great wealth through industrialization and trade, and British merchants invested their surplus capital around the world. Nevertheless, economic indicators began to turn against Britain even during the period of its greatest power. The British share of world trade had declined between 1876 and 1913. Its share of world imports of primary products alone dropped from 30 percent to 20 percent, and its share of world manufacturing exports went from 40 percent to 25 percent.[3] During the war the British essentially liquidated many of their assets abroad to finance the war effort. Even though they won the war, they lost the battle in terms of the strength and competitiveness of their economy. The current account turned negative as the trade deficit worsened, invisibles trade stagnated, and gold was drained out of the economy (see Table 3.1).

British foreign policymakers immediately following the war believed

Table 3.1. British Overseas Trade, 1920–1938 (in millions of pounds)

Year	Merchandise Trade	Investment Earnings	Invisibles Trade	Bullion Specie	Balance on Current Account
1920	−386	+200	+395	+43	+252
1922	−183	+175	+150	+13	+155
1923	−210	+200	+148	+16	+153
1924	−337	+220	+190	+12	+86
1925	−393	+250	+188	+10	+54
1926	−463	+250	+100	−12	−26
1927	−386	+250	+219	−3	+79
1928	−352	+250	+225	−7	+117
1929	−382	+250	+223	+16	+25
1930	−386	+220	+194	+33	−70
1931	−407	+170	+134	+33	−70
1932	−286	+150	+86	−17	−67
1933	−258	+160	+103	−201	−196
1934	−284	+170	+117	−142	−139
1935	−275	+185	+108	−56	−38
1936	−346	+200	+127	−227	−246
1937	−431	+210	+176	−99	−144
1938	−388	+200	+122	+74	+8

Source: Brian R. Mitchell and Phyllis Deane, *Abstract of British Historical Statistics* (Cambridge: Cambridge University Press, 1971), p. 335.

the major foreign issues they faced were how to deal with the United States and Japan in the Far East and how to negotiate Franco-German relations (or nonrelations, really). The United States, an increasingly industrialized competitor, had been pressing for an "open door" in China since the turn of the century in order to generate more trade across the Pacific. With regard to its former continental role, British policy-makers sincerely believed it would be possible to bring Germany back into normal interstate political relations, at the same time as they were reluctant to become directly involved in continental disputes. British policy firmly opposed any type of military guarantees in Europe, thus ensuring continued French intransigence over the German question.[4]

In any case, just after the end of the war, few foresaw the eventual loss of power by the British. After all, Great Britain had won the war triumphantly and still maintained a glorious empire.[5] British statesmen fully expected to lead the economic and naval conferences of the early 1920s that would determine the character of the postwar international political economy. For example, at the Genoa Conference of 1922 British pressure persuaded the participants to reinstate the gold standard, in accord with the preferences of financiers in the City of London. The conference at Genoa represented an attempt to return to the London-centered system of the prewar years. The most significant attempt by Britain to reassert its prewar dominance occurred in 1925 when it restored the convertibility of the pound sterling at prewar rates. This policy had disastrous consequences for the British, however. Gold reserves declined as investors fled the weak British economy for the dynamic and profitable investments of the New York Stock Exchange.

Before the war the world economy had expanded in part because of the growing use of sterling as a key currency, its stability backed by the high standards of British financial houses.[6] Even though Britain lost its dominance in manufacturing by the turn of the century, the growth of world trade put extensive demands on the services provided by the City of London. Britain still perceived itself as the center of the international credit system, and continental states still turned first to London for financial help. For instance, British financiers assisted the new European states established after the breakup of the Austro-Hungarian Empire in setting up central banks and national financial systems. Occupying the center of an international credit system can be a precarious position, however, producing an economy sensitive to external shocks.[7]

British government finances had been devastated by the resources needed to prosecute World War I, and the lack of money increasingly determined British foreign and defense policy during the 1920s and early 1930s. The British Admiralty continually expressed concern about the health of the merchant marine and shipping in general and considered arming them even in peace to supplement government forces. The Treasury Department consistently sought to restrain military spending. By concluding the agreements of the Washington Naval Conference of 1921–22, British policymakers hoped to avoid an expensive naval race with Japan and the United States in the Far East and the Pacific. Domestic issues increased in visibility and importance in government debates even as the influence of the Foreign Office declined. Diplomacy overall was eclipsed.[8]

And yet events throughout the world repeatedly threatened British interests, and government leaders fully expected the next war to be a global one. British policymakers, in the words of Phillip Darby, "were confronted with a political climate less prepared than ever before to see military power as the basis of security, and with defence expenditure as the most obvious target for economies in spending; on the other, a kaleidoscope of threats and problems which, seen through the eyes of British strategists, spanned half the world."[9] The United States, the only other state capable of taking a leading role, meanwhile retreated into isolationism in military and economic affairs. Worse, it participated in the international credit system in a negative manner through its insistence on the repayment of war debts by its former allies.

British commercial interests and sympathetic politicians wanted more than ever to maintain markets abroad, especially in China and southern Europe.[10] The Treasury, the Board of Trade, and the Bank of England were the establishment institutions that pressed most strongly for the liberalization of trade and maintenance of a strong currency. One writer described the City financial-mercantile interests at this time as hierarchical in structure, unified in outlook, and disciplined by an unwritten code.[11] At the same time as business interests united to support expansive foreign economic activity, politicians could count on a growing consensus on retreating from political commitments abroad and avoiding another war at any cost. Great Britain had nothing to gain and almost everything to lose from another war. A Foreign Office memorandum stated, "The fact is that war and rumors of war, quarrels and friction, in any corner of the world spell loss and harm to British commercial and financial interests."[12] Despite this sentiment, Great Britain contributed little to world economic stability during the 1920s.[13] Increasing uncertainty about the political and economic durability of the Versailles settlements that ended the war eventually destroyed business confidence in the system itself.

The wrench in the interwar system was the status of Germany. Economically, it was the largest single debtor of the 1920s, although at the same time, international capital flows favored it.[14] At first, German debts consisted mainly of sovereign obligations, particularly reparations payments, but eventually they included loans from commercial banks and investment houses. Americans and Europeans invested in Germany in the belief that German government spending for reconstruction would be successful and profitable. As the economy weakened, business confidence that the debts would be repaid failed, and capital flows turned against Germany. This led to repeated attempts to renegotiate the reparations payments, linked to negotiations over inter-allied debt, right up to the collapse of the economic system in the Great Depression. The negotiations resulting in the Dawes Plan in 1924 and the Young Plan in 1929, both of which attempted to settle outstanding issues regarding debt and reparations payments, were only temporarily successful. The British, despite repeated efforts, could not bring its allies France and the United States into agreement on the status of Germany.

Thus, both politically and economically, the perception was of a weakened British position in the world. The isolationism of the Americans contributed to a growing concern over the stability of the international system and the possibility that peaceful commerce would not be sustained. Business interests reacted by increasing their demand for protection from international risks throughout this period.

Insurance and Foreign Economic Affairs

We can characterize the period between the world wars by the absence of international political leadership; increasing economic stress, domestic and international; and rising levels of risk. All these structural factors directly affected the individual entrepreneurs and investors engaged in international commerce. Sheer lack of information exacerbated the perception of risk in international transactions. For instance, one analyst noted that the British government had little solid economic information about commercial conditions abroad, even for its prize possession, India.[15]

In the face of such uncertainty, insurers introduced new methods of risk reduction for trading, lending, and investing abroad and directly engaged in economic diplomacy. The centuries leading up to the twentieth had been ones of intense activity in developing financial practices and institutions to support increasing levels of commerce. Britain led the world in developing these new services and supplying them in tandem with its manufactured exports, assuring the place of the City of London as the center of global finance. From 1917 to 1939 British international risks insurers actively participated in the political and economic decisions regarding trade, credit, and investment in the Far East; negotiations over the extension of credit to the Soviet Union; the settlement of debt and reparations issues with Germany; and the fallout from the Spanish Civil War. The insurers began to explore a broader range of potential risks to international commerce beyond war risks on shipping, developing insurance for export credit risks and expanding the risks covered in both political risks insurance and reinsurance policies.

The insurance industry maintained a unique relationship with the British Foreign Office. The international insurers and the diplomatic service both relied on a constant and accurate supply of information about events and personalities in every location of the world. The London insurance market and the Foreign Office regularly exchanged information relevant to each other's interests. In the early period following the war the exchanges between the Foreign Office and insurance underwriters often dealt with the remittance of premiums and claims payments across national borders, what kinds of payments were allowed under the German Peace Treaty, and what money needed to pass through the British Clearing House.[16] The insurers desired to know whether war risk marine insurance was recoverable under the Versailles Treaty. The final peace treaties included provisions regarding such insurance business as the proper division of premium deposits between Austria and the successor states to the Austro-Hungarian Empire.

In addition to such technical inquiries, Lloyd's of London actively pressed the Foreign Office to appoint the people it preferred to British consulates in foreign ports. In return, the extensive network of Lloyd's agents in those same foreign ports collected detailed information on local conditions, which Lloyd's shared with the Foreign Office. The Foreign Office also facilitated the operation of the private insurance market by supplying information on the status of ships after the war. For example, the Foreign Office made available the lists of ships that had been transferred from the Crimea to France in 1923, clarifying ownership, which helped marine insurers settle claims for losses on these ships.[17]

During the 1920s growing trade and investment in the Soviet Union and Asia brought new risk and competition in overseas commerce. The 1930s witnessed an increased concern for political and military crises in the Far East, and also closer to home in Spain. During this period private insurers began aggressively to pursue markets for both export credit insurance and war risks insurance. At the same time, out of its longstanding concern over the continuation of shipping during war and the additional worry over economic competition, the British government for the first time established an export credit and investment guarantee agency. By the end of the decade, as world war engulfed all Europe, the demand for political risks insurance heightened dramatically, revealing both the strengths and weaknesses of the regime. The patterns of commerce had changed, along with the role of the state in promoting it. The commercial insurers confronted a transformed political and economic environment, in which they modified the traditional norms defining and restricting political risks insurance in order to capture new markets. In the delicate balance between strict adherence to a narrow definition of insurable risk and competition to expand their activities, the insurers deeply affected their own financial resources and ultimately changed the relationship between public and private sectors in the provision of international risks insurance.

Credit and Contracts with Russia and Asia, 1917–1931

After the end of the war the economies of Europe and the United States boomed at first. Producers geared up to meet newly released consumer demand, and employment and eventually prices rose as well. The rapid inflation created pressure on governments to rein it in, and British efforts to do so, including fiscal restrictions and higher interest rates, led to a sharp and sudden rise in unemployment. Many people began to lobby for a restoration of the prewar gold standard, which had done so much to maintain stable economic relations and promote trade and investment. It was hoped that the return to the gold standard would allow for lower exchange rates and thus promote exports.[18] By 1924, export levels still had reached only about three-quarters of their prewar volume.[19] In 1925 the government returned the pound to convertibility, but for political reasons did so at high, prewar levels. Unfortunately, the export industries would bear much of the burden of the overvalued currency, limiting their competitiveness and stimulating debate within the government over alternative means for promoting exports.

The experience of World War I legitimated and increased the numbers and types of government intervention in the economy, despite numerous interests arrayed against any expansion of its role. The City financial interests adhered to traditional laissez-faire economic prescriptions for British financial problems and lobbied hard to maintain independence from government strictures. As Peter Gourevitch points out, business circles debated the merits of orthodox policies such as free trade, deflation, and defense of the pound compared with relatively minor deviations in the realm of protectionism and cartelization. In general, the business community rejected government intervention in the economy. It also supported attempts by British policymakers to retain a dominant role for Britain in international politics. For instance, bankers, shippers, and insurers all urged the government to maintain the value of the convertible pound at a high rate, a key symbolic measure of British power.[20]

Despite this general commitment to nonintervention, government leaders debated a variety of proposals for insurance schemes during this time, focusing on two issues: the long-standing concern with the insurance of war risks on shipping and a new concern for insurance on trade as means to support the export industries. As in the prewar debates, officials feared the cutoff of shipping during war not just from enemy actions but from the natural inclinations of business simply to stop operating in a theater of war. In addition, private insurers had made clear that they would not cover war risks once Britain formally declared war, thus further encouraging shippers to cease shipping and leaving a problem for the government to resolve.

Concern by many over opening new markets abroad and retaining access to old ones led to proposals for government loans to merchants conducting business in politically uncertain areas, combined with government export credit insurance. Immediately after World War I the British tried to reestablish the overseas trade of the United Kingdom, at first showing particular concern for trade with central and southeastern Europe. One element of these efforts centered on government authorization for the Board of Trade to grant £26 million in trade credits and to insure or reinsure trade where risks were "abnormal."[21] Thus, the board established the first government export credit and credit insurance program in 1919, eventually known as the Export Credit and Guarantees Department (ECGD) under the authority of the Board of Trade. The founders believed that the government could not let British exports decline further and that providing credit and insurance would promote British trade.

The purpose of the Export Credits Scheme was to extend credits and insurance for those overseas business ventures that a private firm might hesitate to undertake. It was modeled on the export credit insurance program already operated by the Trade Indemnity Corporation (TIC), a private firm that pioneered this market in 1918. A potential exporter might consider a particular transaction too risky for private insurance at a decent rate or for proper financing at all. The ECGD would step in by guaranteeing bills that a bank might be reluctant to discount because of the risk involved. In these cases, the exporter, through a bank, would turn to the ECGD to complete the financing and insurance of the proposed export transactions.[22]

The Export Credits Scheme and its related guarantees (credit insurance) were designed not to compete for business with the private sector. The TIC, for instance, covered domestic business, United Kingdom shipping, and selected other business; merchants who were unable to obtain coverage from TIC could often succeed with the ECGD.[23] Medium- and long-term business was most likely to be covered by the ECGD, whereas short-term projects remained the province of the private market. Both agencies carefully defined their business as complementary and not competitive.

The insurance companies and Lloyd's of London profited from an expansion of business following the war. Lloyd's insurance business in general (not just insurance for international risks) grew tremendously, with its membership doubling and turnover increasing from £3 million to approximately £12 or £13 million pounds by 1922.[24] The overall market for political risks insurance expanded in the 1920s, although no specific figures exist.[25] At the same time, in order to limit their own financial risks, the underwriters of the London companies and at Lloyd's did not always offer every war risk policy they theoretically had on the books. For example, in 1922 Lloyd's did not renew policies in Constantinople because Turkey had rejected the Treaty of Sèvres, and it refused to cover some shipments of war matériel from France. Without overall political guarantees, such as those given in political settlements following the war, many underwriters were reluctant to provide insurance for international risks.

Much of the correspondence between the Foreign Office and the insurers during this period concerned the arms trade. Insurance on arms transfers was a lucrative business during the 1920s. Although this coverage was not explicitly for a "political" risk but simply insurance on property in transit, it had political significance, especially in view of the embargoes the League of Nations and individual states had imposed on arms shipments to certain countries, particularly China. The insurers generally informed the Foreign Office when someone asked for insurance or reinsurance on arms transfers, thus providing the government with a good idea of the pattern of arms sales; the Foreign Office in return informed the insurers of the exact interpretations of agreements and embargoes concerning the arms trade.[26]

One issue that came up repeatedly was how to deal with the new Soviet government. When it came to credit, British policy was to deny any official credits so long as the communists refused to pay the debts of previous governments or otherwise compensate losses. Even had a debt agreement been concluded, however, the officials of the British Board of Trade doubted that any credit should be extended; they felt that there could be no guarantee of business security under the Soviet system, given its repudiation of private property rights. The statutes of the Export Credits and Trade Facilities schemes did not expressly forbid applying them to Russia; successive British governments simply declared that no credit should go to Russia until it had repaid old debts and that guarantees would be useless in the case of a communist economy.[27] This assessment was based both on political fears and on the perception that the Soviet economy was weak and unstable. In the 1920s the rules of eligibility for export trade credit and insurance technically applied to the whole world, but administratively, Russia was ruled out on these counts.[28] Thus, the British government deliberately circumscribed its participation in the market for political risks insurance on Soviet trade and credit.

The Treasury Department, with the backing of the banks and some in the manufacturing community, supported the ban on government sponsored credit to Russia. No private banks granted credits longer than six months.[29] The ECGD Advisory Committee, which approved all credit and guarantees, was made up chiefly of representatives of the banks.[30] The president of the Dresdner Bank feared that the Soviet government might play one country against another and that all states trading with Russia should agree together to refuse credit. Even had the government export credits and guarantees been extended to Russian business, the Board of Trade and the ECGD felt they would be little used. Very high premiums would be charged on these risks, and any bank would feel obliged to discourage its customers from participating.[31]

The doubts about Russian business rested on numerous perceived risk factors. Trade with the Russians meant trade directly with the Soviet government, which had not yet met the conditions for resumption of credit. Also, the type of long-term credits typically requested did not appear to match actual Russian needs. Then as always, the backing for Russian credits depended largely on the agricultural harvest, which remained unpredictable as a source of income. Finally, there existed continuing doubt over whether it would be possible for creditors, including the British government, to take over Russian property in case of default. All these factors, despite the technical feasibility of particular projects, made the political risk too high to countenance.[32] Nevertheless, British manufacturers repeatedly sought out Russian business and even applied for ECGD support for it, although to no avail.

In 1925 several new developments that affected British economic activity generated responses by the insurance community, including the official government guarantee agency. First, this was the year the pound became convertible again, producing heightened concern among export industries over their ability to remain competitive. Second, Britain had embargoed arms sales to China, and the government demanded that insurers also abide by the embargo. Some insurers questioned whether His Majesty's government had the legal power to prevent insurance on arms sent to China; the arms embargo had never been implemented effectively. Lloyd's also inquired as to the government's attitude toward insurance on European shipments of arms—shipments that the British government forbade. Under pressure, the insurers agreed to government demands that they not insure arms bound for China, although they continued to insure arms shipments bound for other places. Third, and most dramatically, unemployment levels reached a politically unsustainable point, resulting in riots and strikes that culminated in the General Strike of 1926.

From 1925 until the close of the decade the perception of instability and economic weakness could be seen most clearly in the financial markets. By the late 1920s all global capital movements had declined by about 35 percent.[33] European stock markets had turned down beginning in 1927. U.S. lending steadily declined in 1928–29, and the reversal of business confidence culminated in the Wall Street crash and the drastic curtailment of capital outflows. U.K. lending also then declined in 1929–30, and finally in 1931 the pound sterling was devalued.[34] In the debates over how to restore the economy the British Treasury opposed the Bank of England in arguing that the bank needed to lower the cost of credit and increase its availability. Instead, political leaders focused on how to stimulate employment and economic growth by rationalizing industry and promoting export growth.[35]

As labor unrest depressed production and exports, some firms were willing to contemplate almost any type of overseas business in order to stay afloat. We can see this most clearly in the hearty welcome given a Soviet trade mission visiting Britain in 1925. British textile machinery producers, who were negotiating with the Soviet trade mission despite all warnings against this business, applied unsuccessfully to the Export Credits Scheme for assistance. They believed that their Soviet contracts provided for a British court decision in the event of default, in which case Soviet property in Great Britain would be liable to confiscation in lieu of repayment. This belief proved to be unfounded, but it reflects the eagerness of British manufacturers to seek out business abroad.[36]

In September 1925 one textile machinery manufacturer successfully concluded a one-hundred-thousand-pound agreement with the Russian trade mission. Even the chairman of the board of that company stated, however, "There is no use blinding our eyes to the fact that trading with Russia today is in the nature of an adventure."[37] Such deals with the depressed British textile machinery industry totaled some eight hundred thousand pounds in the mid-1920s, with options for more. The security offered by the Russians for credit in the financing package for these deals was a guarantee from either the Russian State Bank or Russian Bank for Foreign Trade. Newspaper accounts indicated that the severe slump in the textile industry was leading British manufacturers to make speculative agreements with Russia in something close to desperation.[38]

Despite grave doubts even among the participants, at least one government official speculated that British firms taking Russian orders probably found it very profitable to extend credit for such transactions. City interests remained firmly set against the extension of these credits by the government itself, however.[39] As stated in a memorandum of the Advisory Committee of the ECGD, if the ECGD opened its facilities to Russia, it would look as if the British condoned Russian conduct in seizing foreign property. Such a position would go against British values, for Great Britain stands for "the sanctity of contract in finance and commerce."[40]

Not all groups agreed with the government position on Soviet trade. Workers demonstrating at Birkenhead in June 1925 demanded that the government assist international trade in order to relieve domestic unemployment. They specifically asked that the government reopen negotiations with the Russian government to promote increased trade.[41] Conservative politicians worried that the Labour Party would politically oppose restrictions on Soviet business. Members of the Board of Trade noted that many of the same firms that had lost business from the Russian Revolution were now willing to forgo principle and take the risk of reestablishing trade and investment links with the Soviets. Opposed to these firms were the banks, accused by some of sacrificing commerce and industry for their own interests, which centered on the repayment of debt or compensation for losses. There was particular concern within the ECGD that, were the scheme opened to Russian business, there would be endless trouble every time it turned down a Russian application for any reason.[42] During a period of deep economic crisis the issue of trade with Russia, with all the obvious political risks it entailed, put the government in a difficult position regarding its role in protecting and promoting commerce. Conflicts over relations with the Soviets reflected the deepest political divisions within British society at that time.

Private insurers, though not as directly affected by the political debate, also found Soviet business problematic. Many merchant ships, nationalized by the Soviet government, had been taken from Russian ports and unlawfully detained abroad, leaving their status and the status of political risks insurance claims based on their loss uncertain.[43] All disputes over Soviet business had to be settled in Russia, which made it difficult to pursue claims. Despite these problems, some private insurers covered a portion of Russian business. The Trade Indemnity Company, for instance, insured credit on certain Russian business but compensated for the uncertainty of it by charging extremely high rates.[44] But in general, despite high demand, the commercial insurers limited their involvement in Soviet business transactions.

In the case of credits and credit insurance, both the government and private sector agencies defined business with the Soviets in the 1920s as an uninsurable risk. The government restricted coverage administratively, and the private sector restricted coverage through its pricing policies. Businesses had to bear the risks alone when trading with the Soviets. Since they had such limited access to credit and insurance, British manufacturers concluded few agreements with the new Soviet government, despite their eagerness to do so.

At the same time as these debates over economic relations with Russia, markets in Asia also captured the attention of policymakers and commercial interests. During World War I Britain had sold off many of its investments in Asia to pay for the war effort, so British importance as a source of capital had been eroded. Throughout the 1920s the level of capital outflows from London steadily declined. At first, because of colonial ties, this weakening of Britain's position did not directly affect its economic relations with Asia. The political debate, as noted, was preoccupied with potential threats from Soviet Russia and to a certain degree neglected political and economic developments in the Far East.[45] But Britain found itself increasingly in competition with other states, including the United States, for access to overseas markets, especially in Asia. The political leadership, committed to encouraging British investors and exporters to pursue business in Asia, expanded government export credit and guarantee programs to maintain a foothold against competitors.

The British Admiralty believed one of the main threats to commerce in Asia was the continuing problem of piracy. Standard marine insurance contracts contain protection against piracy, but the dangers to shipping in Asian waters discouraged growing trade. An even more serious problem in the region, however, was Japanese military expansion and occupation, which explicitly aimed to restrict access to Asian markets. The British no longer had the capacity to project military power in the Far East in order to protect their interests. To manage their overseas risks, British trade and shipping had to rely on the private sector insurers for marine insurance, with or without war risks coverage. The ECGD, established principally for export credit and insurance, had only limited ability to address the kinds of political risks facing British business in Asia. The only tools the government had for promoting economic activity in Asia—its navy and its credit and guarantee programs—proved to be ineffective.

Despite problems with government trade credit and insurance for politically risky transactions in the Soviet Union and the Far East, the export credit insurance business grew during the 1920s. The originator of this insurance product, the Trade Indemnity Corporation, continued to expand its business around the globe. Others in Britain and abroad also entered the market. In 1928 the nine private export credit insurers in existence established the International Credit Insurance Association (ICIA) to rationalize the development of credit insurance by harmonizing the terms of contracts and the practices of the industry. The ICIA never gained much authority, however, as the insurers could not reach agreement on the extent of its role. As the government in Britain and then governments elsewhere began to promote exports more vigorously through their insurance programs, the focus of attention would shift to other issues and arenas, as described in the following chapter.

Turning Point: Political and Economic Instability, 1931–1936

Financial collapse in the United States in 1929 radically contracted the outflow of capital from there to the rest of the world, and global economic activity collapsed. British leaders, particularly at the Treasury, worried about the cost and availability of credit for industry. John Maynard Keynes, among others, considered tariffs and export bounties a solution to the economic slump. In a striking reversal of its long-standing position, the British government in 1931 tried to stimulate the economy by devaluing the pound and then letting it float, amid a series of bank failures abroad and payments imbalances at home.[46] In the ensuing years the British turned decisively toward a system of imperial preferences, and many of their former trading partners began pursuing competitive devaluations and tariff retaliation. For Britain, trade in invisibles, including insurance, declined for the next few years and only weakly recovered (see Table 3.1).

As the debate over export credits and insurance for Soviet business continued to demonstrate, it became increasingly difficult to untangle the multiple forces behind British export promotion and risk reduction via its government insurance program. The government authorized greater amounts of export credit insurance in the late 1920s and early 1930s to alleviate the general economic problems of the depression at home, to manage the compartmentalization of global economic affairs caused by trade and tariff wars and rival exchange rate blocs,[47] and to respond to the perception that commerce had become subject to loss and failure from myriad political events. The crisis in Great Britain, as elsewhere, forced the government to intervene directly in the economy to cushion the shocks of a failing system.

Only with the onset of economic depression beginning in 1929 were export credit guarantees finally extended by the ECGD to Soviet business.[48] In 1929 guarantees covered £887,000 in exports; in 1930 this figure rose to £4,841,000 and in 1931 to £8,472,000—an astounding rate of growth. The ECGD estimated that little of this trade would exist without government guarantees.[49] But public protection and promotion of business with the Soviets stirred up much debate in Parliament. In 1930 one critic said, "I think anyone who gives further credits to Russia requires mental treatment"; on the opposite side a supporter of Soviet guarantees declared, "Russia is one of the most wonderful markets in the world."[50] It would not be until 1936 that, by a special White Paper, the Export Credit Guarantee Department finally was permitted to guarantee promissory notes issued by the Soviet government itself (and not just credit extended to British exporters).

Less controversially, government leaders promoted trade in Asia through such efforts as extending agricultural credits to India and Ceylon in 1928 and 1931.[51] But farther east, the confused and conflict-ridden political situation posed numerous dilemmas for British interests. Tokyo accused London of enmity and worried about encirclement by hostile forces, and invaded and occupied Manchuria in 1931. Great Britain advanced a moderate policy of avoiding direct antagonism of Japan; it attempted to maintain its traditional commercial and political ties in southern China and East Asia despite Japanese military involvement in northern China.[52] The United States, meanwhile, continued to have strong economic ties with Japan until the eve of war and sent a trade mission to China in direct competition with British exporters. In response, the British government extended short-term credits and guarantees through the ECGD.

The government expanded and consolidated the Export Credit Guarantees Program over the course of the 1930s in part because of its interest in supporting trade in the Far East. The ECGD supplied financial compensation against the bankruptcy of customers, against transfer risk, and against other credit risks. It often restricted coverage by limiting it to the whole business turnover of a firm, and not just to what the customer considered the riskiest transactions (such "whole turnover" policies are quite common in the private sector as a means of reducing opportunistic behavior by customers). Although it would not cover losses from exchange rate fluctuations, the government was willing to guarantee business against losses from frozen debts. The largest portion of ECGD business was its medium-term coverage on credit, ranging from one to six years in length. This type of credit generally is extended to foreign governments or public bodies. For example, the ECGD covered the financing on the electrification of the Warsaw suburban railway by the British corporation of Metropolitan Vickers and English Electric, totaling £2 million. The participants in negotiations for such credit guarantees include the buyer-government and the British exporters, plus the Foreign Office, Treasury, Board of Trade, Department of Overseas Trade, and City bankers, in addition to the ECGD staff.[53]

Governments throughout the world turned to export credit and guarantee programs as an important tool of foreign economic policy as the depression spread and political crises abroad became common. In 1934 a group of these new public and semipublic agencies came together to form the International Union of Credit and Investment Insurers, commonly known as the Berne Union, as a parallel to the private sector ICIA. The founders viewed it as a forum for cooperation and intended it to provide "discipline" in the market by regulating the terms of export credit insurance so as to limit destructive competition. Initially, the Berne Union dealt only with insurance for commercial risks in transactions involving private buyers. Its influence was minimal, however, its deliberations and decisions largely ignored as governments competed more desperately for collapsing export markets by offering credit and insurance on generous terms.[54]

The British government could respond to the political and economic upheavals in Asia and elsewhere only through economic means, since military intervention was beyond its capabilities and political will. Financial protection, however, could not be entirely successful in promoting extensive economic ties in an area of the world where war and military occupation had become the norm. At the same time, the extension of credit and credit insurance by the government reflected clearly the politicians' concerns over the strength and competitiveness of British industry in overseas markets, especially in Asia.

Insurance and the Onset of War, 1936–1939

Aggression by Germany and Japan in Europe and Asia, the occupation and political collapse of China, and the isolationism of the United States all contributed to the search for ways to continue to maintain economic relations in the face of dire political risk. Once again, the private market and government agencies debated the merits of war risks insurance, both on sea and on land. For both, the stakes were high and consensus among competitors difficult to forge.

The London insurance market, despite the existence of large, sound, and long-lived companies, generally followed the lead of Lloyd's when exploring new markets and setting contract terms. In 1914 Lloyd's had made great profits on its new insurance policies for bomb damage, since the damage had not been as extensive as many predicted. After the war many underwriters began to insure war risks on property such as buildings (land-based war risks) around the world, based on that earlier experience. It was not a large market, and potential customers often had difficulty finding an underwriter willing to cover risks in specific locations at a reasonable price. Demand increased throughout the 1930s, as conflict in Europe seemed to grow more likely. Although technically land war risks insurance could be obtained through Lloyd's, many underwriters feared the effects of potentially large losses on their own financial position and rarely concluded such contracts. Lloyd's underwriters particularly worried about the impact of adverse selection on their portfolio of risks.[55] Their fears turned out to be all too real.

The British government, anxious to maintain and expand the nation's trade and shipping industries, exerted pressure on the private insurance market in an attempt to influence policies and rates, and debated the acceptance of war risks by His Majesty's Government, similar to the pre–World War I debate.[56] As in that earlier debate, political leaders worried particularly about the maintenance of trade in commodities. Lloyd's underwriters could provide some insurance on war risks, but they inquired about the possibility of the government's insuring cotton exports, for instance, against war risks.[57] War risks to property fell outside the purview of the Export Credits Scheme, which covered only export credit risks and not marine or land war risks. Some officials proposed to draft an emergency scheme to reinsure King's Enemy Risks and extend special coverage to colonial and Indian vessels.

The conflicting interpretations of insurable risk, especially war risks on land-based property, became an especially acute point of debate during the Spanish Civil War. The insurance market willingly sold insurance against the possibility of losses from the "civil commotion" in Spain beginning in 1936, for both land- and sea-based war risks. For more than a year, many leading underwriters covered their customers against damage from the civil war, including full insurance against fire damage (a fairly common result of modern warfare). In what seems in hindsight a glaring understatement, one professional journal of the time noted that the underwriters did not fully calculate the extent of possible liability.[58]

While encouraging commercial insurance on British shipping and trade to third countries, the government strongly objected to the insuring by British firms of actual war matériel sold to Spanish forces. It could not forbid such insurance completely, particularly insurance on war matériel transported by truck, since trucking was a legitimate business, but the government contacted Lloyd's of London and the Institute of London Underwriters to convey its position on Spanish insurance. Many private underwriters complied, restricting their coverage. The Eagle Star and British Dominions Insurance Companies, for example, even rejected an application for insurance on the basis of an unconfirmed suspicion that the shipment was destined ultimately for Spanish territory.[59]

In 1937 news reports began to tell of high losses and mounting claims on war risks policies, both marine and land-based. Many underwriters had insured ships trading with Spain against war risks, counting on military protection from British naval vessels stationed in the Mediterranean.[60] The insured ships, from Britain, Spain, Norway, the Soviet Union, and other countries, suffered damage and loss in the conflict when the British navy did not intervene. Spanish insurgents detained foreign ships, leading eventually to claims by insurers against both the Spanish government and the Spanish insurgents. The Institute of London Underwriters reported the seizure of numerous foreign ships chartered or insured by British firms, including those carrying grain cargoes. Lloyd's of London sent a representative to Spain to negotiate directly for the recovery of lost vessels, in a somewhat futile effort to modify potential losses to Lloyd's. The insurgent government issued a statement to foreign companies that fire claims paid to workers' committees in government territory would not be recognized, causing confusion among all claimants and companies.[61]

Faced with such confusion, British underwriters from Lloyd's and the companies cooperated in setting up a facility, the Association of Foreign Insurance Companies, to assist in recovering property and establishing the accuracy and payment of claims.[62] This organization would operate in insurgent-controlled territory and develop procedures to maintain insurance activities under wartime conditions. The association had to negotiate with an insurgent government that, in an effort to obtain cash, tried to compel the insurance companies to accept full liability for damage to property in areas under its control.

The land-based war risks policies led to the most bruising losses for insurers. The Spanish Civil War was notable for innovations in warfare that led to massive aerial bombardment of cities and towns and destroyed lives and property that would not have been at such great risk in earlier wars. Modern technology and tactics made it increasingly difficult to delineate the line between the war zone and civilian territory. At this point, it became clear that land war risks insurance in particular had become a gamble, pure and simple, as insurers had no ability to estimate scientific probabilities for the likelihood and extent of potential loss.

By 1938 the losses on land war risks policies had mounted drastically, although only one year before they had been highly profitable. The same was true for credit risks: whereas in 1936–37 the claims made to the Trade Indemnity Corporation, for example, had been quite low, one year later they had swung around and were unusually high.[63] The experience of the ECGD with transfer risk reinforced the view that the Spanish debacle offered important lessons.[64] The ECGD reviewed its 1936–37 losses and discovered that all its claims were for Spanish transfer problems. Department officials noted, "It was pointed out that in the light of the experience of last year, Transfer Risk might lead to heavy calls on the Department's funds, and had served to underline the wisdom of the general commercial view that political risks were outside the scope of private insurance enterprise."[65]

Adverse selection incentives, which led the riskiest customers to seek insurance, had exacerbated Spanish losses. In 1938 the International Credit Insurance Association warned its members to avoid covering different contracts and different customers that might aggregate into a portfolio of risks vulnerable to the same cause of loss.[66] Good business practice mandated diversification of the portfolio of risks held by any one insurer, but unfortunately, the types of insurance and credit guarantees customers desired at that time appeared to encourage concentration of risk. The ICIA believed the difficulty of determining the boundaries of a credit insurance contract was linked to the lack of clarity in insurance practice regarding the division of losses between the private sector and the general public, a division it viewed as rooted in social norms. Its 1938 report forthrightly stated that the effects of a calamity on both the creditor and the credit insurer depend on the policy of the community regarding loss and liability.[67] In other words, individual contracts must be considered to be backed by the customs and norms of the particular society of which the participants are members.

Even as they insured land war risks in Spain, many underwriters were insuring the same type of risk in England. As the scale of war damage in Spain became clear, some British underwriters realized that a war in their own country, which was much more industrialized and densely populated than Spain, would be absolutely devastating to property on land. In 1936 the chairman of Lloyd's, Neville Dixey, first raised the issue with the Committee of Lloyd's of excluding land-based war risks from all insurance policies. In order to work, such an exclusion clause would have to be accepted by all underwriters, both at Lloyd's and in the companies, both in Britain and abroad. Dixey then opened negotiations with underwriters at Lloyd's and at the companies.[68] As the negotiations were taking place, claims for losses on land war risks in Spain kept piling up, underlining the potential for unsustainable loss if a major war broke out. The Spanish trouble gave a "nasty jar" to insurers granting wide cover against general and civil war.[69]

The fiasco of Spanish land war risks convinced leading insurance underwriters that such risks just were not insurable. Leading Lloyd's underwriters lobbied other insurers to modify their insurance practices and to join in eliminating land war risks insurance from their business. The result was a near total ban on land war risks insurance, implemented and enforced by the London insurance market. Lloyd's of London convened a committee that, with support from the management of the largest British companies, such as the Commercial Union, Royal Exchange Assurance, and Eagle Star, drew up and promoted what became known as the Waterborne Agreement.[70] All major European insurance companies signed it; as the Board of Trade reported, "the British insurance interests had with much difficulty and with considerable labour convinced their foreign confreres of the impractability of war risks insurance and had persuaded them to co-operate in not writing this particular risk."[71] Sea-based war risks, however, could still be covered, since ships had the option of simply sailing out of harm's way.[72]

The agreement would be adhered to for more than forty years, monitored by a committee of insurers based at Lloyd's. If one insurance company began selling land war risks policies again and did not suffer immediate and horrendous losses, the other insurers would feel compelled to compete in this market, too. This is a classic case of an environment structured so that strong incentives exist to defect from the agreement, though all would benefit by adhering to it. Defection has been rare, however, owing to the central influence of the leading underwriters, particularly at Lloyd's, who maintain discipline by denying access to its reinsurance facilities and other services. In addition, the agreement was to a certain extent self-enforcing, since the ultimately high costs of pursuing land war risks business could outweigh any short-term profits. Hundreds of insurance firms around the world eventually signed the agreement, largely because of pressure from the major British companies and Lloyd's.

Within the international risks insurance regime, participants had defined a strong norm in which war and civil war risks for land-based property were defined as uninsurable, since no reasonable limits could be set in establishing the terms of the insurance contract. A clear-headed analysis could only conclude that the concentration of risk in such business was overly high, considering the immovability of buildings on land. Additionally, the costs of administering a war risks program would probably be relatively high, since the problem of adverse selection in this case appeared too great. Simple geographic diversification of holdings by commercial interests and insurers might be a preferable strategy, although the prospects of a truly global war were not entirely reassuring on this point. Few statistics existed at the time to guide calculations of real probabilities of loss, and previous experience of war could provide little guidance since modern weapons could destroy much more effectively and devastatingly than those of the past.[73]

The British government generally supported the ban on insurance against land war risks. In 1937 the Board of Trade discussed with disfavor an association that was advertising the sale of war risks insurance, despite general agreement that these risks were uninsurable.[74] The secretary of this insurance association, in a letter to the Board of Trade, claimed, "It is difficult to believe that as Insurance Companies and

Lloyd's Underwriters and the Government have all refused to devise a scheme which would provide some measure of compensation or insurance for loss of property by acts of War, that your Department should regard with disfavor a Mutual Scheme among property owners to do their best in their own modest way to spread among themselves such loss as they may sustain through acts of War."[75] Interestingly, the records of the Board of Trade mentioned that it might be difficult for the government to state on the floor of the House the real reason why such an association was worse than useless: the horrific level of damage likely to result from a modern war.

The Experience of State Insurance within a Private Regime

An economist would say that any product or service could be, and would be, sold if given the correct price. An ICIA report of 1938 concurred, declaring, "Taking a long view, it will probably always be better to grant the assured at high rates as extensive cover as possible, than cheap but ineffective cover."[76] The private underwriters themselves generally disagreed, however, and even the government insurance agency strictly limited its coverage.

The impact of the economic crisis in 1930 had forced many business groups to reassess their traditional policy positions; even the shipping and banking sectors, long proponents of laissez-faire, pressed for new approaches. Business leaders accepted the idea of greater intervention by the state in the economy and questioned the value of strict reliance on market forces.[77] The same interests that had been lobbying for more trade liberalization in the past, however—the Treasury Department, the Board of Trade, and the Bank of England—continued to press for open markets and attempted to appease Germany and Japan by holding out the prospect of mutual gains from trade.[78]

State export guarantees remained controversial. Some questioned whether taxpayers should underwrite the export and reexport of colonial produce, which had turned out to be a major part of the guarantees business. Others questioned whether or not there was conflict inherent in underwriting exports of similar products from different, competing colonies (for example, Sudanese versus Indian cotton). Still others wished to determine whether the guaranteeing of colonial products helped those products compete with British goods, although colonial produce sold directly to foreigners did not in fact compete with

United Kingdom trade. The main colonial products at this time were rubber, sold mainly to Russia under a specific trade agreement, and tea, sold primarily to the United States and Canada and therefore probably not requiring guarantees. Finally, some persons involved in the debate expressed concern at the possibility that government insurance would compete with the facilities of the City financiers and insurers.[79]

The ECGD reached the legal limit of the amount of credit it could cover in September 1938. The Treasury Department insisted it could not exceed the £50 million restriction that had been set, although a recently concluded Anglo-Turkish agreement required £45 million by itself.[80] At the same time, supporters of the ECGD pointed out that the chief "weapon" of Great Britain against totalitarian states was financial assistance to foreign countries, such as Greece, Portugal, and China.[81] The ECGD declared in a ministerial brief that the government guarantee "allows British heavy industry to maintain its place in foreign markets from which otherwise in the virtual cessation of foreign lending it might be excluded."[82]

In 1938, when the ECGD reached its limits, the Board of Trade and the Committee of Imperial Defence suggested expanding the agency's authority to cover armaments.[83] Support also came from within the ECGD, as the ban on covering arms was viewed as an obstacle to the effective functioning of the agency. ECGD officials believed their decisions should be made on a commercial basis, whereas the arms ban clearly came from political motivations. Such political decisions could be made only with the approval of the Foreign Office and therefore should be kept separate from regular business.[84]

At the end of the 1930s a ministerial brief summed up the experience of state-supplied export guarantees by stating that the program had been politically popular, successful, costless, and in ever greater demand.[85] Nevertheless, as conflict broke out in Europe, promoting export credit insurance became more and more difficult.[86] The same tensions that would result in a world war also stimulated the demand for insurance and guarantees for overseas commerce, but made it increasingly difficult for public and private agencies to insure property and credit against a wide array of political risks.

The debate over private versus public supply of political risks insurance in Great Britain often centered on access to information. The International Credit Insurance Association, though weak in many ways, provided a means to exchange information on creditors and decrease the costs of monitoring contracts. But the ECGD theoretically had access to more information than private agencies and thus could be allowed to take on more risks than the private firms.[87] Some went so far as to claim that the City no longer could estimate the risks in foreign trade, following the economic devastation of the depression.[88]

One analyst of the insurance market believed that inadequate coverage by the private market was probably the reason behind the government's eventual decision to expand the ECGD program to include expropriation insurance (as opposed to credit insurance or war risks insurance). For instance, Lloyd's of London began selling limited expropriation insurance only in the 1930s.[89] The ECGD had an advantage in being backed by the revenue of the state, assisted by the Treasury, Foreign Office, and Board of Trade, and thereby better able to obtain quality information. Supporters claimed that government guarantees helped encourage and stabilize British trade during a difficult period.[90] The ECGD's success rested, according to its supporters, on such practices as lending on business grounds alone and maintaining secrecy about individual contracts and the amount of credit extended to individual countries.[91]

Nevertheless, the political upheavals of the late 1930s led the ECGD to implement various exclusion clauses to avoid covering catastrophic risks. Private firms, such as the Trade Indemnity Corporation and Credit Indemnity, did not always limit their losses in this way except for the exclusion of land war risks. Credit Indemnity, however, obtained government reinsurance of its risks. Exclusion clauses generally name political risks such as war, sometimes civil war, revolution, insurrection, riots, and credit repayment moratoria as outside the scope of insurance coverage.[92] Creditors and insurers before 1945 also had to cope with sovereign agencies that responded to crisis by canceling or reducing debt payments. Some governments delayed repayment by imposing a moratorium on their loan payments. Insurance and guarantee contract exclusions denied coverage in these circumstances.

Insurers, both public and private, clearly feared that though many risks are local and can be spread through portfolio diversification, modern war itself could not be localized. The high concentration of losses from modern war could bankrupt an insurer—even one backed by the government. Predictable risks can be managed by government agencies through traditional insurance techniques, such as the use of short-term or high-priced policies or of clauses that terminate the contract under specific circumstances (although a customer can also use that clause to cancel, especially if the high-priced risks decline in probability). These techniques, however, also decrease the incentives for exporters and investors to seek insurance and guarantees to manage their risks and may lead to an outcome contrary to what government officials perceive as being in the national interest, that is, maintenance of trade and investment relations in politically turbulent conditions.

Despite all the concerns about the viability of insurance against war risks when war is imminent, numerous marine war risks associations existed just before British entry into World War II. Most of these were mutual associations among shipowners instead of independent insurance companies. On the eve of conflict in 1938 many underwriters still concluded insurance contracts for the shipping business, often agreeing to cover war risks. After Munich, however, the underwriters, bedeviled by uncertainty, became increasingly reluctant to commit themselves to provide cover for war risks at low peacetime rates. At the same time, naturally enough, the merchants insisted on obtaining war risks insurance at low and stable rates that would allow them to make future commitments themselves.

The British government felt compelled to intervene once again, as it had just before the outbreak of war in 1914. This time Parliament authorized the Board of Trade to reinsure King's Enemy Risks, leaving the marine insurers themselves to handle the content and price of the direct insurance. The minute Germany invaded Poland, however, the government reverted to a program of direct war risks insurance. It split war risks on cargo with Lloyd's and the companies, with the cargo coming in and out of Britain primarily insured by the government and the overseas business covered by the private market. The participants intended to make certain both that British trade continued and that British insurance would remain competitive against foreign insurers.[93]

In addition, the British government agreed in 1939 to establish a Commodities Insurance Scheme under the War Risks Insurance Act, followed two years later by the War Damage Act, which introduced direct compensation for damage to buildings, land, and business from enemy acts. In all these schemes Lloyd's played a leading role in placing and administering the insurance. The government also cooperated with the mutual war risks associations in various financial arrangements and in reinsurance.[94] Despite the massive destruction that devastated most of the European continent by the end of the war, most private insurers and the government schemes profited from their war risks business.[95]

Most governments that had established export credit and insurance agencies during the 1920s and 1930s suspended their activity entirely for the duration of the war. In 1942 a group of British commercial insurers suggested that government leaders should consider establishing a supranational insurance body, to be called the International Insurance Company, to take care of risks on a global basis. That idea was not further developed; after World War II, as described in the following chapter, the insurance of global risks would be divided among the commercial insurers and reinsurers and among separate and independent national export credit insurance and investment guarantee agencies.[96]

Testing the Limits of Insurable Risks

The lack of stability between the world wars manifested itself in a number of ways: the inability to maintain a stable international monetary system, the aggressive expansionism of Germany in Europe and Japan in the Far East, and of course the financial collapse in New York and the global depression that followed. The decline of British stature in the world, as reflected in its weakened trade position, heightened the perception of risk in overseas commerce.

Between the two world wars the international risks insurance regime still primarily consisted of the commercial insurers, despite the new presence of government agencies in one corner of the business—export credit insurance. The regime itself, particularly its norms, developed during this time in response to dire experience. First, the commercial insurers began experimenting with new products, selling insurance for political risks on trade credit and expanding the use of reinsurance. Then they began to relax their judgment regarding what was an insurable risk and covered property and buildings on land against the damages caused by war. The damage ultimately landed in the bank accounts of the insurers, who had to pay out huge claims on Spanish Civil War losses. In response, the insurers established a rule against insurance of land-based war risks. In the 1938 Waterborne Agreement we see a restricted definition of insurability that set limits on the private insurers for decades to come.

An ICIA report acknowledged at the time that perhaps perceptions had to change regarding what constitutes a catastrophe, particularly given the differences among societies in which projects are insured. "In certain hard-boiled countries, especially in South America, a revolution, for instance, is not so overwhelming an evil; it may be much more harmless than a bad harvest."[97] The report argued that even nonviolent changes may be catastrophic, such as increases in tariffs or the imposition of a boycott. Furthermore, governments themselves posed nonmilitary threats in the form of expropriations of property and persecution of minorities.[98] This report put forth the idea that the international risks insurers that had limited their business to marine war risks should expand their conception of insurable political risks at the same time as they definitively excluded one risk—land-based war.

In a departure from earlier liberal commitments, the British government itself began to extend credit and insurance to stimulate exports during this period. In establishing the ECGD, the founders explicitly attempted not to compete with the private market. The agency's policies covered the long-term contracts and political risks that were generally in limited supply from private underwriters. The practices of the ECGD conformed to those of the London market, following its lead in designing policies and exclusion clauses. Separating the sphere of activity of each set of actors in the insurance arena was considered mutually beneficial. The commercial insurers supplied only a part of the insurance desired by commercial interests and thus left a large amount of coverage to be supplemented by public agencies.

One interesting aspect of the development of the public-private nexus in insurance affairs in the interwar years was the close cooperation between the British Foreign Office and the London insurers, especially Lloyd's. Often the private insurers were the tool for carrying out government policy, formally or informally. For example, in 1939 some suggested that illegal immigration into Palestine could be restrained by refusing insurance on ships engaged to transfer emigrants, or possibly the underwriters could disclaim liability in case of a loss.[99] Insurers also helped monitor arms embargoes by providing information to the government about the transportation of weapons, based on what they insured.

The structure of incentives facing private actors in the early twentieth century, combined with the hierarchy and concentration of the industry itself, facilitated the establishment of regime norms of nonsupply that encouraged the entrance of state agencies into this market on a cooperative rather than competitive basis. This trend would change in the latter half of the twentieth century, as we see in the following chapter.

4/ *Redefining Risk and Responsibility, 1979–1989*

The relative decline of the United States in the 1980s produced a flurry of historical comparisons with the decades of British decline.[1] Like Great Britain before it, the United States ceased to be the dominant capital-exporting country; its trade position deteriorated; increasingly powerful states challenged its hitherto dominant position; and its ability and willingness to live up to political and security commitments seemed to waver. The main U.S. protegé in the Persian Gulf, Iran, unexpectedly collapsed in revolution in 1979, with no direct U.S. intervention, and political upheaval was followed by a long war between Iran and Iraq. The Middle East peace talks dragged on interminably. Recurring trade conflicts with Japanese and European allies increasingly strained relations. And then the Soviet Union went from "evil empire" to political disintegration within only a few years, transforming the shape of world politics.

From 1979 to 1989, as the context of world affairs changed dramatically, the demand for and supply of international risks insurance fluctuated within an overall upward trend. The institutional center of the insurance regime shifted decisively toward the public sector and away from private insurers, particularly in the area of investment guarantees. Commercial insurers redefined insurable political risks to expand their business, changing long-held attitudes and practices regarding prudent underwriting. Financial upheavals strained the resources of the primary actors, weakening the cohesiveness of industry interests and pushing state agencies toward a more active involvement in the management of international risks.

Prelude to Change, 1945–1979

Between World Wars I and II, as described in the previous chapter, private insurers restricted the supply of specific kinds of international risks insurance, leaving an unmet demand that exacerbated a deteriorating environment for foreign economic transactions of all sorts. The extensive and ongoing exchange relationships among firms, especially in the acknowledged capital of world insurance—London—became the foundation of a private international risks insurance regime. The participants established a norm of nonsupply of land war risks insurance and restricted sales of certain kinds of political risk insurance.[2] The main agency of British government insurance, the Export Credit Guarantees Department (ECGD), limited the scope of its programs to areas where private property rights were clear and emulated the practices of the private sector through a narrow definition of insurable political risk and a narrow view of its mission. The political failures of the 1920s reinforced the strength of the private insurance regime; the insurance failures of the 1930s consolidated a regime of selective nonsupply.

At the end of World War II the establishment of a postwar economic order dominated by American power seemed to presage a period of peace and stability in which political risks would be insignificant and the need for the international risks insurance regime described above would be minimal. Instead, the era of decolonization led to increased interest in incorporating peripheral regions into the world economy, despite the uncertainty and risks attached to this process. Foreign investors did not believe the Bretton Woods regime would protect their investments in developing countries. As Helen Hughes notes, "a broad network of public insurance and guarantees therefore began to be laid down by both the industrial and developing countries to stimulate capital flows."[3] Hermes in Germany, CoFACE in France, the ECGD in England, and the U.S. Export-Import Bank and Overseas Private Investment Corporation (OPIC) all provided varying forms and levels of export credit insurance and investment guarantees.[4] Yet this government "safety net" remained weak and fragmented, and it only fitfully expanded until the 1980s.[5]

Private insurers only occasionally supplied international risks insurance, as part of their marine underwriting business. The Suez Crisis stimulated development of specialized political risks insurance policies, separate from marine and other insurance lines. Stephen Merrett, of Merrett Syndicates at Lloyd's of London, is sometimes credited with initiating the first political risk policies in 1972, along with Hogg Robinson brokers.[6] In 1974 the American International Group (AIG) tentatively entered the market, and a number of others began to offer political risk coverage by the end of that decade: the Insurance Corporation of North America (INA), Swett and Crawford, Chubb, CIGNA, and the American Foreign Insurance Association (AFIA).[7]

No intergovernmental institutions regulate the global insurance business, though some international public and private institutions have promulgated nonbinding policies and guidelines. The Berne Union and ICIA played a weak role in developing norms and regulations for export credit insurers, both public and private. Regional associations exist, such as the Interamerican Federation of Insurance Companies and the Commission Européenne d'Assurance.[8] The United Nations Conference on Trade and Development (UNCTAD) has been debating insurance issues since its founding in 1964, with little effect. Its main goals have been to encourage the development of indigenous insurance capacity in developing countries and to assist governments in monitoring the solvency of local firms.[9] Both the Organization for Economic Cooperation and Development (OECD) and the European Community established guidelines for the insurance industry, but they applied primarily to insurance on local risks, not transborder ones.

The industry has been self-regulated at the international level, primarily through the actions of "lead" insurers. The political risks insurance industry has objected strenuously to any proposals for international standards and multilateral regulation. Leading representatives have argued effectively that market forces already regulate the industry and that it would be impractical if not impossible for more than one hundred countries to agree on one set of standards.[10] The industry favors self-regulation through developing standard contract terms that define insurability and manage opportunistic behavior and through establishing cooperative associations to handle common problems.

Despite the existence of government political risk agencies and the relatively long history of private political risks insurance, many of the corporations that invested overseas after World War II remained surprisingly reluctant to consider such insurance as a means of protecting their "bottom line." They feared a host country government would not look kindly on a corporation whose executives bought insurance that implied the government was unstable or unable to maintain political control of the country. Government-supplied political risks insurance appeared even worse, since it would identify the corporation too closely with its home country government, which could be a liability in dealing with nationalist political leaders.[11]

These attitudes began to change during the 1970s, when the perception of political risk began to soar. By the beginning of the 1980s most managers accepted the need to incorporate risk management techniques, including political risks insurance, into strategic planning. Three trends lay behind this change. First, technological complexity in modern production increased the size and value of each commercial transaction. New technologies made possible, for instance, the high-tech services of computerization and the more low-tech benefits of containerization of cargo shipping. These advances make it possible to exchange goods and services on a much larger scale than previously possible, increasing the potential loss on each transaction from any one adverse event. Insurers called this trend the advent of "jumbo risks," exemplified by modern jets, offshore oil platforms, telecommunications satellites, and even the U.S. space shuttle.[12] Technological change did not directly affect the perception of risk, but it clearly increased the value of what was at stake in risky environments.

Second, the perception of risk was directly influenced by the belief that major political powers, especially the United States, had lost control over events. The "lift-off" in the perception of political risk can be traced directly to the fall of the shah of Iran, which seemed to signal the end of U.S. power.[13] The collapse and overthrow of the shah's government electrified corporate executives, both in the United States and around the world.[14] Until then they had firmly believed that trade and investment in a country so closely supported by the U.S. government could not possibly be subject to political risks. In fact, businessmen considered transactions in Iran almost risk-free; Iran had a better credit rating than the United Kingdom at one time.[15] The Iranian oilfields were shut down, the U.S. government did not intervene militarily, and the Saudi Arabians did not take up the slack in oil production. Suddenly, the world faced a second oil crisis—and a new understanding of political risks. Nearly $4 billion in foreign investments was seized; most of it was uninsured.[16]

As one business reporter put it, insurers viewed the fallout from the Iranian Revolution as both a "bonanza and nightmare."[17] A leading private underwriter publicly declared that developing country governments no longer feared retribution from the great powers when pursuing anti-Western and anti-business policies.[18] And by 1985 an executive of Conoco, a major U.S. multinational corporation, felt compelled to comment: "The United States, in recent years, has been perceived as relatively less able or willing to defend many of its interests in an effective way. There is an aura of perceived impotence relative to our actual versus our verbal responses to phenomena such as terrorism, Soviet adventurism, and unfair trade practices. This perception, in various instances, reduces foreign inhibitions relative to putting pressures on U.S. multinationals."[19] With their expectations upset by events, corporate executives turned to their traditional suppliers of property insurance and demanded they offer political risks insurance policies for projects in the Middle East and other developing regions.

Finally, the third force that affected the perception of international risks was the dramatic change in international financial markets. The Bretton Woods currency system collapsed, ushering in a new era of floating exchange rates and unprecedented volatility in currency markets. The first oil crisis exacerbated financial instabilities by instigating simultaneous inflation and recession in the industrialized economies. The massive recycling of "petrodollars" restructured global financial flows and stimulated the expansion of international and offshore banking.[20] In the 1970s the amount of loans made through the Euromarkets exceeded any previous lending spree.[21] As government control over international financial affairs seemed to decline, financial and political risks became more and more entwined.

Changing perceptions of political risk ultimately affected the norms and financial resources available to insurers, which in turn changed the supply of political risks insurance and the regime that supported it. Even before the crises of the 1980s ambitious underwriters responding to the demands of their customers began to press against the boundaries of regime norms, with contracts that skirted the limits of what was ordinarily permissible in areas such as financial guarantees and war risks. They wanted to redefine what political risks were insurable and further expand the market, thus upsetting the existing balance between government and private sector activity.

In 1977 Stephen Merrett, a leading political risk underwriter at Lloyd's, described insurable political risks as including strikes, riots, civil commotions, and malicious destruction but deliberately excluded kidnap and ransom risks because he did not think they should be insured.[22] Merrett discussed terrorism only in the context of marine political risks and did not mention land war risks, which fall under the Waterborne Agreement.[23] Over the course of the next decade insurance underwriters would expand the definition of insurable political risks, even questioning the strictures of the Waterborne Agreement.

The specific events or policy changes that had the most significant impact on international risks insurance during the 1980s fall into three broad categories, each of which is treated separately below. First, the deregulation of financial markets in the United States and Great Britain, followed closely by deregulation elsewhere, increased the incentive for insurers to treat their business as a source of investment income instead of strictly as an insurance mechanism. Second, the debt crisis in the developing world and the increased political concern over competitiveness in the developed countries pushed many governments to intervene more actively in managing the risks of overseas lending and investing. Third, the continuing conflict in the Persian Gulf challenged the ability and willingness of insurers to continue providing insurance for marine war risks. These combined to affect the demand for international risks insurance, the resources of insurers both public and private, and the norms that guide the regime, especially regarding insurability of risks. The decade was capped by the dramatic collapse of communism in Europe and breakup of the Soviet Union, which produced expansive new opportunities and risks that would reinforce the trends already set in motion, as discussed in the final chapter.

Collateral Damage: Financial Deregulation and Commercial Insurers

The wave of financial deregulation that has swept one country after another in the past two decades affected the commercial insurance industry through several avenues. As U.S. financial institutions challenged the dominance of London in global finance, American insurers increasingly participated in international markets. At the same time, one of the leading institutions of the London market, Lloyd's, suffered internal conflict and massive losses, partly because of the temptations of playing loosely in a financial boom. One of the few restraints on the private insurers was the influential role of conservative reinsurers in holding to a restrictive definition of insurability. Finally, financial deregulation facilitated the ability of traders, investors, and lenders to develop new alternatives to insurance to manage their financial and political risks.

A 1984 cover story in *Business Week* boasted, "[New York] has taken the crown away from London and ended 300 years of European dominance of world financial markets. It has become the capital of 'capital.'"[24] Until recently, however, U.S. insurers lagged behind the banks in entering global markets. The British insurers simply dominated the industry so effectively that most U.S. firms did not pursue it. After all, the U.S. market itself was so large and dynamic they did not feel compelled to go abroad for business in order to be profitable. Federal legislation put regulatory authority over insurance in state hands, exempted the industry from antitrust legislation, and prohibited agreements with foreign organizations on rates and contract clauses.[25] That ensured a fragmented, decentralized system in which small firms predominated, reinforcing the domestic orientation of most U.S. insurers.

First the United States and then Great Britain began lifting regulatory restrictions on banks and stock markets beginning in 1975 and culminating in the "big bang" in the British market in 1986; deregulation opened up a new era of global financial markets. One of the immediate results was a boom in mergers and acquisitions, particularly among financial firms—including insurers. Within the European Community, insurance companies were involved in more than one hundred mergers and acquisitions in the mid-1980s alone.[26] Insurance brokerages aggressively pursued mergers and acquisitions opportunities, and many U.S. firms keenly sought out British partners.[27]

The foreign business of many American insurers was often handled through consortia, which also merged during the 1980s. The most prominent were the American Foreign Insurance Association (AFIA), which acted as the foreign department for a group of property and casualty insurers, and American International Underwriters (AIU), which acted as a general agent abroad for a group of nonlife insurers.[28] In 1984 CIGNA merged with the AFIA, thus strengthening CIGNA's participation in international markets.[29] AIG, one of the most internationally oriented of United States–based insurers, absorbed the AIU.[30] Eventually, aggressive American firms also would acquire British brokers, underwriters, and insurance firms.

In a second trend the private insurers were emboldened to explore political risks insurance more intensively. Although Lloyd's of London has a long history of involvement in international markets, most of its underwriters shied away from specialized political risk contracts until the 1970s.[31] In 1971 Julian Radcliffe, a junior underwriter at Lloyd's, suggested that the large amount of business transactions being concluded in the Middle East faced political risks that the insurers might cover. In the next few years he and others began experimenting with independent political risk policies. At that point, Lloyd's and the U.S. investment guarantee agency, OPIC, entered into an unusual alliance.[32] Lloyd's announced that some of its syndicates, along with twelve U.S. companies plus Skandia and the government of Abu Dhabi, had agreed to reinsure the portfolio of investment guarantees held by OPIC so that OPIC would be able to expand the amount it could insure directly.[33] On the expiration of the agreement, both sides felt the cooperative arrangement had been successful but also believed they could operate sufficiently well on their own. This agreement constituted a unique partnership between a government agency of one country and firms based in another country, with the private sector insuring the government agency.[34]

The impetus for this reinsurance joint venture came from the American side, but through the successful operation of this agreement the London insurers gained further experience in underwriting political risks and began to see this area as a potential profitable market. When demand for political risks insurance surged after 1979, growing numbers of underwriters became more flexible in defining insurable risks, even as others adamantly maintained traditional views, especially regarding political risks. Reasons given for opposition to private political risks insurance were the expected problems with developing country judicial systems, the difficulty of distinguishing commercial from political risks (even in OECD countries, where state intervention in the economy had become common), and the perceived increase in volatility of production throughout the 1970s, boding ill for the future.[35]

Those willing to step into this business carefully designed their pricing structure and contract terms to protect their financial health and restrain opportunistic behavior. For instance, the insurer might set the price to vary with the value of goods insured and the perceived riskiness of the location and project type; in addition, the customer might be required to cover all transactions under one policy, and not just selected—and clearly risky—ones. This new willingness to cover political risks came just as the demand for such insurance exploded and the insurance industry itself began to feel the effects of the financial revolution.

In 1978 AIG/AIU launched the first substantive political risks insurance program by a United States–based firm. Over the next five years its political risk business would grow by approximately 30 percent per year.[36] AIG aimed to offer a substitute to the public insurance agencies.[37] By the mid-1980s a few large U.S. insurance corporations such as CIGNA, Continental, and Chubb sometimes offered selected types of political risk cover, including export credit insurance. Many multinational corporations wanted to work with only one multiline insurance company for all their worldwide insurance needs, and they encouraged their traditional insurers to offer a wide array of products.[38]

Transnational businesses pressed their insurers to relax restrictions on specialty products, including land war risks cover and financial guarantees.[39] Some Lloyd's underwriters and other insurers were willing and able to cover new forms of international risks. The category of political risk grew to include (at various times) war risks, terrorism, kidnap and ransom, currency inconvertibility, and contract frustration and rejection insurance; contract frustration risks became one of the fastest growing portions of the political risks market.[40] Nevertheless, most underwriters continued to maintain that financial risks such as currency inconvertibility were not insurable.[41]

Some underwriters began skirting the provisions of the Waterborne Agreement without directly repudiating it, in an effort to satisfy their customers' demands.[42] Nonsignatory firms and government agencies became more willing to cover certain land war risks in selected regions of the world. In the mid-1980s the Chubb insurance group covered land war risks, although only in conjunction with its regular property and casualty coverages, in order to reduce the overall riskiness of their portfolio of insurance contracts.[43] By the middle of the decade some underwriters openly urged that the Waterborne Agreement be reviewed, and brokers regularly asked insurers for cover on war risks on land, though with the proviso that nuclear war and major-power war were excluded.[44] Those supporting this more expansive approach to insurability argued that underwriters have become more sophisticated since the 1930s, that they have more skill in setting the parameters of coverage and correctly establishing the price for a policy, and that they know more now about how to control opportunistic behavior. They also have become more adept at attracting customers to contracts that are hedged about with limits and exclusions, through providing ancillary services such as information on business and political conditions in foreign countries or training in loss prevention techniques. All this seemed to indicate that the restrictions agreed to in the 1930s had become outdated by the 1980s.

International business became very interested in obtaining international risks insurance just as many insurers became caught up in the "casino capitalism" of the 1980s.[45] The temptation to tangle in the new financial whirl would later come to haunt many insurers, especially Lloyd's of London. Lloyd's, designed for an earlier era, had long been in need of reform, given the expansion in the number of members over the years plus the increasing competitiveness of the business. The system at Lloyd's relied on being able to attract outside "names" to put up their personal capital, with unlimited liability, while the active underwriters actually managed the business.[46] For many, Lloyd's became a financial investment and not an insurance concern.

Lloyd's prided itself on its commitment to regulating its own affairs, which was affirmed repeatedly by Parliament. As things began to go sour for Lloyd's, one of the early investigative committees in 1980 stated, "Since the continued success of Lloyd's as an international market for insurance is important to the national interest, it is of national importance that Lloyd's should have an efficient system of self-regulation."[47] The form this self-regulation takes is of numerous market agreements that govern different types of underwriting within Lloyd's, with certain ones given formal legal force but most functioning through informal pressure on underwriters. This informal pressure can be quite effective. Typically, an insurance contract has many different underwriters and different syndicates each taking a percentage of the business; the threat of exclusion from these multiparty contracts can be used to discipline unruly underwriters and apply pressure to conform. These pressures seemed to fail in a devastating manner in the early 1980s.

The new financial era posed numerous temptations for insurers to pursue aggressive and in some cases unscrupulous or corrupt practices, eventually leading to disaster.[48] Scandal followed on fraud which followed on negligence as the insiders at Lloyd's grew "greedier and greedier and greedier," as one of those insiders himself reported.[49] Many individuals began to join Lloyd's solely because of tax considerations, and the inflow of new money led some underwriters to seek quantity and not quality in their insurance business. A number of Lloyd's syndicates and managing agents have since been accused of segregating these outside or nonunderwriting names into high-risk syndicates, which experienced extensive and often unbearable losses.[50] Some syndicates reinsured their risks, and those reinsurers turned around and reinsured their own, in a chain or "spiral" of reinsurance; the same piece of business might go through the same syndicates and companies several times, providing premiums and commissions to all. When disaster struck, all those insurers and reinsurers would pay and pay again—and those disasters occurred in the 1980s.[51] This system did not diversify risk—a bedrock principle of insurance—but concentrated it among a relatively small number of underwriters.[52]

Every impulse toward more profound changes in the structure and functioning of Lloyd's in the 1980s foundered against the barriers put up by supporters of the status quo. Numerous official and semiofficial reports over the years analyzed the situation and recommended stronger self-regulation. The Lloyd's Act of 1982 initiated mild reforms intended to strengthen self-regulation, but it did not prevent the rogue behavior and resulting litigation that followed. The market at Lloyd's has been brought low by the reputation-shattering financial scandals and legal battles of some of its member syndicates throughout the 1980s and into the 1990s.[53] Five years after the limited reforms were implemented, the Neill report pointed out the need for investor protections for Lloyd's similar to those imposed on other financial institutions by the Financial Services Act of 1986, from which Lloyd's had been exempted. Another five years later three reviews—the Walker, Rowland, and Morse reports—criticized Lloyd's management for insufficient regulation. The system has had to reform itself finally, under pressure internally from its own members and externally from the political outcry against the existing system.[54] These problems, combined with the effect of huge losses on the financial capacity of Lloyd's, have weakened its role within international insurance markets, although perhaps not irretrievably.

When the surge in political risk business began in 1979, the insurance market as a whole had become an extremely attractive source of profits. The financial deregulation that had started in the United States stimulated a major boom in financial markets during the 1980s. Attracted by high returns and low barriers to entry in the insurance industry, too many new entrants quickly caused a problem of overcapacity and a competitive lowering of prices to untenable levels.[55] Insurers discovered they could invest the influx of premium income in financial instruments whose returns dwarfed anything they could obtain from selling insurance itself; high investment returns allowed insurers to push the underwriting cycle to new extremes as they drove prices downward, writing contracts that covered marginally insurable risks and lowering prices below actual costs (referred to as "cash-flow underwriting").[56] The explosive growth and profitability of financial investments perverted the insurance market by turning it into a cash cow, to be milked of premium income that could then be invested.[57] The problem was particularly acute for the reinsurers, which reportedly had a 100 percent overcapacity in 1982 and thus would be especially vulnerable in a downturn.[58]

This dynamic affected all lines of insurance, though international risks insurance prices remained relatively stable from 1982 to 1986, since it is a specialized type of insurance and demand for it remained high. CIGNA estimated in 1984 that it had issued more than two hundred political risk policies in two and a half years, totaling $2.25 billion in liabilities.[59] At times, the company supplied insurance for contract frustration coverage in Iran and Iraq, which were in the midst of a long conflict, for premiums up to 8 percent of the value of the project, a tremendously high price. As one insurer commented, "We can pick and choose the risks that we want; we get more proposals than we know what to do with."[60]

The temptations of cash-flow underwriting affected the international risks insurers for a brief period in the mid-1980s, but by then the boom was unsustainable; there no longer existed those high investment returns to offset low prices.[61] The London political risk market began to contract because of mounting claims for losses, reduced reinsurance capacity, and a weakened world economy.[62] In the wider insurance markets the softening of prices as the underwriting cycle deepened was accompanied by extensive and unanticipated losses, especially from product and pollution liability claims.[63] Until about 1985, as Antony Baker notes, "the most important single factor concerning the world insurance market has been overcapacity."[64] But the increased capacity chased too little premium income and experienced heavy underwriting losses in every country. By 1985 the industry as a whole was reaching financial exhaustion.[65] Two years later potential customers began to express concern that the number of political risk underwriters was declining in both the U.S. and London markets even as contract terms were becoming quite restrictive.[66]

Restraints on commercial insurers came primarily from the industry itself, and not from governments or other external forces. Since many international risks policies involve very large projects with the potential for huge losses, most insurers do not have the financial capacity to cover them alone or are reluctant to have one jumbo risk that soaks up their resources and decreases dramatically the diversification of their portfolio. On truly expensive projects the lack of even a small but crucial reinsurance percentage can scuttle the deal, and an esoteric specialty with a narrow market may close down completely without reinsurance. The insurers absolutely must reinsure their political risks, and therefore the reinsurers set the limits of what the direct insurers can cover.[67] The major reinsurers, such as Lloyd's, Swiss Re, and Munich Re, play a key role in the expansion or stagnation of a particular line of new insurance and have been reluctant in general to cover political risks.[68]

Many analysts have wondered about the security of reinsurance contracts, however, since major projects may require numerous layers of direct and reinsurance contracts. The direct insurers generally arrange a commercial reinsurance treaty for both domestic and foreign business, with a separate treaty for political risks reinsurance, typically through Lloyd's. Often, on large transactions, multiple reinsurers each take a small percentage of the overall contract, making it extremely difficult to determine who is ultimately responsible for paying claims. In response to these concerns, the U.S. government has demanded more control over reinsurance, but the German and Swiss governments have not been interested in taking action. One observer familiar with the reinsurance business held the opinion that the major reinsurers, such as Swiss Re, would make sure no crisis occurred by stepping in to reorganize the market if there were a serious problem.[69]

The role of reinsurance in driving the insurance industry became politically sensitive during the 1980s. In 1984, at the height of the market, CIGNA could not assume new political risk business in the Philippines and some Latin American countries because of its reinsurance treaty limits.[70] In the mid-1980s many reinsurers pulled back from covering certain kinds of risks, including political ones, as interest rates dropped, investment income declined, and losses mounted.[71] As a result, the supply of private sector insurance for political risks began to contract. When CIGNA attempted to write a policy insuring Citibank's loans to five developing countries, the reinsurers claimed this move violated the terms of their reinsurance treaty, and made it impossible for CIGNA to conclude the deal.[72] As one insurance industry expert criticized, the reinsurance companies come in at the height of the market but are the first to clench when things go sour.[73]

Even as direct insurers sought to expand coverage of political risks, and reinsurers began reining them in, the financial deregulation of the 1980s led to new and increasingly sophisticated tools for managing risks which competed with insurance products. Futures and options markets expanded rapidly, along with the use of computers for program trading. Used "properly," their advocates argued, these financial instruments could prevent portfolio losses and hedge the investor's risks; as one commentator put it, "so grand was the feeling of invulnerability that someone named this new strategy portfolio 'insurance.'"[74] Unlike insurance, however, these techniques produce real losses and no compensation in a financial collapse.

One indirect measure of the increased perception of risk in foreign transactions was the sudden emergence of a commercial market for political intelligence, which contributed to the range of new methods for managing the risks of international commerce. In the early 1980s "political risk analysis" sprang up as a specialty service designed to gauge the likelihood of war, revolution, and political and economic turbulence. The ability to predict where and when a risky event might occur became a salable service, and political scientists and others styled themselves "political risk analysts." At first corporations established in-house political risk analysis units, but recession and downsizing during the course of this difficult decade led them eventually to contract with outside consultants for this service.[75] Over time the more sophisticated analysts came to recognize that war and similarly traumatic destabilizing events are less likely to occur than problems due to economic nationalism or changes in regulatory regimes.[76]

Investors also began to safeguard their rights through complex legal arrangements that entangled their enterprises deliberately in a network of economic and political relationships.[77] Some of this network reflected the increasing complexity of intercorporate relationships generally. For instance, much of the credit extended to firms today is guaranteed unofficially when parent corporations lend to buyers, associated corporations, and subsidiaries. Richard Stern notes, "By creating a solid network of rights through agreements with private parties, the investor circumscribes the actions which a sovereign government may take vis-à-vis the enterprise without trespassing a right of the investor."[78]

Traditional foreign direct investment began to give way to new financial techniques, products, and organizational strategies, for example, capital for a project may be raised from a number of sources, such as suppliers, banks, bond issues, joint venture agreements, and new financial instruments.[79] Political authorities in the main financial centers lifted regulatory restrictions from traditional financial institutions and decided either not to regulate or to regulate only lightly such relatively new entities as offshore corporations. Many banks began to offer some form of financial guarantees.[80] Finally, many of the largest multinational firms began to self-insure, avoiding the costs of outside intermediation of their risks. They sought out "alternative insurance" by hiring consultants to tell them how to manage their own risks, which often meant consciously retaining a portion of them. Some firms set up a subsidiary company to hold the financial reserves it set aside in case of a loss, creating a "captive" insurance company that could also compete with traditional insurers for outside business.[81] Small companies, unable to retain large risks or set up captives, banded together in risk-retention groups or mutual insurance societies. These captives and risk-retention groups could skim off the high-quality risks and leave the regular insurers with the worst ones.[82]

The percentage of commercial insurers engaged in specialized political risk underwriting expanded and then declined in the period studied here; overall it remains a relatively small portion of the global insurance industry.[83] By the end of the 1980s, many insurers in the United States and United Kingdom were reducing their political risk business in response to the effects of loosened underwriting norms on their financial capacity. Lloyd's suffered claims for losses in Cuba, Libya, Nicaragua, Sudan, Vietnam, and Iraq, inspiring all underwriters to make their contract terms more restrictive. Furthermore, despite an increase in demand from their customers, Lloyd's underwriters cannot underwrite financial guarantees or export credit insurance. Nevertheless, the capacity of the London market to cover political risks such as confiscation, nationalization, expropriation, and deprivation expanded approximately ten times in the 1980s.

By the early 1990s there were only about six major private international risks insurers: Lloyd's, AIG, PanFinancial, Citicorp Trade Indemnity, and the relatively new PARIS.[84] Lloyd's and AIG dominate this group, in part because of their expertise.[85] AIG, CIGNA, and Zurich Insurance are also very active in global policies, which are sold to multinational corporations and which "top off" their local policies around the world. Estimates indicate the private sector insures annually only about one-quarter to one-fifth as much as government agencies, collecting about $100 million in premiums compared with the $400 to $500 million collected by government schemes.[86]

At the same time as the private sector insurers suffered through a severe underwriting cycle, the economy at large went through a bitter recession, resulting ultimately in a more active role for public sector insurance agencies for a period of time. The conservative agenda of the Reagan and Thatcher administrations prominently included a commitment to less government intervention in and regulation of the economy.

Ballooning budget deficits during a recessionary period reinforced this trend toward limited government. At the same time, intense competition for global markets and the pressure to revive sluggish economies produced calls for government support of national industry, if not directly through nationalization then indirectly through some sort of industrial policy. Philip Cerny argues the deregulation of the 1980s preceded or masked policies of reregulation that were more pro-competitive and designed to facilitate market activity instead of substitute for it.[87] This occurred within the context of national political debates that increasingly focused on what Paul Krugman critically called an obsession with competitiveness.[88] One way governments could facilitate foreign trade, credit, and investment in response to competitiveness concerns was by expanding their programs for export credit insurance and investment guarantees.

Expanding Public Responsibility for Foreign Risk: Competition and the Debt Crisis

The demands by international businesses for more protection abroad coincided with several larger trends. First, the threat of expropriation and nationalization of foreign assets actually declined over the course of the 1970s and 1980s. Instead, potential threats became more murky, as host country regulatory changes incrementally chipped away at ownership and control.[89] In response, investment guarantees designed to protect foreign property rights became complex instruments of corporate and national policy. Contract repudiation and home government export controls emerged as significant political risks.[90] Second, the international monetary system became more politicized and unstable, as governments could and did manipulate exchange rates in response to current account imbalances. That made it increasingly difficult to distinguish between the normal costs of business (commercial risk) and costs incurred from political intervention (political risk); thus, foreign exchange difficulties began to creep into the category of political risks, as defined by both private and public agencies. Third, competition for export markets heated up tremendously and became a particular concern of the United States as its preeminent position in the world economy seemed to erode.[91] Competition provided further justification to support and expand existing programs of government insurance for trade, credit, and foreign investment. Finally, the developing country debt crisis shocked the international financial community with the revelation of how fragile the system was, and it became a forceful impetus for change. The crisis also affected the attitudes of developing country governments toward foreign investment, as they welcomed foreign investors in a wave of economic reform that swept across the globe.[92] Resolving the problems of competitiveness and the debt crisis both involved gathering political support for an expansion of the public sector's role in protecting business from international risks.

Estimates by industry observers indicate that privately written gross premiums for political risks and trade risks insurance experienced a boom from 1978 to 1984, growing from around $15 million to $150 million.[93] The value of the business covered by the private underwriters ranged in the millions. During this same period, however, the members of the Berne Union (public sector agencies) covered business valued at approximately $200 billion, with the total volume of guarantees outstanding estimated at around $350 billion.[94] The value of international risks underwritten by the public sector dwarfed that of the private insurers.

Even though the commercial insurers became more willing and able to cover political risks, many multinational corporations expected their governments to assist them when they faced political difficulties in foreign markets.[95] Nearly all major industrialized countries have established some form of export credit and/or investment guarantee insurance agency, as have many of the developing nations, as one response to business demands. These programs generally are supported by bilateral interstate treaties that provide for protection of foreign investor rights and determine the conditions for resolving disputes. Most public agencies work closely with the commercial insurers, dividing the market between them in complementary fashion, with some states administering their government programs through commercial insurers or through public-private joint ventures.[96] Because of their historic position as leading centers of international insurance, the following discussion is limited to the British and American contexts; both countries have an active group of commercial political risks insurers plus long-standing government schemes.

Political supporters of government insurance view it as a public responsibility and even a public good, despite the fact that the benefits are captured almost exclusively by individual private actors. They argue that insurance can be used as foreign aid to promote business in less developed countries, to promote exports and investment abroad to strengthen the national economy,[97] to provide for national security by securing a steady supply of vital raw materials, to strengthen the market for goods and capital without regulating or nationalizing industry, to discourage foreign governments from arbitrarily expropriating foreign assets, and to counter the subsidies of competitor governments.[98] This array of arguments provides numerous bases on which to marshal political support. Both the United States and Great Britain designed their programs, especially the investment guarantee ones, with a strong foreign aid component. In the 1980s much of the rationale for the continuation of these programs centered on competition and countering subsidies.

Opponents view the programs as "expensive, difficult to control, and subject to political and economic pressures which have tended to subvert their objectives."[99] They are often attacked for "subsidizing success," as Feinberg labeled it, since their programs seem to benefit primarily large and already successful transnational corporations.[100] Many policymakers view investment guarantee programs simply as a tool of foreign policy and development aid, which makes them inevitably become controversial; as Lipson has shown, they are intimately connected to the expansion of Western concepts of property rights, which may infringe on the sovereignty of weaker states.[101] Export credit and export credit insurance programs are a tool of foreign *economic* policy, promoting the competitiveness of national industry against well-financed foreign competitors.

Two issues dominated the political debates that influenced changes in the role of government in international risks insurance over the course of the decade: competitiveness and the debt crisis. The political debate in Washington and London at that time centered on the pressing need to expand trade, as a response both to the fallout from the debt crisis and to general international competitive pressures that had produced record-breaking trade deficits in both countries. At the same time, the Reagan and Thatcher administrations preferred a market-oriented solution to economic problems and strongly resisted direct government intervention in the economy. During the first years of the debt crisis official export credit and insurance actually declined.[102] In 1981 the Reagan administration attacked the U.S. Export-Import Bank, the main source of government export credit and insurance, by threatening to cut back its funding significantly. Strong opposition emerged, however, stimulated by widespread concern over the subsidized credit and insurance offered by competitor governments; instead of cuts, the program received a new infusion of cash.[103] The expansion of export credit and investment guarantee programs during an era of tight-fisted government could be seen as a middle ground between doing nothing and implementing an interventionist industrial policy, which were the two alternatives dominating discussions. Protecting business from foreign risks would be a means of expanding economic activity in a way that supported the market instead of supplanting it.[104]

The intense pressure to increase exports produced a situation in which governments competed among themselves, particularly in the industrialized countries, to provide subsidized export credit and insurance. As each country matched the terms of the others, it became a losing strategy for all except the exporters. The major trading states repeatedly attempted to negotiate an end to this destructive competition, trying to diminish or eliminate the subsidy element in export credit and insurance. They produced only weak codes in the OECD and the GATT and a number of minimal and unenforced "gentlemen's agreements."[105] The Berne Union failed in its efforts to promote standard contract terms. Most of the negotiations revolved around the distortion of product markets created by government-subsidized interest rates for export credit; little attention has been paid to the effect of government insurance on the direction of trade and investment.[106] Without a negotiated solution, these agencies would be tempted to undermine their financial stability by loosening underwriting standards and enlarging the subsidy element of their policies.

At the same time as concerns over competitiveness absorbed great attention in negotiations among the industrialized countries, a different concern suddenly became the central element in relations between the industrialized and the developing world: the debt crisis. In 1982 the Mexican government formally announced it could not make the next installment of its debt payments and threatened default. The debt crisis shocked the business community by forcing it to confront an unexpected form of political risk in foreign transactions: the threat of governments declaring themselves insolvent and potentially undermining the global financial system. This realization galvanized the international financial community, especially major money center banks in the United States that had lent more than their capital base and underestimated their accumulated risk in developing nations. In the following years one debtor state after another balanced precariously on the edge of default, with governments, international organizations, and major commercial creditors attempting to avoid both default by governments and financial collapse by major banks. The crisis forced major banks to cooperate in rescheduling debts, elevated the International Monetary Fund (IMF) and World Bank into monitors and enforcers of debt agreements, and imposed stringent policy reforms on debtor nations in order to wring out a steady flow of funds from debtors to creditors.[107]

At the beginning of the debt crisis many observers were fairly sanguine about the outcome, despite their initial shock at the weak position of both banks and debtor countries. One analyst argued that more than 75 percent of the debt actually was "covered" in some fashion—by private and public insurance and guarantees, by the implicit or explicit backing of parent corporations, by foreign buyers' credits and loans to other associated corporations, and through the willingness of the IMF and World Bank to intervene in debtor nation affairs to prevent default.[108] Another observer claimed that in 1981, just before the Mexican default threat, 68 percent of loans to developing nations, excluding members of the Organization of Petroleum Exporting Countries (OPEC), were guaranteed.[109]

Instead of a quick resolution to what seemed to be a temporary cash-flow problem, with risks to creditors and investors minimized by various forms of direct and indirect insurance, the more immediate result of the crisis was that almost all capital flows to the debtor states ceased. Private direct investment dried up, new lending simply became part of the rescheduling of existing debt, and trade flows dramatically reversed as debtor states pumped up exports to gain hard currency. By the middle of the decade most business executives believed the extensive political and commercial risk in debtor nations outweighed any calculation of potential gains from doing business there. Without any new money the debtor countries sank into a recession that would stymie all efforts to resolve the crisis.

Private sector solutions to managing the risks involved in the financial crisis failed to evolve, despite the high level of coordination among banks in rescheduling debt.[110] For instance, Citibank hailed as innovative its insurance policy covering $900 million of its $12 billion in loans to five of its largest debtors. As Citicorp vice-president Thomas Jones said, "We wanted to show that someone was willing to share the risk, that the banks are not facing a doomsday scenario."[111] The insurer, CIGNA, had to back out of the deal in large part because of the reluctance of reinsurers to participate in the risk. The private insurers that had covered exports and short-term credit on transactions in Africa and Latin America suffered a series of losses that began to grow in size and number as the debt reschedulings began to expand beyond sovereign debt to include commercial debt and even trade credit.[112]

The solution that many policymakers would grasp hold of by the mid-1980s paralleled the response to concerns over international competitiveness: expand insurance and guarantee programs, in this case explicitly to address the issue of political risk. National programs already insured a portion of the debt previously incurred, and policymakers hoped that continued coverage by these official organizations would encourage renewed private lending and investment. Furthermore, this plan dovetailed with concurrent concern over promoting exports and investment, with the goal of reducing the trade deficit, expanding employment, and increasing corporate profitability. At the same time, the program to insure exports and investment would, it was hoped, encourage continued trade with debtor nations and facilitate the resumption of foreign investment.

Both the British ECGD and the U.S. ExImbank had suffered a marked deterioration in their financial resources due to the record number of claims caused by debt reschedulings and delays in payment. By the mid-1980s government export credit insurance agencies in the United States, United Kingdom, Germany, Japan, and France were in deep financial trouble. In 1983 the United States–based Federal Credit Insurance Agency (FCIA), a joint subsidiary of about fifty companies that insured U.S. multinationals against commercial and political risks and participated in Export-Import Bank operations, suffered such losses—over $200 million from 1983 to 1985—that it abandoned the business and simply became the administrator of ExImbank insurance.[113] The continuing debate over whether the private sector could or should take over the export credit insurance and investment guarantee business erupted once again, as it had repeatedly since the agencies' inception.[114]

The ECGD and ExImbank both raised premiums and instituted stringent underwriting standards in an attempt to recoup their losses and establish more stable financing. They also decided not to resume operations in countries renegotiating their debt until two to three years had passed. The ECGD came "off cover," as it is called, for trade credits to most debtor nations and required its existing customers to remain meaningfully at risk in all transactions, that is, the ECGD would no longer insure 100 percent of any project, as it had at times in the past. This tightening of insurance terms, especially the increase in premiums, backfired by driving away the highest quality business—the classic adverse selection problem. By 1986 the U.S. ExImbank had a deficit of

$333 million and the ECGD had an accumulated deficit of $1,109 million.[115] These massive deficits undermined both agencies financially and politically.

Despite these losses, the directors of these agencies came under political pressure to resume cover even in countries in the midst of a debt renegotiation, instead of waiting for the final agreement, because the cessation of capital flows to the debtor nations continued to strangle their economies. The conservative administrations in Britain and the United States put pressure on the agencies to behave more commercially, however.[116] The proposed reforms were opposed by U.S. bankers and exporters, who did not want to see the subsidy element of ExImbank's programs reduced.[117] Both the ECGD and the Export-Import Bank underwent significant restructuring that allowed them to expand their programs—for instance, to cover import credits, project financing, and small business transactions—but also reduced the subsidy element. The ECGD also considered separating commercial and political risk policies at the request of its customers.[118] In 1986, in order to promote exports, Congress infused the Export-Import Bank with new money and made a commitment to its overall expansion.

Four years into the debt crisis a study by the IMF demonstrated significant if incremental changes across many national export credit and insurance programs. These agencies increased the flexibility of their terms in response to the lack of resolution of the developing country financial crisis. The report notes, "Over the period since mid-1982, both official and bank creditors have been asked in certain cases to make a concerted effort to provide financing for the adjustment programs of debtor countries."[119] Export credit flows increased in the mid to late 1980s, as did guaranteed bank credits and official export credit insurance.[120]

Even with the reforms, the weakened public agencies had left a potentially lucrative market underserved and open to commercial exploitation. At the beginning of the decade one industry observer described the political risks insurance market as dominated by one regional and fourteen national agencies, with scarcely any participation by private companies.[121] Within a few years the private sector successfully captured a portion of the market for export credit and foreign investment insurance, although often with severe policy restrictions and high premiums.[122] The public export credit and insurance agencies continued to struggle politically and financially throughout the 1980s, despite reforms, caught between pressures to expand and a larger trend toward government downsizing and privatization.[123]

The London-based Trade Indemnity Corporation actively pursued international markets in the early 1980s. It successfully persuaded a significant number of firms to consider insuring their entire business operations for both political and commercial risks, arguing that even the industrialized countries posed substantial risks from fluctuations in economic performance and regulatory reforms. TIC's export credit insurance business increased solidly during the middle of the decade and seemed to symbolize the strengths of the private sector: competitive terms, strong underwriting norms and practices, and expertise in evaluating risks.

Private insurers devised sophisticated contracts to protect themselves as much as the insureds. Different underwriters offered different policy terms and contracts, but all attempted to insulate themselves from opportunistic behavior by customers. For instance, an underwriter could insist on "whole turnover" cover, which insures the entire business of a customer and not just the high-risk transactions. Some underwriters sought partnerships to coinsure projects, and for complex and high-value projects, reinsurance is vital. Most underwriters require that the customer be "meaningfully at risk" on each transaction and must endure a waiting period before a claim will be paid. In contrast with the public agencies, the commercial firms insured export credit risks fairly successfully.

One of the more interesting developments to come out of the debt crisis and competitiveness concerns of the 1980s was that government leaders in both the developed and developing world accepted a larger public role in guaranteeing foreign investments, not just insuring exports. This could be seen most clearly in the United States. The U.S. government supplies investment guarantee insurance for American firms on projects in low-income countries through an agency that is separate from its export credit and insurance programs—OPIC.[124] OPIC investment guarantees are limited to three basic categories: expropriation, currency inconvertibility, and political violence, including (since 1981) civil strife and terrorism.[125] OPIC operates as an independently financed agency of the government, subject to periodic congressional reauthorization and backed by the full faith and credit of the U.S. government.[126] Congress designed OPIC to be used as a foreign policy tool, for economic development and support for U.S. business operations abroad. At every reauthorization, however, one of the main issues raised in congressional debate is whether the private sector could—and should—do the same job, especially given the profitability of OPIC's operations.[127]

OPIC operates under customary insurance principles, despite its foreign policy mandate. It manages moral hazard and adverse selection problems through excluding certain risks, waiting one year before paying a claim, and covering less than 100 percent of a loss. The program diversifies its business across investors and nations and is required by law to limit how much of its liability is to any single investor. OPIC can provide guarantees only when the government of the host country has signed a bilateral investment protection treaty with the United States, which provides a second layer of legal "insurance" against expropriation risk.[128]

Congress has put further political limits on OPIC operations in order to pursue foreign policy goals. OPIC statutorily cannot provide guarantees for investments in countries with high per capita income[129] or to communist countries, and the Department of State occasionally rejects a proposal because of human rights violations in the host country. To avoid controversy, the agency shuns military projects and foreign investments that are politically sensitive, including those that seem to be exporting jobs from the United States or building up competing foreign industries. OPIC officials' efforts to expand into trade promotion, a natural corollary of some of its investment programs, has occasionally caused friction with the International Trade Administration and the Export-Import Bank. Finally, OPIC cannot provide guarantees for projects that might increase unemployment or worsen the balance of payments.

On the other side of the transaction, some developing country leaders have objected to being labeled "less developed" or have refused to accept the terms of the bilateral investment protection treaty, which is required for OPIC-guaranteed projects. Many developing country leaders are sensitive to the idea that investment guarantees reflect a negative judgment about their political system or leadership. They also perceive investment treaties as an instrument for imposing Western notions of property rights or judicial remedies. These treaties and guarantees may be viewed as violating the autonomy of developing country governments. The Mexican government, for instance, has jealously guarded its sovereignty and would not consider an investment treaty with the United States until recent negotiations for a North American

Free Trade Agreement (NAFTA). Thus, the scope of OPIC programs has been restricted both geographically and politically, owing to the policies of both the United States and developing country governments.

Despite these political and financial limits, OPIC officials had acquired a degree of experience in political risk underwriting by the 1980s, through the agency's own projects and through observing the commercial insurers. OPIC has modeled its policies in large part on the norms and practices of the private sector and has attempted to restrain opportunistic behavior by investors. OPIC does not pay claims to those who deliberately aggravate the political situation in a host country or in any way cause that government to abrogate the terms of the original business contract; an unscrupulous investor seeking to abandon a sinking project might act provocatively as a way of exiting the contract, leaving OPIC to pick up the costs. The success of this restriction depends, however, on the ability of OPIC officials to determine whether or not a firm has caused its own losses. One could even imagine a host government and a foreign investor colluding for the host to take over an ailing firm, to the benefit of both.[130] The backlog of disputed claims under OPIC perhaps demonstrates the extent of this problem.

The Reagan administration, despite its commitment to reducing the role of government in the economy, rejuvenated OPIC and expanded its programs in the face of intense anxiety over U.S. competitiveness in global markets, a need to shore up the economy at home, and especially pressure to direct capital toward the debtor nations. Like the Export-Import Bank, OPIC restructured its programs to conform more to commercial practices by reducing subsidies, tightening underwriting standards, and generally becoming more market-oriented than before. The Reagan administration appointed a marketing expert to direct the agency, and in 1988 Congress voted to expand OPIC programs further. One innovation is that OPIC now has the authority to coinsure projects with private firms, in line with the administration's privatization mandate, which it had not done since its initial experiment with a British consortium in 1971. Although it was first perceived as being a service for major multinational corporations, OPIC also attempted to expand its contacts with small businesses during this period; they accounted for about one-third of its projects by the mid-1980s.

Given the profitability of OPIC but the restrictions on where and how it could operate, one would expect to see numerous commercial insurers competing for the same business.[131] A recent analysis of this question argued that the ability of OPIC to access State Department and CIA information sources gives it an advantage over commercial insurers. Similar access to information also provides advantages to other national insurance schemes. Furthermore, the author points out that OPIC underwriters understand how to structure a contract to limit opportunistic behavior and can diversify the agency's portfolio widely, despite being limited to investments in low-income countries. The informational advantage of a government agency may not in fact be so great, however. Many insurers, such as those at Lloyd's, have extensive intelligence capabilities and great depth of experience in understanding international risks.[132]

Any government agency such as OPIC, however, operates with one distinct advantage: the full faith and credit of the government. Thus, any claim for loss is essentially backed by unlimited reserves. Considering the size of possible losses today and the long-term nature of many contracts, it is extremely difficult for commercial insurers to maintain reserves of sufficient size to cover all contingencies, even with coinsurance and reinsurance. Commercial insurers are also much less likely to favor long-term projects of ten years or more; unlike a government agency, there is no guarantee a private firm will be in business that long. The result is that the international risks insurance market is divided between private and public agencies, with the latter specializing in large projects and long-term contracts.

The debt crisis frightened off foreign investors and cut off commercial lending to the heavily indebted countries in the 1980s when the political and financial risks involved became obvious and overwhelming. The efforts of governments to stimulate renewed lending and investment through their insurance and investment guarantee programs generally failed. Under Michel Camdessus, the IMF reconsidered its commitment to requiring full repayment of the debt and began to support the previously unthinkable—debt relief—as a way to generate economic growth. The World Bank also responded innovatively; bank staff, led by Ibrahim Shihata and others, lobbied for the establishment of a multilateral investment guarantee agency. Bank staff members pinpointed noncommercial risks as a significant impediment to foreign investments, as revealed by discussions with business representatives and by their awareness of the growth of private political risks insurance and the political risk analysis profession. They also pointed out that the inadequacies of national investment guarantee agencies, particularly in their spread of risk, led increasing numbers of them to look for reinsurance to diversify their portfolios. Additionally, bank staff noted the growing number of bilateral investment protection treaties, increased membership in the International Centre for the Settlement of Investment Disputes, and the establishment of new national investment guarantee agencies—all indicating that governments and investors sought financial and legal protection for international commerce.[133]

After negotiations among the major capital exporting nations, many of the capital importers, and representatives of the business community, the World Bank established a new subsidiary in 1988, the Multilateral Investment Guarantee Agency (MIGA).[134] The MIGA provides investment security similar to that of OPIC or ECGD for projects in which the states involved have ratified the MIGA treaty. It provides guarantees against what it defines as noncommercial risks, specifically currency transfer, expropriation and legal/administrative infringements of investor rights, armed conflict and civil disturbance, and investment-related breach of contract by the host government. Note that this is a very broad definition of political risks. It also supplies advisory and promotional services to member countries to help create a "responsive" investment climate, and considers this function one of its distinctive features.[135] Unlike national programs, the MIGA can guarantee investments for projects involving more than two countries and covers both new investments and expansion of existing ones, including privatizations. The MIGA does not compete with national guarantee agencies and can coinsure or reinsure with them. It also is able to work with private political risks insurers.

The MIGA is the first relatively successful attempt to establish multilateral protection for international investment, which has always been difficult and highly sensitive since host governments must agree to abide by rules on the treatment of foreign property.[136] World Bank officials, and not government leaders in the United States or other capital-exporting nations, initiated the discussions that led to the creation of the MIGA.[137] World Bank President A. W. Clausen lobbied in favor of it from the beginning of his term. In a 1985 speech he pointed out, "Political risk is clearly an obstacle, and a significant one, to international investment in the developing countries. The establishment of investment guarantee programs in all the industrial countries, the increasing sophistication of political risk analysis, the emergence of a private market for political risk insurance—these developments all confirm the importance of political risk to many investors. Investment insurance can, by pooling risk, reduce it and translate it into a limited, manageable cost."[138]

A report in *The Economist* in 1986 argued that the World Bank should promote the private sector—which is exactly what the MIGA would do—as a direct way to help the world's poor and "mollify the anti-aid dullards in [the U.S.] Congress."[139] The Reagan administration supported the MIGA Convention negotiations despite its wariness regarding government intervention in the market and in the face of heavy opposition, especially from the AFL-CIO, which argued that efforts to support foreign investment were tantamount to promoting the export of manufacturing jobs from the United States. In the end, the United States made the first capital contribution to the MIGA and has the greatest amount of voting power in MIGA decision-making processes.

The MIGA may represent a new stage in the development of an international risks insurance regime. The resources of this agency are potentially much larger than those of the private sector or individual state agencies. Its guarantees may be perceived as relatively neutral politically, coming from a multilateral agency and not from a particular government, although its activities in promoting a favorable business climate may be criticized for priveleging business over labor and the poor.[140] One of the main questions for those establishing the MIGA is the extent to which it succeeds in stimulating new or additional capital flows (the "additionality" issue).[141]

Under the impetus of the debt crisis and growing national economic competition, the market for public and private international risks insurance expanded. The dynamics of markets for trade credit insurance differ from those for investment guarantees, however, because of differences in the degree of flexibility of the underlying insured value—loans are much more flexible financial instruments than direct investments, or less asset-specific. It is relatively simple to cancel a trade transaction, whereas foreign direct investments are more difficult to abandon. These differences also are connected to the amount of leverage of the participants; one analyst notes the "threat of retaliation from the world banking community if one of its own is violated, versus the minimal backup accorded a single industrial corporation."[142]

The Ultimate International Risk: War, Trade, and Marine Insurance

Despite the shift in financial power to New York, the London market still sets the rates and terms for marine insurance worldwide, since most ships insure with London companies. Marine insurance, the oldest type of insurance, now is an absolute requirement for all shipping and is not considered an optional enhancement. If the London insurers significantly raise the premium on insurance for a voyage to a particular destination or along a particular route, all legal shipping potentially can be choked off.

Marine insurers jointly regulate the terms they offer customers through the Joint Hull Committee, in which they have formulated "understandings" to underwrite business at rates and terms proposed by the committee. In the 1970s the two oil shocks and the economic stagnation that followed led to a worldwide shipping slump and a softening, or lowering, of the price of marine insurance. The Joint Hull understandings were intended to forestall the kind of vicious competition that deepened the underwriting cycle in other lines of insurance.[143]

Most shipowners have their vessels insured under a worldwide trading warranty, which automatically excludes areas of conflict. Shipping in politically disturbed areas requires a special rate quote to cover political risk.[144] The Middle East has consistently been the "hot spot" where rates fluctuate wildly. In September 1970, for instance, the Institute of London Underwriters announced it would raise rates on voyages to the Middle East by about 400 percent.[145] Shipowners traditionally have established protection and indemnity mutual clubs in an effort to control costs and insure themselves against risks that insurance underwriters considered uninsurable or insurable at very high rates.[146]

Lloyd's underwriters' decisions on raising and lowering marine insurance rates deeply influenced shipping through the Persian Gulf during the Iran-Iraq War in the 1980s. Approximately one-sixth of world petroleum passes through the gulf, which was threatened when Iran began attacking neutral shipping (the "tanker war"). When the tanker war began, Lloyd's underwriters first doubled the price of marine political risks insurance in the gulf but did not withdraw from the market entirely; later they lowered war risk rates in response to competition in the London market. By 1985 marine underwriters had paid out around $1 billion in losses.[147] Some underwriters even continued to insure trade and shipping with Iran itself, in the belief (later proven accurate) that, despite the lame response by the United States to the Iranian Revolution and the lack of direct intervention in the Iran-Iraq War, the United States would always maintain a certain degree of stability in the gulf.

Both the Soviet Union and the United States maneuvered for advantage during the conflict, while many of the most vulnerable oil-importing states, such as Greece, the Netherlands, and Japan, stood on the sidelines hoping for a resolution to the conflict. Eventually, the

Reagan administration decided to step in directly, both to protect international navigation and to support the wider goal of ending the war and protecting the security of friendly Arab states. The United States agreed to protect Kuwaiti neutral shipping, first through a controversial program of "reflagging" tankers and ultimately by providing military escorts. In this case, the continued availability of private insurance before U.S. intervention helped minimize disruptions in oil markets. Fortunately, this conflict did not evolve into another great-power war but instead remained relatively contained within the region.

When Iraq invaded Kuwait in 1989, insurance rates on shipping in the region again surged upward in response, initially by about 2,000 percent. Both the airlines and the Pentagon brought up the issue of whether the government should provide insurance against war risks.[148] Once the lines of conflict were clearly drawn, however, many were surprised to see commercial rates drift down again. The underwriters looked on the military mobilization of the United States and its allies, sanctioned by the United Nations, as providing greater protection to shipping, although it raised the possibility that this could become a great-power war. The availability of insurance did not decline significantly, and the fear that shipping through the gulf would be halted by the war proved unfounded.

Years before the Persian Gulf conflict Arab investors and governments responded to what they perceived to be manipulation of insurance rates by London marine underwriters by forming a collective Arab insurance group to cover regional risks, perhaps seeking the same success as the oil cartel. The Inter-Arab Investment Guarantee Corporation, established in 1974 and made up of twelve Arab members, competed unsuccessfully with London insurers to cover shipping in the gulf. The corporation, established for political reasons, could not effectively control the opportunistic behavior of its member-customers or its costs and generally remained outside the established international risks insurance regime. Although the corporation did not succeed, today one of the larger international insurance companies is the Arab Insurance Group (Arig), which buys insurance internationally to retail among Arab nations.[149]

The political risk surrounding such events as the Iran-Iraq and Persian Gulf wars make them interesting cases for the study of insurance and its role in facilitating economic transactions, especially shipping, during outbreaks of violence.[150] Marine war risks insurance supports continued shipping along dangerous routes worldwide and today is especially important for Southeast Asian shipping, which suffers from extensive piracy, with literally hundreds of vessels attacked in the 1990s, including oil tankers.[151] Local governments have been unable or unwilling to take the military actions that would eliminate piracy, and marine insurers willing to insure against it have found steady business. In 1980 the marine insurers themselves set up and financed the Far East Regional Investigation Team (FERIT) to police the Southeast Asian seas, seeking to restrain fraud and piracy.[152] The private insurers have been instrumental in maintaining global transportation despite clear threats.[153]

The Institutions of International Risks Insurance

During the 1980s the overall level of demand for international risks intermediation increased, as technology transformed the nature of the modern economy, the political-economic power of the United States was challenged, and financial markets underwent rapid and amazing structural changes. Political and economic events in the Middle East, Persian Gulf, and Latin America fed the perception of increased risk. At the same time, as developing country markets contracted in mid-decade, many exporters, investors, and lenders attempted to withdraw to the safety of the industrialized markets. These changes ultimately established a new environment for international economic activity and produced conflicting trends within the public and private sectors in the international risks insurance regime. These trends reflect the intersection of demand, norms, and resources in driving the institutional division of the market between public and private sector agencies.

The supply of international risks insurance fluctuated over the course of the 1980s. In many cases public agencies were the primary source of these fluctuations. For example, the U.S. public export credit agency had authorizations for export credit insurance of $4,108.4 million in 1979, peaking in 1985 at $6,444.0 million and hovering in the range of $4,300.0 million for the rest of the decade. Its guarantee program on medium- and long-term business fluctuated between $600.0 and $2,509.7 million, with most years around $1,300 million. In 1990, however, its authorizations for guarantees expanded to $3,382.7 million and then doubled and tripled over the next few years.[154] The British ECGD continued to lose money, and in 1991 the government sold off its short-term export credit insurance business.[155] The MIGA only truly launched its operations in 1988 and initially provided guarantees on just a few projects. Its business expanded dramatically in the early 1990s, however, though it is still small relative to its potential.[156]

The level of privately placed political risks insurance is more difficult to establish. One analyst estimated that the private political risks insurers annually cover only one-fourth to one-fifth of what the national insurance schemes cover.[157] There is general agreement that the private political risks insurance market took off during the early part of the 1980s. Later in the decade it contracted somewhat along with the rest of the insurance market, particularly in response to the withdrawal from the market of the reinsurers.[158] Individual companies and underwriting syndicates at Lloyd's entered and exited the business regularly, with only a few maintaining a continuous presence.

The degree to which there is unmet demand for insurance, or transactions for which international risks insurance is not supplied by either public or private agencies, cannot be directly determined. When a firm believes there is unacceptable risk on a prospective transaction, it has a number of options other than buying insurance, including abandoning the project—an alternative chosen by many commercial banks with regard to Latin American debtor states. Some corporations have restructured their business in ways that reduce their risks in developing countries.[159] Some developed new financial and organizational techniques to reduce or redistribute their risks, such as strategic alliances, joint ventures, and new forms of investment that do not involve ownership control and its commercial and political risks.[160] Others sought new ways to manage political risk among the burgeoning number of clever financial alternatives invented during the 1980s, including self-insurance and complex hedging strategies. The turmoil in financial markets increased corporate awareness of risks in general, and many firms are devising comprehensive company-wide policies to address all risks, especially financial ones.[161] Firms also simply lobbied for government protection, both directly through diplomatic intervention and increasingly through expanded insurance and guarantees for exports and investments abroad.

Just as the financial sector as a whole reorganized and became more concentrated in terms of the size and number of major players but less centralized in terms of geographical place, so did the insurance industry. Many corporations and brokerage houses merged or were acquired by others, and some went out of business. The large multinational broker became a leader in placing international business, including the specialized coverage of political risks, putting together global insurance and reinsurance programs for multinational companies.[162] Within Lloyd's, syndicates and managing agencies grew in size and number, as did the non-Lloyd's company market.[163] Lloyd's itself began to lose its position at the center of the industry, however, and London was replaced as the center of finance by New York.

The relaxation of regulatory controls on the major financial markets in the early 1980s increased the perception of risk in foreign transactions and the demand for insurance. At the same time, it encouraged abandonment of standard insurance practice as insurers—for a time—could rely on income from investments instead of from their underlying insurance business. This development resulted in two trends among international risks insurers: losses on insurance business by both public and private insurers, undermining their financial capacity; and increasing competition from new insurers, such as captives and mutual insurers, and from public agencies now mandated to become more commercially competitive. The nonlife insurance industry as a whole made few profits on its underwriting throughout the 1980s, and many companies went bankrupt.

The response of the commercial sector eventually was to raise prices and restrict coverage, especially for political risks. In many cases, these actions were stimulated by the unwillingness of reinsurers to participate in covering political risks, which limited the financial capacity of direct insurers. Public sector agencies responded in a wide variety of ways: the United States reinvigorated its programs to deal with debt and competitiveness problems, and the United Kingdom privatized the Export Credit Guarantee Department because of budget deficits.

Overall the private market today is a limited one, for several reasons: the historical dominance of a few major players such as Lloyd's (despite its current weaknesses) and AIG, the expertise that is needed to underwrite international risks correctly, high losses that have undermined capacity, and the reluctance of reinsurers to participate in this market. The commercial insurers also tend to set premium rates in response to factors beyond a simple calculation of the probability of loss. Insurers raise and lower rates because of changes in their own resources or to encourage or discourage certain kinds of business in order to balance their portfolio of risks.[164] Insurers also carefully limit their contracts through various exclusion clauses, so their insurance may not be the total coverage against risks that the customer may demand.[165] In the mid-1980s one analyst observed, "The private market relies on OPIC to pick up the mainstream of the business, and to develop a general interest in it, and then fills the niches where it has an advantage."[166]

Government insurance programs potentially have much deeper sources of financial support and access to a wider array of information regarding conditions in a foreign country than do commercial insurers. In addition, almost all government programs contain a subsidy element. They are often limited by political restrictions that may make it difficult to diversify risks sufficiently or even pool a sufficient number of risks, but that may be offset by their access to detailed information about foreign politics, on which they can base predictions of risks. Even as the commercial insurers displayed a new willingness to cover some "exotic" risks at reasonable prices in the early years of the decade, many international firms turned increasingly to government agencies for export credit insurance and investment guarantees for their largest, long-term projects in foreign countries. As a 1984 British report stated, "there is no evidence that the private sector could provide the equivalent of ECGD's existing services, or that the bulk of ECGD's activities could be transferred to the private sector."[167]

Government agencies found themselves under conflicting pressures from their political masters to expand their business without reaping politically untenable losses. In response, the government agencies in the United States and Great Britain implemented more commercially competitive practices, carefully judging the insurability and probability of loss for different projects and countries and trimming back the subsidy component of their programs. A close examination of the ECGD,[168] ExIm, and OPIC insurance operations indicates that aid and foreign policy goals have been weakened in favor of maintaining a commercially oriented management policy (though the foreign policy aims have by no means been eliminated). The public and private agencies seemed to be converging in their underwriting norms and practices.

The public insurance and guarantee agencies found new purpose in the global debt crisis. Over the course of the decade, in response to the continuing problems of debtor nations and the desire on the part of creditor states to resolve them, the insurance and guarantee agencies extended their business, on a case-by-case basis, resuming cover in debtor nations even before debt reschedulings had been completed. Reforms early in the decade pushed the agencies, especially in the United States, to become more like those in the private sector. Given expanded resources, they were able to extend cover for long-term risks that the private sector no longer could or would insure. As Lipson notes in reference to the banking community, "the limits to private voluntary cooperation help to explain the changing role of international institutions in the debt crisis."[169]

Like the private sector, the state agencies have limits on programs, both from the nature of insurance and as a response to political pressures. Legislatures established export credit and investment guarantee agencies principally to fulfill foreign policy goals, perceiving them as useful for foreign aid and development programs. Over the course of the 1980s such programs became increasingly identified with competitiveness issues, as many countries sought to expand their exports. The investment guarantee programs also came to be viewed as an instrument for expanding free markets and capitalism in general. In contrast to earlier eras, there was relatively little political demand to institute government insurance on the basis of national security. National agencies quickly became embedded in the insurance regime's network of extant rules, procedures, and customs, and officials often turned to the private sector for assistance in administering or designing their programs, even moving toward cooperative agreements to coinsure or reinsure projects.

The flexibility of the international risks regime in the 1980s contrasts with the rigidity of the late 1930s, when the debacle of the Spanish Civil War led to the withdrawal of the commercial insurers almost entirely from certain political risks markets. This flexibility comes primarily from the government export credit and investment guarantee agencies, however. Commercial insurers, having entered the political risks insurance market more aggressively after 1979, faced a double set of losses. First, they found themselves presented with claims for losses on white elephant projects in the Middle East which had been financed during the oil price boom that collapsed a few years later, revealing a steady accumulation of risk in places such as Iraq and Saudi Arabia. Second, the debt crisis demonstrated they had not adhered to the most basic norms and practices of the insurance business and had actually reduced the spread of their risk globally. Both illustrated the dangers of adverse selection, in which those businesses likely to be good risks (i.e., unlikely to suffer losses) forgo insurance while the bad risks come to dominate the insurer's portfolio.

The private and public sector agencies perceive their roles as complementary. As one prominent private insurer states, "there are occasions when we are competitive, but on the whole we try to be a complementary alternative and to fit in with the government schemes."[170] The trade-off between public and private provision of insurance is a function of the limitations each sector puts on its policies. The private political risks market is limited: war and inconvertibility coverage is rare, the time period of the contract is short, and the capacity to cover large projects or numerous small projects in one country is restricted. Commercial policies, however, are flexible with regard to the terms and countries of coverage, and the contracts are relatively easy to negotiate and conclude. Public agencies are deliberately designed to offer policies that cover war and inconvertibility and have long terms and high values. But coverage is generally restricted on a political basis, and concluding the agreement requires an extensive bureaucratic process.[171] Neither government agencies nor private ones cover all the risks facing corporations in their international transactions.[172] Private insurers attempt to delineate a clear line between the kinds of transactions the public agencies should insure and the kinds of policies they themselves offer; at the same time, the definition of that line has not remained fixed.

The norms of the international risks insurance regime established in the first part of the century came under attack in the early 1980s, as commercial insurers redefined insurable political risks. In the early part of the decade private insurers offered coverage for confiscation, expropriation, and nationalization. Over the course of the 1980s an increasing number began to expand political risks to include contract frustration and inconvertibility. Some underwriters debated the utility of the fifty-year-old Waterborne Agreement and sought to relax its provisions. While the norms concerning insurability became more flexible, the accepted consensus on appropriate insurance practice weakened, as cash-flow underwriting dominated the insurance industry in the early part of the decade, leading eventually to great losses. The international risks insurance regime, first established one century ago, had fundamentally changed by the end of the 1980s, with the private insurers occupying one narrow part of the market and the big public sector agencies occupying another corner.

5/ *The Infrastructure of Global Capitalism*

The development and evolution of an international risks insurance regime over the course of the twentieth century depended on the initiative and authority of the private sector participants. The insurance underwriters in London and elsewhere made crucial decisions about what would be insured, how it would be insured, and by whom. The public authorities, concerned with national security and economic well-being, looked on the management of political risks as an important factor facilitating foreign commerce but proved reluctant to become participants themselves; they eventually joined the regime as junior partners. The commercial underwriters and government agencies carefully separated their business from each other, viewing their operations as complementary and not competitive. Both adhered to standard industry norms in designing their insurance contracts, and both believed that many international risks could not be insured. By the end of the century a marked shift had occurred in the relationship between the public and private sectors in providing insurance and managing the risks of international commerce. Changes in demand, industry norms, and the financial resources available to the insurers transferred greater influence over the regime to public sector players.

What Changed? The Influence of Demand, Norms, and Resources

The three periods examined here—1870–1914, 1917–39, and 1979–89—represent three cases where we could expect the overall demand by business for protection from international risks to be high. All three time periods include military conflicts, with demand naturally increasing most sharply on the outbreak of war among the great powers in the earlier two periods. In the final case, demand dramatically rose at the beginning of the decade in response to revolution in Iran and fluctuated in response to political changes in the Persian Gulf region. The character of demand, however, evolved over the course of the twentieth century. In the earlier period business interests looked on war risks for shipping as the main threat to international commerce, which made it fairly simple to divide protection tasks between the government, which maintained the navy, and the private sector, which could supply insurance. International risks in the 1980s included a much wider range of threats to trade and investment, such as rejection of contracts already concluded, foreign exchange controls, and other problems that straddle the border between political and commercial risks.

In the earliest decades of the nineteenth century insurers categorized political risks as an adjunct to marine insurance, which covered many different perils encountered at sea. By the end of the century, in response to the threat to shipping from imminent conflict among the great powers, the private sector separated war risks from other marine insurance in order to protect themselves from the financial consequences of modern warfare. This also enabled them to monitor the behavior of customers, by establishing standard exclusions in the marine insurance contract and restrictive limits on political risks policies. Political leaders in Great Britain, the main case discussed here, expressed deep concern about the inability of shippers to buy sufficient insurance against war risks, viewing it as vital to the maintenance of shipping in time of war. Both commercial insurers and policymakers doubted the wisdom of government participation in the war risks insurance market; they defined the role of public authorities in a limited manner, expecting them to be concerned primarily with maintaining a powerful navy to protect shipping. Only the outbreak of war persuaded the government to set up a temporary insurance program for war risks.

The political and economic instabilities of the interwar years generated great demand for insurance against international risks, and the private sector responded by expanding its willingness to cover new risks besides marine war risks. The 1920s and 1930s, with the threat of war a constant companion to efforts to recover from economic collapse, produced new developments in the insurance market. Increasing risk had brought about innovations in the 1920s, including the first tentative efforts by the British state to supply long-term trade credit insurance and the entrepreneurial efforts of commercial insurers to cover land war risks. The industry, however, still lacked the knowledge and sophistication to safeguard itself against its own risks. The Spanish Civil War demonstrated this, with its massive losses to insurers. These losses led them to instigate a regime of selective nonsupply of war risks insurance. The British public insurance agency, the ECGD, supported this withdrawal from the market but could not by law extend its own limited program to respond to the resulting unmet demand. At the start of World War II British political leaders finally agreed to provide war risks insurance but remained reluctant to infringe too heavily on private territory; the insurance program was carefully designed not to compete with the private sector and was abandoned at the end of the war.

In the 1980s the cooperative relationship between government and private sector insurers began to change. Though both sides declared their compatibility, most states increased the size and scope of their programs, despite a political environment committed to a minimal government role in the economy. In the United States the Export-Import Bank and OPIC gained increased funding, new missions, and congressional and administration support. At the same time, the political debate in the United States reflected concern over whether OPIC programs in particular promote the loss of American jobs. In Great Britain similar doubts dogged the ECGD. International competition heated up in the private sector with the weakening of the influence of Lloyd's of London, the periodic entry of major U.S. insurance companies into the political risks field, the growing influence of major European reinsurers, and the general competitive environment facing all industries at a time of recession and restructuring of the economy. The debt crisis and the Iran-Iraq War demonstrated the possible uses of insurance in encouraging trade and investment in high-risk environments. On the whole, however, the private insurers remained uncertain of their commitment to supplying political risks insurance, despite protestations to the contrary. They often restricted their coverage and entered and exited the market repeatedly. By the end of the decade government insurance and guarantees had become common, partly in response to the weakness of the private sector, and a multilateral source of investment guarantees had been established.

In order to support the industry, the insurers had to develop norms and techniques that would protect themselves as much as their customers from financial loss, and these norms influenced the extent to which they would participate in the market. They needed to design contract terms that would minimize opportunistic behavior on the part of customers. Ancillary services were needed for the industry as a whole, as well as mechanisms of cooperation that would restrain the dire results of overcompetition among insurers. In maintaining their own financial health, the private insurers rarely could meet the full demand for insurance from their corporate customers, leading to market failure. In response, the political authorities did not necessarily step in to force changes in the norms and practices of the insurers in an effort to support foreign commerce.[1] The state supported the decisions on insurability determined by the commercial underwriters; the role of public authorities was to sanction the legal and institutional structures put in place by the commercial underwriters and then make a decision on whether or not the government should provide the "missing" insurance. Officials creating government programs relied heavily on the private sector for assistance in the design and execution of public insurance and appropriated many of the common practices of the industry.

The financial resources of the private and public insurers determined their participation in political risks insurance. In the 1980s, financial deregulation and the development of new financial instruments undermined the existing private sector players. While some insurance corporations profited immensely, others collapsed under the weight of their losses. In the case of Lloyd's, mismanagement and corruption exacerbated its problems. The public sector did not remain immune to attacks on its resource base. In Britain and the United States budget problems combined with a monetarist ideology to shrink the government role in the economy. Export credit insurance and investment guarantees were not eliminated immediately, though, since their supporters successfully characterized them as market-making institutions. The result was the expansion of an increasingly competitive government program to support trade, investment, and credit in foreign markets.

The twentieth century saw two parallel and occasionally intersecting trends: the deeper participation of the insurance industry in services that directly supported global trade and investment, and the increasing propensity of states to use economic tools to attain national ends. The latter trend fits what Philip Cerny calls the "commodification" of the state, as states become entrepreneurs, leading to "a new blurring of the distinction between public and private and a more, rather than less, active role for the state in promoting capitalism, going far beyond the notion of limiting 'market failure' or counteracting crisis tendencies."[2] Policymakers continue to debate whether or not government should provide insurance and guarantees for international economic transactions. Economists argue against them as ineffective, inefficient, and a drain on the treasury.[3] R. Michael Allen and W. Kip Viscusi, in an analysis of government programs, maintain there are no economic grounds for government insurance and that government programs do not even work well as a foreign policy tool. They admit that insurance and guarantees may allow a state to deal with a foreign policy problem at arm's length, influencing events without direct intervention, but they also note as a potential problem the principle of subrogation, in which the insurer gains legal title to anything of value it can recover after it pays a customer's claims; if the government is the insurer, this could lead to increased involvement in the affairs of the host country, contrary to the original intent.[4]

Those who favor limited government programs point out that the power of a sovereign government to recover losses in foreign countries clearly exceeds that of the private sector. Moreover, backing a guarantee program with the full faith and credit of the government reduces the amount of financial reserves that must be held, an option not available to private insurers. Government agencies also have access to superior information sources on political events abroad, and may be better able to calculate political risk probabilities. Finally, the private insurers do not always step in to respond to all demands for protection, especially when they involve large-scale and long-term projects in developing countries. In general, the public agencies insure risks that the commercial insurers themselves find too risky or simply beyond their financial capacity.

These trends occur within the context of a shift in power from Great Britain to the United States, the increasing participation of Pacific rim countries in the world political economy, and a decrease in the usability of force to promote economic aims. At the same time, as international interdependence binds together once-separate economies, governments have less ability to affect the level of political risk even though they acknowledge that its existence might hinder the further expansion of commerce.[5] The infrastructure the state provides its citizens to carry out economic activities now goes well beyond the traditional government role in defense and transportation to include a much broader range of economic services, but those services still tend to stop at the national border. Promotion of foreign commerce through programs that facilitate market activity but do not directly intervene in the affairs of another state, and that therefore do not violate sovereignty, have become a substitute for more aggressive state protection of foreign commerce.

The trends set in force in the 1980s continued into the 1990s, as new crises and challenges emerged. There are now two new types of international risk that concern insurers. One is the result of the wave of free market reforms that have swept the world in the past decade, dramatically capped in eastern Europe by the fall of the Berlin Wall. The process of reform is fraught with political pitfalls. The other is the risk of both catastrophic and incremental loss associated with the modification of the environment by human behavior. In the former case, both state and multilateral agencies have used expanded insurance and guarantee programs to overcome the perception of unusually high levels of political risk in newly reforming economies, especially those in the former Soviet bloc. In the latter case, private sector insurers and reinsurers have become concerned about the long-term risks to property that global warming represents, although they have yet to determine the appropriate response to the problem.

Where Are We Going? Political Risk and Economic Reform

Two sources of political risk that have dominated the news in the 1990s are the transformation of the former Soviet bloc and its opening to economic ties with the West, and the rise of so-called emerging markets among the newly industrializing countries. The dramatic collapse of communism and the transition to a market economy is both an opportunity and a risk for foreign commercial actors. Some states, such as Hungary, Poland, and the Czech Republic, have made great progress toward establishing a stable political and economic system. But the level of uncertainty about the political environment varies dramatically across the former Soviet bloc states. Laws, regulations, and legal enforcement of rights are weak and ineffective. In some places the path from communism may not be an irreversible one.

The dire need for capital to finance the transition is obvious to all observers, as both modernization and privatization must go forward simultaneously and on a scale never seen before. The situation is ripe for producing both great wealth and great loss for those foreigners willing to conduct business there. Given the scale of need and the high level of political risk, and the threat to global stability if the transition does not succeed, the governments in the West responded to the changes with large transfers of aid and expanded programs to encourage exports and investment in order to stimulate the new private sector. This environment provided opportunities for the programs of the newly established MIGA, and also led to the creation of a separate development bank for central Europe.

The first response of many countries, including the United States, was to provide investment guarantees to persuade investors to increase their investments beyond what they might have planned (often called "additionality"). Both OPIC and ExImbank now legally can operate in central Europe, Russia, and the former Soviet republics. One of OPIC's first steps was to negotiate bilateral agreements with all the former Soviet republics which provide for private property and subrogation rights and clearances for OPIC operations. OPIC management has established a special investment guarantee program for eastern European economies, complementing the new ExImbank funding. Bilateral agreements between the United States and Poland and Hungary include explicit investment guarantees as part of aid and investment packages, to be funneled through OPIC and the ExImbank. In 1990 one of the first major post–cold war investments was the acquisition by General Electric of a partial interest in the Tungsram Company of Hungary. OPIC provided investment guarantees, and MIGA reinsured OPIC's risks for $30 million and twenty years.[6]

Since 1992, political restrictions on ExImbank financing of projects in the former Soviet Union have been lifted by repeal of the Stevenson and Byrd amendments.[7] Covering political risks is now a large part of ExIm's business, particularly as developing and transitional economies privatize such large enterprises as telecommunications and banking systems. Since these enterprises are no longer owned by the sovereign government, commercial banks want guarantees before they lend.[8] ExImbank business in Russia is viewed as supporting the administration's efforts to stabilize the Russian economy and, through that, the Russian political system. Those in favor of lifting all restrictions on East-West trade, and especially opening up access to credit and guarantees, argue that ExImbank facilities would be used not to dispense aid but rather to make U.S. firms competitive. In 1994 the president of ExImbank pledged to pursue new programs aggressively while reducing the subsidy element in ExIm's lending and guarantees; the year before, the bank had administered a record number of loans and guarantees totaling $15 billion. The president stated, "We're trying to do more in high-risk countries, where private lenders won't go."[9]

Other Western lenders, in the year before the revolutions in eastern Europe, had opened up billion-dollar lines of credit to the Soviets, backed by official guarantees.[10] After the collapse of the Soviet Union the Russians, realizing that foreign investors would need some sort of assurance that the changes were permanent, discussed setting up an insurance company, backed by jewels and precious metals, to cover economic transactions against Russian political upheaval.[11] The German government has offered both trade credit insurance and investment guarantees to its eastern neighbors, significantly expanding its existing programs.[12] In 1996 alone, German companies exporting to the Commonwealth of Independent States were protected by approximately $1.5 billion in export credit guarantees from the German agency Hermés; most of it covered trade between eastern German companies and Russia.[13]

The creation of MIGA came in perfect time to address the risks inherent in investment in the former communist states. Its supporters believe it is ideally suited to assist in the transition, since it was specifically designed not only to provide investment guarantees but also to help improve the investment climate in general—which is the essence of the market-oriented reforms being undertaken in eastern Europe. One problem with MIGA programs, however, is that they tend to favor large transnational corporations and foreign investors over the small businesses and social programs that may be vital to the process of change.[14]

Stunned by the scale of the problems of transition and the capital needed to reinvigorate eastern economies, the Europeans led in the establishment in 1990 of the European Bank for Reconstruction and Development (EBRD), headquartered in London. The EBRD is similar to the MIGA and World Bank combined but is specifically designed to promote trade and investment in eastern Europe. It is especially interested in projects that support the private sector and increase foreign investment.[15] Critics of the EBRD have questioned whether it is effective and whether the overlap and conflicts between its programs and advisers and those of the World Bank group lead to confusion for the recipient country.[16]

American insurers represented at a meeting of the International Insurance Council in 1990 claimed that the focus for the future should be on the wider "new" Europe with no east-west divisions. James Smith, of AIG, predicted that the political pressures in central Europe would stimulate further European integration, providing great opportunities for business. With the collapse of communism in Czechoslovakia,

CIGNA quickly began negotiations to establish operations there. Allianz, a major German insurer, has actively pursued joint ventures with state insurance companies in central European countries. Chubb and Son, under the leadership of Henry G. Parker III (founder of the International Insurance Council), aggressively sought out eastern markets and even before the breakup of the Soviet Union arranged a joint cooperation agreement with Ingosstrakh, the Soviet insurer, to coinsure U.S.-Soviet joint ventures.[17] These industry representatives noted at the time that establishing property values for insurance, settling losses, and ascertaining "insurable interest" would be a challenge in this region.[18]

In 1993, at a conference on investment in the states of the former Soviet Union, the participants pointed out approvingly the relative strengths of different organizations involved in supplying insurance on commercial transactions in that region. The representative from MIGA, for instance, explained that private insurance is probably most suited for short-term projects with high expected returns and for trade-related risks. MIGA and EBRD, on the other hand, are best suited to provide guarantees on long-term investment projects. One insurance broker pointed out that private insurance companies fill some of the gaps left by public agencies because, as he put it, they "do not have to march to the tune" of international organizations, U.S. government agencies, or the AFL-CIO.[19]

In aid programs everywhere, support for the private sector has been a keynote of the 1990s. World Bank president James Wolfensohn has stated his view that the institution should be a partner both to developing countries and to private capital, applauding the efforts of bank affiliates such as the MIGA. The bank itself now provides partial political risk guarantees for private sector projects. A CEO at the World Bank/IMF annual meetings in 1995 agreed, stating that "guarantees are better at mobilizing private capital than direct loans."[20]

Although much attention has been focused on eastern Europe, dramatic reforms have been implemented elsewhere, too. Another source of disturbance to the system has been the growth and volatility of emerging markets, particularly in Latin America. Between 1989 and 1995 private capital flows to developing countries grew from $41.9 billion to $247 billion, with easily reversed equity capital the largest portion. The unsustainability of these flows was demonstrated by the crash of the Mexican financial system—twice. The United States led a financial rescue effort both times, which involved extensive use of government guarantees. The use of guarantees in this instance, however, cannot be described simply in terms of insurance. The risk of disaster in the Mexican case, and in projections about possible future cases, appeared to be disastrously high, potentially exceeding the resources of private and public insurers, central banks, and the international financial institutions. Therefore, all possible resources had to be brought to bear, blurring the distinctions between insurance and lender-of-last-resort financing. One economist commented, "The idea behind both plans was to come at financial markets with an overwhelming show of financial force that will convince them not to pull all their money out of Mexico and other emerging markets. . . . But the irony in both cases is that to save capitalism and free markets, we will have to have government step in and assume the risk of Wall Street bondholders."[21]

After the Mexican bailout Michel Camdessus, managing director of the IMF, proposed a new program to lend on a short-term basis to countries experiencing sudden capital flight. This plan is seen by some as essentially providing "insurance" for emerging markets to prevent a crippling loss of confidence.[22] Additionally, the IMF has become more active in trying to ameliorate systemic financial risk through closer monitoring and surveillance of member countries. In his opening address to the World Bank/IMF annual meeting in October 1995, Camdessus recommended, "More than ever before, countries need tightly disciplined macroeconomic policies to maintain a stable environment for investors, whether domestic or foreign."[23]

New Risks: Global Environmental Degradation and the Role of Insurance

One new and unusual area for insurers is environmental risks. The global banking and insurance industries are waking up to the threat of global warming, which may have devastating effects on their business. As the *Washington Post* noted, "the financiers have come to realize that they have at risk literally trillions of dollars worth of insured property and long-term investments."[24] In the past decade the insurers and reinsurers have suffered record-breaking losses stemming from an unusual spate of severe natural disasters—hurricanes, floods, and earthquakes. The causes of these disasters and the large scale of the resulting losses are not completely natural, however. Weather patterns are affected by changes humankind makes to the environment, including global warming, which may lead to an increase in calamitous weather. In addition, the settlement and concentration of human activity, especially in urban areas, means that the scale of loss in any given disaster will be large. In response, Swiss Re and about thirty other insurers recently signed an accord with the United Nations committing them to help reduce environmental risk and address climate change.[25] In many ways, financial institutions such as insurers appear to be more amenable or flexible in the face of dramatic change than many other corporations—or even governments, for that matter. They have responded to new risks with both traditional and innovative programs.

Another point at which insurance and the environment intersect is in the role of insurance in distributing the costs of pollution and environmental cleanup. Under the current system, business buys insurance to cover the expenses of an accident such as an oil spill and then after an accident the courts decide on liability. In recent years courts in the United States have broadened liability beyond what the insurance underwriters thought they were contracting for in their policies, leading to an imbalance between the premium rates they charged and their ultimate liability. Today some observers worry that the insurers, feeling the threat to their financial stability, will withdraw from the market entirely, as they did in the mid-1980s. Lloyd's, for instance, was threatened with collapse, since it provides the majority of pollution and environmental insurance. Mark Spalding notes, "The question then arises as to what will happen when the next infamous event occurs? Lloyd's insures ships bearing toxic or other waste; ships, trains and trucks carrying hazardous chemicals and products; coastal property at risk of being destroyed by storms and rising sea levels due to global warming; waste treatment and storage facilities; and nuclear facilities."[26] In order to control its losses on this type of business, Lloyd's proposes to spin off its environmental and other liabilities into a separate company, to segregate old losses from new claims.

The insurers have tried to limit their environmental liability in several ways. On occasion they have simply refused this insurance, essentially deeming pollution risks uninsurable because of the reinterpretation of their policy contracts by the courts. They have also attempted to develop new contract terms, such as the "claims made" policy, which limits coverage to claims that are filed during the term of the insurance contract. Finally, they have simply raised the price for pollution and environmental damage insurance. The effects on society as a whole are uncertain. As Spalding argues, it could be a good idea to raise insurance rates, forcing out of business the frequent polluters who cannot afford the high premium rates their bad practices entail and essentially making polluters internalize the costs of environmental damage. The lack of insurance or its high costs may also prompt more effective environmental protection to prevent losses from occurring. Unfortunately, the unavailability or high costs of insurance may simply mean that a lot of business will be uninsured; when accidents occur, someone else will have to pay for the cleanup, which often comes down to public money.[27]

Profound change in the former Soviet bloc, plus free market reforms around the globe, create an expanded menu of opportunities and risks for the global investor, trader, and lender. And now the definition of political risk may increasingly include the risks of change in the natural environment.[28] The international risks regime has continued to evolve in response to these new risks. In the area of threats to foreign investment, government guarantee programs have taken a lead role along with new multilateral institutions. In the area of environmental threats, the commercial underwriters have taken some relatively bold steps to deal with an emerging and complex issue. In general, these trends reflect the declining coherence of the regime itself as we reach the close of the twentieth century.

International Regimes and International Protection

The issues of protection and private authority raised by the development of an international risks insurance regime pose some interesting questions. For instance, at what point are trade-offs made between force and finance, and who makes those trade-offs? Many political economists have concentrated on force versus finance as a domestic problem, along the lines of guns versus butter. The problem of what happens when protection is provided solely by the private sector, even in foreign jurisdictions, raises an even more difficult calculus.

The differences between the early part of the century and the later part are significant, especially when we consider that constant crisis in the 1980s did not break down into global war, as occurred twice before. The 1930s case, for instance, demonstrated clearly the limits of nonmilitary protection in a military world, as modern warfare outstripped the capacities of private insurers. In contrast, the risks of war today can be included in a portfolio of risks; in fact, military protection may be limited in an increasingly nonmilitary world. The changes of the 1990s reflect a new relationship between economic and security concerns. It may be that we have entered a stage in which the "rise of the trading state" is accompanied by the elaboration of private networks that provide authoritative guidance in particular areas of the global economy.[29] The issues of protection raised by the internationalization of markets for capital, labor, and goods and services combined with a declining threat of world war would be illuminated by a more complete examination of the changing nature and purpose of military protection and foreign economic policy.[30]

This examination of international risks insurance also directs attention to the problems of focusing on traditional state-centered models of development to explore modern changes in the international political economy. The state in the past has been viewed as the primary enforcer or protector of private transactions, particularly through the exercise of military power. Yet throughout history the state has rarely been entirely effective in providing such protection for international commerce.[31] The foregoing analysis of the international risks insurance regime, which discusses both the role of insurance itself and the activities of the insurers as active agents in world affairs, demonstrates the need to explore non-state-centered accounts of the development of the international political economy. Such an exploration sheds light on the issue of what alternatives exist to reduce or redistribute the risks of commerce and thus facilitate its continuation.

Regime theorists are correct in their assessment of the importance of international institutions "after hegemony," but they neglect empirical examination of the private sector as generating and maintaining international regimes, such as the one for international risks. Regime theorists who concentrate their attention on the role of the state in establishing and maintaining the framework of international economic activity ignore the role of business actors in negotiating institutions that structure the choices available to political actors. Charles Lindblom described the privileged position of business within domestic society, but we need a better understanding of the equivalent at the global level.[32] We have only a weak grasp of how business diplomacy fits into traditional conceptions of foreign policy and international political economy.[33]

The relationship between corporations and states can be either independent or instrumental.[34] States can appropriate the principles and norms developed in the private sector to support their aims in regulating economic activities. In some cases, the corporate community may be enlisted directly to implement particular programs or functions. But corporations are not always the servants of state policy. They influence state preferences by forming coalitions within the domestic political system or by creating transnational coalitions. Private corporate regimes can directly affect state interests by changing the policy options available to countries, particularly through their market power. Self-organization within the private sector can either facilitate or obstruct the pursuit of state welfare goals, and in any case cannot be ignored.

The relationship between corporations and other actors in society is an asymmetrical one. Corporations have more resources and influence than social interest groups and thus are able to establish institutions that are relatively independent of states. They are capable of constraining state behavior through their market power, as noted in much of the literature on business-government relations. Their position is further reinforced by a prevailing liberal ideology in dominant states in the system today, which cordons off some activities from government intervention.

The existence of private corporate regimes raises anew the problems of transnationalism and interdependence first noted decades ago.[35] The central problematic of most analyses of multinational corporations is the extent to which the interests of states and firms coincide or conflict and whether states or firms have greater power over outcomes. In other words, corporate private regimes may matter because they are "bad," changing the costs and benefits of different courses of action for both states and individuals. Therefore, systematic analysis of corporate regimes may tell us about the conditions under which states opt out of or are too weak to affect decisions in particular issue areas. In the case of international risks, the existing regime structured the choices available for public action by deciding what risks were insurable—thus either leaving some risks to be borne solely by those engaged in commerce or forcing the government to relieve the effects of market failure.

Further examination of intermediary institutions, such as banks and stock markets, is warranted to explore the ways in which networks of private cooperation overlap and intertwine. To what extent do these networks increase the efficient distribution of flows of global capital and goods? The private regime established by the insurance industry may be replicated in other areas. In fact, the financial revolution of the 1980s opened the way for the financial sector to become ever more global and encompassing. Clearly, there is some potential for the embedding of the insurance regime within a larger international financial framework.

Increasing technological interdependence, global ecological crisis, and evolving international social norms make it more and more difficult for states to control their environment. Options once available are often now out of reach, and the line between public and private realms of activity has become blurred. Issue areas that once were distinct have begun to overlap in significant ways. Every regime is embedded and entwined with others. Or, as Ulrich Pfister and Christian Suter put it, "we understand the long-term structural change of international financial relations to move from a non-cooperative system with no capacity for self-organization or self-reflection, such as a perfect market system, toward a social system composed of cooperative subsystems capable of self-organization and self-reflection."[36]

We can view the insurance regime as part of a larger historical progression within global society. In the past, when the perception of risk increased, the participants either would require greater compensation for participating in a transaction or simply not participate at all. Such increases in risk led in time to demands for intermediary forms of protection, such as credit insurance and guarantees, on new loans and investments. This stage produced a network of insurance providers. As the environment in which economic activity takes place deteriorates, insurance agencies have tended to restrict the terms and increase the price of insurance. When the demand for international risks insurance exceeded private sector supply, the result often has been state intervention to underwrite new transactions, establish property rights and obligations, and stand behind the traders and investors. If international risks reach the point of outright conflict or war, private and public commercial and financial techniques may no longer be viable. Insurance can facilitate trade in risky environments, but it cannot counter the effects of a complete breakdown in order.

Over the course of centuries the level and type of risk that could be borne by the private sector has been extended by the development of intermediary institutions such as insurance. Societies first went through periods in which trading was a gamble, pure and simple, with no way to protect against the risk of loss except through brute force. Eventually, however, merchants developed such basic financial institutions as banking and insurance as intermediaries in transactions which shared the risks of commerce. During the twentieth century the demands of creditors and investors led to further expansion and refinement of the institutions of risk reduction. The intermediaries, state and private, developed and codified the terms and conditions under which different financial instruments would be sold. The private sector established the initial conditions for insurance operations, and the state originally entered only to remedy a perceived market failure. The variability of the private market justified continued state intervention but only in selected types of risks. The state role in export credit insurance and investment guarantees is in some sense equivalent to the state role as lender of last resort.

The insurance industry plays an unusual role in society. Although it is a profit-making business, it is also an important market-supporting institution that facilitates economic activity. The service it provides results in benefits to more than simply the participants in each transaction. The benefits accrue to society as a whole; as *The Economist* notes, "insurers are not only economic agents. Far more than other financial institutions, they are also seen as bound by an implicit social contract to make their product available to those [who] need it."[37] As governments became more active in support of the domestic economy in the twentieth century, policymakers grew more interested in the potential of government insurance to support and expand the market, especially in international transactions. Raymond Barre once declared, "We are living in a world where uncertainty is growing and risks are becoming ever more extensive. At the same time, we note an upward trend in the demand for security. To what extent can the demand for security be met by the State without slowing down or hindering the adaptations made necessary and inevitable by the far-reaching changes in the world?"[38] And to what extent can adaptations to global capitalism proceed without the security provided by the private sector, alone or in concert with the state?

Underlying the growth and further institutionalization of the international risks insurance regime is a troubling question. While unrestrained political risk—chaos and war—clearly limits economic growth and development, it is not clear that making economic consequences predictable for one group promotes overall economic growth for the larger society.[39] The movement toward a global system of international property rights and the recent emphasis in so many countries on providing an attractive business climate, undergirded by insurance and guarantees, may force governments to abandon policies widely supported within their societies in favor of encouraging foreign economic interests.

We cannot understand institutions of production and exchange apart from the institutions we have designed to protect them. In turn, the character of protection affects the institutions of production and exchange.[40] It is doubtful whether the globalization of trade and production could have progressed so far without the availability of protection, both by the state and, when that fails, by private sector services. In the past century the organization of economic activity has been transformed by the application of modern technology and managerial techniques. Karl Polanyi describes the links between trade and war before the twentieth century: "Trade had become linked with peace. In the past the organization of trade had been military and warlike, it was an adjunct of the pirate, the rover, the armed caravan, the hunter and trapper, the sword-bearing merchant, the armed burgesses of the towns, the adventurers and explorers, the planters and conquistadores, the manhunters and slave traders, the colonial armies of the chartered companies."[41] The private networks of international insurance may tie trade with peace more closely than ever before as the socialization of risk moves forward.

Notes

Chapter 1. The Search for a Sure Thing.

1. The Citibank policy applied only to problems of inconvertibility, in which the debtor has local currency but cannot exchange it for dollars, and not to default or debt repudiation. Michael Isikoff, "Crises Spur Growth of Political Insurance," *Washington Post,* November 18, 1984, F3.
2. Richard N. Cooper, "Managing Risks to the International System," in Richard J. Herring, ed., *Managing International Risk: Essays Commissioned in Honor of the Centenary of the Wharton School, University of Pennsylvania* (Cambridge: Cambridge University Press, 1983), p. 23.
3. Many of the most profound differences among scholars concerning the nature and functioning of the international system hinge on differing perceptions of the degree of "anarchy" that exists, defined as the lack of governing institutions at the global level, and what this means for the behavior of states. For a short selection from among the extensive literature on this topic, see Kenneth Waltz, *Theory of International Politics* (Reading, Mass.: Addison Wesley, 1979); Robert O. Keohane, *After Hegemony: Cooperation and Discord in the World Political Economy* (Princeton: Princeton University Press, 1984); Kenneth Oye, ed., *Cooperation under Anarchy* (Princeton: Princeton University Press, 1986); David A. Baldwin, ed., *Neorealism and Neoliberalism* (New York: Columbia University Press, 1995); Alexander Wendt, "Anarchy Is What States Make of It: The Social Construction of Power Politics," *International Organization* 46 (Spring 1992): 391–426.
4. There exists an extensive literature in international relations on international regimes and institutions, discussed more fully in the following chapter. Two edited volumes that summarize the earliest and latest approaches are Stephen D. Krasner, ed., *International Regimes* (Ithaca: Cornell University Press, 1983),

and Volker Rittberger, ed., *Regime Theory and International Relations* (Oxford: Oxford University Press, Clarendon Press, 1993).

5. The international relations literature is replete with explorations of the relationship between system structure, particularly hegemony, and the stability of the international economic system. See Charles Kindleberger, "Dominance and Leadership in the International Economy: Exploitation, Public Goods, and Free Rides," *International Studies Quarterly* 25 (June 1981): 242–54; Robert Gilpin, *The Political Economy of International Relations* (Princeton: Princeton University Press, 1987); Keohane, *After Hegemony;* John Kroll, *Closure in International Politics: The Impact of Strategy, Blocs, and Empire* (Boulder: Westview Press, 1995).
6. Kenneth Oye argues that it is difficult to distinguish between public and private spillovers in international affairs. He focuses on what he calls "divertable externalities," in which spillovers can be privatized. The opposite situation, in which private activity generates public goods externalities, is the case with international risks reduction. Kenneth Oye, *Economic Discrimination and Political Exchange: World Political Economy in the 1930s and the 1980s* (Princeton: Princeton University Press, 1992).
7. This book focuses on one way to reduce or redistribute risks without using force. This is not to claim, however, that force is totally irrelevant to dealing with risks; on the contrary, it is because political officials sometimes will not or cannot use force that alternatives within the private sector must be developed.
8. Martin Shubik, ed., *Risk, Organizations, and Society* (Boston: Kluwer Academic, 1991); Horst Siebert, "Risk Allocation in Large-Scale Resource Ventures," *Kyklos* 40, 4 (1987): 476–95.
9. In a discussion of risk and uncertainty, Oliver Williamson argues that when environmental risks are so difficult to define that you cannot design an insurance contract for the occurrence and nonoccurrence of them, then that is true uncertainty, not risk. See Oliver Williamson, *Markets and Hierarchies: Analysis and Anti-trust Implications* (New York: Free Press, 1975), p. 24.
10. Frank Knight, in 1921, wrote the first comprehensive economic analysis of risk, focusing his attention on this "entrepreneurial" risk. Frank Knight, *Risk, Uncertainty, and Profit* (Boston: Houghton Mifflin, 1921).
11. Classical economic models imply riskless choice; others assume risk aversion on the part of the average person or variations in attitudes toward risk. Contemporary research indicates individuals are risk averse when they expect to gain and risk seeking when they expect to lose; see Daniel Kahneman and Amos Tversky, "Prospect Theory: An Analysis of Decision under Risk," *Econometrica* 47 (March 1979): 263–91; George Quattrone and Amos Tversky, "Contrasting Rational and Psychological Analyses of Political Choice," *American Political Science Review* 82 (September 1988): 719–36. Gary Becker and Isaac Ehrlich argue that attitudes about risk depend on market opportunities, in "Market Insurance, Self-Insurance, and Self-Protection," *Journal of Political Economy* 80 (July/August 1972): 623–48. Business research indicates that risk attitudes vary systematically across different types of managers; those in charge of managing risk for the corporation tend to be more risk averse than other

managers. See Gordon C. A. Dickson, "A Comparison of Attitudes toward Risk among Business Managers," *Geneva Papers on Risk and Insurance* 7 (April 1982): 89–97.

12. Much of the literature on risk dwells on various schemes of classification, of varying utility. See, for instance, Peter G. Moore, *The Business of Risk* (Cambridge: Cambridge University Press, 1983); Thomas L. Brewer, ed., *Political Risks and International Business* (New York: Praeger, 1985); Shubik, *Risk, Organizations, and Society;* David A. Jodice, compiler, *Political Risk Assessment: An Annotated Bibliography* (Westport, Conn.: Greenwood Press, 1985).

13. Jodice, *Political Risk Assessment,* p. 5.

14. Charles Lipson points out that we can analytically distinguish between commercial and political risks, but in practice it may be impossible to tell them apart. See *Standing Guard: Protecting Foreign Capital in the Nineteenth and Twentieth Centuries* (Berkeley: University of California Press, 1985).

15. M. J. Peterson, personal communication.

16. Christine R. Hekman, "Evaluation of Risk in International Portfolios," in Carl Beidleman, ed., *The Handbook of International Investing* (Chicago: Probus Publishing, 1987), p. 258.

17. I use the terms "political risk" and "international risk" interchangeably, since the political risks I am interested in are those involved in transnational economic activity.

18. These strategies are not limited to the management of specifically international risks but can be applied to local risks also.

19. Becker and Ehrlich, in "Market Insurance," discuss self-insurance as a means to reduce the size of a loss and self-protection as a way of reducing the probability of loss, both of which I regard as self-help.

20. Alan Rugman analyzes such strategies in *International Diversification and the Multinational Enterprise* (Lexington, Mass.: Lexington Books, 1979).

21. When trends move differently in different countries, risk is diversifiable, but when trends are correlated, it is not. Global integration is decreasing diversifiability across states. Hekman, "Evaluation of Risk"; Theodore H. Moran, "International Political Risk Assessment, Corporate Planning, and Strategies to Offset Political Risk," in Fariborz Ghadar, Stephen Kobrin, and Theodore H. Moran, eds., *Managing International Political Risk: Strategies and Techniques* (Washington, D.C.: Ghadar and Associates, 1983), pp. 158–66.

22. An interesting self-help method involves transforming a lumpy project into a flexible and mobile one. For instance, some investors have built floating storage and packing plants, particularly for use in the Middle East cement industry. If the political situation deteriorates, the entire facility can be physically floated out of range. George E. Cooper, Jr., "Political Risk and Methods of Reducing It: The Case of Trading Companies," in Ghadar et al., *Managing International Political Risk,* p. 35.

23. Probably the largest insurance loss to date occurred in 1992 when the Alpha Piper oil platform exploded in flames.

24. Kenneth Arrow, "Insurance, Risk, and Resource Allocation," in *Collected Papers of Kenneth J. Arrow The Economics of Information* (Cambridge: Har-

vard University Press, Belknap Press, 1984), pp. 77–86. Note that much of world trade today consists of intrafirm transactions, in contrast to the interfirm exchange of traditional economic theory.

25. The literature on the modern corporation is too extensive to list here, but see especially Alfred D. Chandler, Jr., *The Visible Hand: The Managerial Revolution in American Business* (Cambridge: Harvard University Press, Belknap Press, 1971); John H. Dunning, *The Globalization of Business* (New York: Routledge, 1993); Rugman, *International Diversification;* and Williamson, *Markets and Hierarchies.*

26. The transactions costs approach has been used to explain why market exchange has been replaced by the hierarchical organization of the firm. See Ronald Coase, *The Firm, the Market, and the Law* (Chicago: University of Chicago Press, 1988); Oliver Williamson, *The Economic Institutions of Capitalism* (New York: Free Press, 1985); Williamson, *Markets and Hierarchies;* and Gary J. Miller, *Managerial Dilemmas: The Political Economy of Hierarchy* (Cambridge: Cambridge University Press, 1992). For a critical discussion of transactions costs, risk, and uncertainty, see Cento G. Veljanovsky, "The Coase Theorems and the Economic Theory of Markets and Law," *Kyklos* 35, 1 (1982): 53–74.

27. Raymond Vernon, "Organizational and Institutional Responses to International Risk," in Herring, *Managing International Risk,* p. 194.

28. Charles Oman has made the best attempt to trace these changes in investment patterns; see *New Forms of International Investment in Developing Countries* (Paris: OECD, 1984) and *New Forms of Investment in Developing Country Industries: Mining, Petrochemicals, Automobiles, Textiles, Food* (Paris: OECD, 1989).

29. Many corporations today turn over such typically internal functions as accounting and data processing to outside firms. The growth of the so-called service economy reflects these changes (and not necessarily increases in fast-food employment). Producers increasingly turn to specialized firms to provide these business services efficiently and effectively, particularly for their global operations. This strategy ultimately may reduce the ability of the firm to manage risk through internal structural change, though it may increase its overall efficiency, flexibility, and profitability. See Orio Giarini, ed., *The Emerging Service Economy* (Oxford: Pergamon Press, 1987).

30. Information industries can be seen as indirect intermediaries, supplying the information that risk managers use to develop business strategy. The modern political risk analysis industry (part of the information industry) provides assessments of the probability of loss due to political actions. These firms generally do not bear any direct liability themselves, although some may bundle their information and expertise with other services, including insurance. See Jodice, *Political Risk Assessment.*

31. A nice summary of the market failure literature and its application to international political economy is found in Ruben P. Mendez, *International Public Finance: A New Perspective on Global Relations* (New York: Oxford University Press, 1992).

32. Rent seeking, as defined by Krueger, referred to the use of resources by a firm to lobby government for such trade privileges as an import license. This generates a scarcity premium between the domestic and world price of the good and thus is a waste of resources and a detriment to society. Anne O. Krueger, "The Political Economy of the Rent-Seeking Society," *American Economic Review* 64, 3 (1974): 481–87. See also Robert D. Tollison, "Rent-Seeking: A Survey," *Kyklos* 35, 4 (1982): 575–602.
33. Michael Loriaux, in an interesting analysis of French financial liberalization, argues that changes to the expected wealth of individuals lead them to political action instead of adjustment to their new economic circumstances; their demands for state intervention to maintain income and benefits can be viewed as a form of insurance. *France after Hegemony: International Change and Financial Reform* (Ithaca: Cornell University Press, 1991).
34. See Philip G. Cerny, *The Changing Architecture of Politics: Structure, Agency, and the Future of the State* (London: Sage, 1990).
35. John H. Dunning, "The Changing Domain of International Business Activity," in Lee Preston, ed., *Multinational Enterprises in the Global Economy* (College Park, Md.: CIBER Maryland, 1994), pp. 75–88.
36. Cerny, *Changing Architecture of Politics.*
37. Douglass C. North, *Institutions, Institutional Change, and Economic Performance* (Cambridge: Cambridge University Press, 1990), p. 126.
38. Robert O. Keohane, "Realism, Neorealism, and the Study of World Politics," in Keohane, ed., *Neorealism and Its Critics* (New York: Columbia University Press, 1986), p. 7. This emphasis has been changing, with the revival of the study of international organizations in general and nongovernmental organizations and individual action in particular. See, among others, James Rosenau, *Turbulence in World Politics* (Princeton: Princeton University Press, 1995); Thomas Risse-Kappen, *Bringing Transnational Relations Back In: Non-state Actors, Domestic Structures, and International Institutions* (Cambridge: Cambridge University Press, 1995).
39. Karen Orren used this phrase in a different context, in a refutation of the absence of feudalism in America. Karen Orren, *Belated Feudalism: Labor, the Law, and Liberal Development in the United States* (New York: Cambridge University Press, 1991), p. 5.
40. I draw on the discussion of the historical development of the private/public distinction in Claire Cutler, "Global Capitalism and Liberal Myths," *Millennium* 24, 3 (1995): 377–97; see also Claire Cutler, Virginia Haufler, and Tony Porter, "Private Authority and International Regimes," paper presented at the Workshop on Private Regimes, San Diego, April 16, 1996, and conference, "Private Power, Public Power, and International Regimes," University of Victoria, August 26–27, 1996.
41. Susan Strange, "Protectionism and World Politics," *International Organization* 39 (Spring 1985): 234.
42. Douglass C. North, "Transaction Costs in History," *Journal of European Economic History* 14 (Winter 1985): 558. See also Cutler, "Global Capitalism and Liberal Myths"; Anne-Marie Slaughter, "International Law in a World of Liberal States," *European Journal of International Law* 6 (1995): 503–38.

43. This phrase is taken from the title of a collection edited by James Rosenau and Ernst-Otto Czempiel, *Governance without Government: Order and Change in World Politics* (Cambridge: Cambridge University Press, 1992).
44. See Beth Yarbrough and Robert Yarbrough, "International Institutions and the New Economics of Organization," *International Organization* 44 (Spring 1990): 255–56; Tony Porter, *States, Markets, and Regimes in Global Finance* (New York: St. Martin's Press, 1993).
45. Jonathan David Aronson, *Money and Power: Banks and the World Monetary System,* Sage Library of Social Research, 66 (Beverly Hills, Calif.: Sage, 1977), pp. 18, 185.
46. The literature on hegemonic stability proposes a relationship among leadership, interstate cooperation, and a stable liberal economic order. This literature is extensive; see, among others, Charles Kindleberger, *The World in Depression* (Berkeley: University of California Press, 1973 and 1987); Robert Gilpin, *U.S. Power and the Multinational Corporation* (New York: Basic Books, 1975); Arthur Stein, "The Hegemon's Dilemma: Great Britain, the United States, and the International Economic Order," *International Organization* 38 (Spring 1984): 355–86; Timothy McKeown, "Hegemonic Stability Theory and Nineteenth-Century Tariff Levels in Europe," *International Organization* 37 (Winter 1982): 73–92; Keohane, *After Hegemony;* David A. Lake, "International Economic Structures and American Foreign Economic Policy, 1887–1934," *World Politics* 35 (July 1983): 517–43.
47. See John Stopford and Susan Strange, *Rival States, Rival Firms: Competition for World Market Shares* (New York: Cambridge University Press, 1991).
48. See Carol Heimer, *Reactive Risk and Rational Action: Managing Moral Hazard in Insurance Contracts* (Berkeley: University of California Press, 1985).
49. See the following chapter for a more complete discussion of norms and regime theory.
50. The reputation and trust of economic partners are key elements supporting efficient economic exchange, as noted in the "new institutionalism" literature. Institutions enforce reputation and trust and forestall the temptation to cheat by establishing a long-term continuing relationship that is a valuable asset to both partners. Insurance actually sidesteps the problem of cheating by reducing the costs it imposes, thus encouraging exchange. This works only if the partners believe the insurer is reputable and trustworthy, however. See Paul Milgrom, Douglass North, and Barry Weingast, "The Role of Institutions in the Revival of Trade: The Law Merchant, Private Judges, and the Champagne Fairs," *Economics and Politics* 2 (March 1990): 1–23; Karol Soltan, Virginia Haufler, and Eric Uslaner, eds., *New Institutionalism: Institutions and Social Order* (Ann Arbor: University of Michigan Press, 1997).
51. Exchange refers to immediate transfer of property rights, whereas contract involves future performance. Armen Alchian and Susan Woodward, "The Firm Is Dead; Long Live the Firm: A Review of Oliver E. Williamson's *The Economic Institutions of Capitalism,*" *Journal of Economic Literature* 26 (March 1988): 66–73.
52. For more on the concept of moral hazard, see Kenneth Arrow, *Essays in the Theory of Risk-Bearing* (New York: North-Holland, 1974); Heimer, *Reactive*

Risk; Chunchi Wu and Peter F. Colwell, "Moral Hazard and Moral Imperative," *Journal of Risk and Insurance* 40 (March 1988): 101–17; Becker and Ehrlich, "Market Insurance."

53. An excellent discussion of how decision makers attempt to transform "reactive risks" (or moral hazard) into "fixed risks" can be found in Heimer, *Reactive Risk.* See also Arrow, *Theory of Risk-Bearing.* On the problem of monitoring, see Williamson, *Economic Institutions of Capitalism;* Alchian and Woodward, "The Firm Is Dead."

54. Insurance can be considered a quasi-public good because it serves a wider function in society than a simple exchange of services; it supports the market system in general by facilitating investment and exchange in risky environments. See Duncan Snidal, "Public Goods, Property Rights, and Political Organizations," *International Studies Quarterly* 23 (December 1979): 532–66. The entire distinction between "public" and "private" goods is open to debate, however, and certainly the development of insurance itself demonstrates the extent to which these two have not always been distinct. Some institutions are neither purely "state" nor purely "market." Jesse Malkin and Aaron Wildavsky, "Why the Traditional Distinction between Public and Private Goods Should Be Abandoned," *Journal of Theoretical Politics* 3, 4 (1991): 355–78; see also Elinor Ostrom, *Governing the Commons: The Evolution of Institutions for Collective Action* (Cambridge: Cambridge University Press, 1990).

55. In the field of public finance, government intervention is warranted and even efficient when it resolves such market failures. Market failures occur when public goods or externalities exist, when an industry is organized into a monopoly, when markets are nonexistent or incomplete, or when there is a failure of information supply. For this argument as applied to international affairs, see Mendez, *International Public Finance,* p. 49. Insurance markets can fail because of the incompleteness of markets when some types of insurance are not offered, the problems of information asymmetry, and the perception of insurance as having public goods characteristics.

56. Essentially, the insured avoids the probability of a large loss by substituting the certainty of a small one—that certain small loss being regular payment of money to the insurer. Kenneth S. Abraham, *Distributing Risk: Insurance, Legal Theory, and Public Policy* (New Haven: Yale University Press, 1986), pp. 1–2.

57. Among others, see Virginia Haufler, "Learning to Cope: Risk Management in History," paper presented at the Washington International Theory Seminar, Washington, D.C., May 5, 1995; Robert S. Lopez and Irving W. Raymond, *Medieval Trade in the Mediterranean World* (New York: Columbia University Press, 1955); Frederic Lane, *Venice: A Maritime Republic* (Baltimore: Johns Hopkins University Press, 1973); Giuseppe Stefani, *Insurance in Venice: From the Origins to the End of the Serenissima,* 2 vol., trans. Arturo Dawoson Amoruso (Trieste: Assicurazioni Generali, 1958); Solomon Huebner, "The Development and Present Status of Marine Insurance in the United States," *Annals of the American Academy* 26 (September 1905, whole no. 90): 241–71; M. M. Postan, *Medieval Trade and Finance* (Cambridge: Cambridge University Press, 1973); H. A. L. Cockerell, "Marine Insurance," in H. A. L. Cockerell and

Edwin Green, *The British Insurance Business, 1547–1970: An Introduction and Guide to Historical Records in the United Kingdom* (New York: Holmes and Meier, 1976), pp. 3–17.

58. David Mayers and Clifford W. Smith, Jr., *Toward a Positive Theory of Insurance,* Monograph Series in Finance and Economics, 1 (New York: Salomon Brothers Center for the Study of Financial Institutions, 1982). Mayers and Smith base this list on their argument that insurance assists a corporation in managing principal-agent issues by reducing contracting costs.
59. North, *Institutions,* p. 31.
60. Adam Smith, *An Inquiry into the Nature and Causes of the Wealth of Nations* (1776; rpt. New York: Modern Library, 1937), p. 109.
61. Many insurers are mutual insurance companies, in which the customers are also the "owners" of the firm. Liability for loss is transferred from the individuals to the group as a whole; the individual still retains a percentage of the liability, but any losses are proportionately less and thus less likely to bankrupt the individual.
62. North notes that one of the main innovations promoting the mobility of capital was the transformation of uncertainty into risk. This occurred through the development of both insurance and portfolio diversification, which reduced the costs of exchange. *Institutions,* p. 126.
63. The mortality tables used by life insurance companies represent one of the earliest attempts to systematize knowledge of the human life span. Given a person's age, the life insurance underwriter can estimate the statistical probability of that person living a stated number of years into the future. The insurance premium, or price, is set according to this statistical probability. As Adam Smith argued, the value of risk "admits of such a gross estimation as renders it, in some degree, reducible to strict rule and method." *Wealth of Nations,* p. 714.
64. In 1977 Jonathan David Aronson bemoaned "The paucity of research on the political influence of international banking, insurance, construction, transport, consulting, advertising, and other services." Aronson, *Money and Power,* p. 16. Since then there has been an explosion of interest in the banking industry and monetary system, and a fair number of analyses of the services industries in general, the latter spurred by the Uruguay Round negotiations over barriers to trade in services. Nevertheless, insurance is still a neglected field in political science. See, however, Aronson himself, "Banking and Insurance," in Susan Strange and Roger Tooze, eds., *The International Politics of Surplus Capacity: Competition for Market Shares in the World Recession* (London: George Allen and Unwin, 1981), pp. 111–24; Susan Strange, "The Risk Managers," manuscript, 1996; and, in a notable exception, Charles Lipson, who discusses U.S. expropriation insurance within the context of a broader analysis of the development of protection for foreign capital, in *Standing Guard.*
65. These company histories provide fascinating glimpses of business life in earlier times and give us insight into the development of modern capitalism. See, among others, Frank Spooner, *Risks at Sea: Amsterdam Insurance and Maritime Europe, 1766–1780* (Cambridge: Cambridge University Press, 1983); Barry Supple, *The Royal Exchange Assurance* (Cambridge: Cambridge Univer-

sity Press, 1970); P. G. M. Dickson, *The Sun Insurance Office, 1710–1960* (London: Oxford University Press, 1960); Bernard Drew, *The London Assurance: A Chronicle* (Oxford: Kemp Hall Press for London Assurance, 1928); D. E. W. Gibb, *Lloyd's of London: A Study in Individualism* (London: Macmillan, 1957); Godfrey Hodgson, *Lloyd's of London* (New York: Viking, 1984); A. F. Shepherd, *Links with the Past: A Brief Chronicle of the Public Service of a Notable Institution* (London: Eagle and British Dominions Insurance Co., 1918); and Oliver M. Westall, ed., *The Historian and the Business of Insurance* (Manchester: Manchester University Press, 1984).

66. For instance, Lawrence G. Brandon, *Sound a Clear Call: Unveiling the Future of the Insurance Industry* (Malvern, Pa.: CPCU-Harry J. Loman Foundation, 1984); John F. Dobbyn, *Insurance in a Nutshell* (St. Paul, Minn.: West Publishing, 1981); Mayers and Smith, *Toward a Positive Theory of Insurance;* Post, *Risk and Response.*

67. Kenneth Arrow once claimed that "insurance is an item of considerable importance in the economies of advanced nations, yet it is fair to say that economic theorists have had little to say about it." Arrow, "Insurance, Risk, and Resource Allocation," p. 78. But see Becker and Ehrlich, "Market Insurance"; John H. Dunning, *Insurance in the Economy,* Occasional Paper 34 (London: Institute of Economic Affairs, 1971); Irving Pfeffer, *Insurance and Economic Theory* (Philadelphia: S. S. Huebner Foundation for Insurance Education, 1956); and Jean-Jacques Laffont, *The Economics of Uncertainty and Information,* trans. John P. Bonin and Helene Bonin (Cambridge: MIT Press, 1989).

68. Robert L. Carter and Gerard M. Dickinson, *Barriers to Trade in Insurance,* Thames Essay 10 (London: Trade Policy Research Centre, 1979); Organization of European Cooperation and Development, *International Trade in Services: Insurance—Identification and Obstacles* (Paris: OECD, 1983); Antony M. Baker, "Liberalization of Trade in Services—The World Insurance Industry," in Orio Giarini, ed., *The Emerging Service Economy* (Oxford: Pergamon Press, 1987), pp. 193–212.

69. This general inattention should not obscure the work of those who have addressed one or another aspect of international insurance. The number of such works has increased as the industry itself became more determinedly international and as political attention began to focus on barriers to trade in services and to the movement of foreign capital. See Hardy F. Glass, compiler, *International Insurance: A Tribute to Professor Alfred Manes* (New York: International Insurance Monitor, 1960); Leon H. Doman, *Supra-national Regulation of Insurance: The Effects of International Treaties and Agreements on Insurance and Reinsurance* (New York: Worldwide Research Corp., 1966); Giscard d'Estaing, *Financement et garanties du commerce international* (Paris: Presses Universitaires de France, 1977); Manfred Holthus, Dietrich Kebschull, and Karl Wolfgang Menck, *Multilateral Investment Insurance and Private Investment in the Third World* (Hamburg: Verlag Weltarchiv, 1984); Organization for Economic Cooperation and Development, *International Trade in Services: Insurance;* and Henri Loubergé and Pierre Maurer, *Financement et assurance des crédits à l'exportation—Aspects théoriques et pratiques en vigueur dans les pays européens* (Geneva: Editions Droz, 1985).

70. Insurers do not typically group these different types, or "lines," of insurance, although they all belong to the larger category of international risks.
71. This list, though not comprehensive, includes some sources of loss that were not always considered insurable political risks, such as the calling of financial guarantees. The rest of this book discusses the changing definition of insurable political risk as part of the overall evolution of insurance.
72. The list of possible sources of loss due to political risk under this heading may include insurance on nonrecovery of debt for the export of goods and services, making good on breach of contracts for exports, lack of profitability of such a contract, and failure of export promotion campaigns. Most public and private agencies do not cover all these all the time.
73. Data on political risks insurance are notoriously suspect, since such information is considered highly sensitive and is not publicly available. As one analyst has noted, an understanding of trends in political risks insurance is hampered by this lack of hard data, and anecdote and opinion about its development and evolution often conflict. Stephen J. Kobrin, *Description and Analysis of the U.S. Market for Political Risk Insurance for Overseas Investments in Developing Countries* (OPIC Contract 85-C-015, April 24, 1986).
74. Frank Spooner used such archival material to explore economic trends in the late eighteenth century, in *Risks at Sea;* the insurance records are one of the few sources of data that cover long periods of time in a relatively consistent manner.
75. Janice E. Thomson's work on mercenaries and pirates challenges the traditional conception of public versus private authority by examining the process by which such activities came under the exclusive authority of the state. *Mercenaries, Pirates, and Sovereigns: State-Building and Extraterritorial Violence in Early Modern Europe* (Princeton: Princeton University Press, 1994). See also Cutler, "Global Capitalism and Liberal Myths."

Chapter 2. Creating an International Risks Insurance Regime.

1. See Virginia Haufler, "Learning to Cope: Risk Management in History," paper presented at the Washington International Theory Seminar, Washington, D.C., May 5, 1995.
2. But see Charles Lipson, "Banker's Dilemmas: Private Cooperation in Rescheduling Sovereign Debts," in Kenneth Oye, ed., *Cooperation under Anarchy* (Princeton: Princeton University Press, 1986) pp. 200–225. The literature on regimes is extensive; see, among others, Stephen D. Krasner, ed., *International Regimes* (Ithaca: Cornell University Press, 1983); Arthur Stein, "Coordination or Collaboration: Regimes in an Anarchic World," in Krasner, *International Regimes,* pp. 115–40; Robert O. Keohane, *After Hegemony: Cooperation and Discord in the World Political Economy* (Princeton: Princeton University Press, 1984) and *International Institutions and State Power* (Boulder: Westview Press, 1989); Duncan Snidal, "The Limits of Hegemonic Stability Theory," *International Organization* 39 (Autumn 1985): 579–614; Volker Rittberger, ed., *Regime Theory and International Relations* (Oxford: Oxford University Press,

Clarendon Press, 1993). Susan Strange wrote a now-classic critique of regime theory as an American fad, yet that fad has lasted more than a decade and reached across the Atlantic to the European scholarly community. "Cave! hic dragones: A Critique of Regime Analysis," in Krasner, *International Regimes,* pp. 337–54.

3. See Keohane, *After Hegemony.*
4. Mark Zacher, "Toward a Theory of International Regimes," in Robert L. Rothstein, ed., *The Evolution of Theory in International Relations* (Columbia: University of South Carolina Press, 1991), pp. 119–38.
5. Young does not directly analyze nongovernmental organizations as a powerful influence within regimes. Instead, he argues that the rules and conventions of a regime apply to states but that the activities of a regime may include private entities. Oran Young, *International Cooperation: Building Regimes for Natural Resources and the Environment* (Ithaca: Cornell University Press, 1989), p. 13. See also Peter Haas, "Do Regimes Matter? Epistemic Communities and Mediterranean Pollution Control," *International Organization* 43, 4 (1989): 377–404; Ernst Haas, *When Knowledge Is Power* (Berkeley: University of California Press, 1990); Martha Finnemore, "International Organizations as Teachers of Norms," *International Organization* 47 (Autumn 1993): 565–98; Peter Haas, Robert Keohane, and Marc Levy, eds., *Institutions for the Earth* (Cambridge: MIT Press, 1993).
6. See Robert Keohane, "International Institutions: Two Approaches," in Keohane, *International Institutions and State Power,* pp. 158–79; Young, *International Cooperation;* Haas et al., *Institutions for the Earth;* John Gerard Ruggie, ed., *Multilateralism Matters: The Theory and Praxis of an Institutional Form* (New York: Columbia University Press, 1993).
7. Debora L. Spar, *The Cooperative Edge: The Internal Politics of International Cartels* (Ithaca: Cornell University Press, 1994).
8. See John Stopford and Susan Strange, *Rival States, Rival Firms: Competition for World Market Shares* (New York: Cambridge University Press, 1991). There exists a large literature on relations between states and firms within a number of different traditions. The dominant points of departure within international relations are the dependent development framework, bargaining theory, and the political economy of trade. Among many, see Richard Barnett and Ronald Muller, *Global Reach: The Power of the Multinational Corporations* (New York: Simon and Schuster, 1974); Raymond Vernon, *Sovereignty at Bay* (New York: Basic Books, 1971) and *Storm over the Multinationals* (Cambridge: Harvard University Press, 1977); Robert Gilpin, *U.S. Power and the Multinational Corporation* (New York: Basic Books, 1975); C. Fred Bergsten, Thomas Horst, and Theodore H. Moran, *American Multinationals and American Interests* (Washington, D.C.: Brookings, 1978); Peter Evans, *Dependent Development: The Alliance of Multinationals, State, and Local Capital in Brazil* (Princeton: Princeton University Press, 1979); Theodore H. Moran, *Multinational Corporations: The Political Economy of Foreign Direct Investment* (Lexington, Mass.: Lexington Books, 1985); Stephen Kobrin, "Testing the Bargaining Hypothesis in the Manufacturing Sector in Developing Countries," *International*

Organization 41, 4 (1987): 609–38; Robert Cox, *Production, Power, and World Order* (New York: Columbia University Press, 1987); Helen Milner, *Resisting Protectionism: Global Industries and the Politics of International Trade* (Princeton: Princeton University Press, 1988); and Benjamin Cohen, "The Political Economy of International Trade," *International Organization* 44, 2 (1990): 261–81.

9. Krasner, *International Regimes,* p. 2.

10. Volker Rittberger and Michael Zürn, *Towards Regulated Anarchy in East-West Relations—Causes and Consequences of East-West Regimes,* Tübingen Arbeitspapiere zur Internationalen Politik und Friedensforschung, 11 (Tübingen: Arbeitsgruppe Friedensforschung, 1989).

11. "International regimes represent the strongest form of cooperation between independent states short of formally giving up part of their sovereignty." Rittberger and Zurn, *Regulated Anarchy,* p. 17; see also Volker Rittberger, ed., *Regime Theory and International Relations* (Oxford: Oxford University Press, Clarendon Press, 1993).

12. Claire Cutler, "Global Capitalism and Liberal Myths," *Millennium* 24, 3 (1995): 377–97.

13. See Virginia Haufler, "Crossing the Boundary between Public and Private," in Rittberger, *Regime Theory and International Relations,* pp. 94–111. There is an increasing literature on the role of nongovernmental organizations in international affairs, referring not to firms but to such organizations as Greenpeace. In the past decade there has been a noted upsurge in the influence of such nongovernmental organizations (NGOs), as formerly domestic organizations have sought out transnational activities; as governments and international organizations have delegated tasks to them, especially in the area of poverty alleviation; and as these organizations have become a more visible and integral part of international negotiations, such as those over the environment and women's rights. See Finnemore, "International Organizations"; Paul Wapner, "Politics beyond the State: Environmental Activism and World Civic Politics," *World Politics* 47 (April 1995): 311–40.

14. Tony Porter, in *States, Markets, and Regimes in Global Finance* (New York: St. Martin's Press, 1993), argues that cartels are in fact a form of private regime, in contrast to the argument presented here.

15. Paulo Sylos-Labini, "Oligopoly," in John Eatwell, Murray Milgate, and Peter Newman, eds., *The New Palgrave: A Dictionary of Economics* (New York: Macmillan, 1987), 3: 701–4.

16. Leonard W. Weiss, "Cartel," in Eatwell et al., *New Palgrave,* 1: 372–74.

17. On the internal politics of cooperation within a cartel, see Spar, *Cooperative Edge.*

18. Zacher, "Theory of International Regimes," uses the term "jurisdictional competencies" to refer to "the right of states to legislate and have enforcement powers in other geographical areas" (127). In a private regime we can see analogous behavior in the negotiated agreements among firms that establish the boundaries of correct behavior and the sanctions for misbehavior.

19. This statement applies generally, but not to specific cases. For instance, the British fire insurance companies essentially operated a cartel for Latin American

fire insurance until the nineteenth century. In the 1980s some reinsurers were accused of collusion over liability insurance in the United States; in this case, however, the collusion was over withdrawing from the market, not monopolizing it.

20. The focus of this book is the international risks insurance sector, though the story of insurance must obviously include the development of the entire industry; until recently, however, only marine insurance and reinsurance were international in their operations.
21. Donald N. McCloskey, *Enterprise and Trade in Victorian Britain: Essays in Historical Economics* (London: George Allen and Unwin, 1981); Gilpin, *U.S. Power and the Multinational Corporation,* pp. 81–183.
22. Andrew Gamble, *Britain in Decline: Economic Policy, Political Strategy, and the British State* (Boston: Beacon Press, 1981), p. 85; Paul Kennedy, *The Rise and Fall of the Great Powers* (New York: Random House, 1987); Kennedy, *Strategy and Diplomacy, 1870–1945* (London: George Allen and Unwin, 1983); and Kennedy, *The Realities behind Diplomacy: Background Influences on British External Policy, 1865–1980* (London: George Allen and Unwin, 1981).
23. Phyllis Deane and W. A. Cole, *British Economic Growth, 1688–1959* (London: Cambridge University Press, 1962), p. 28.
24. Paul Kennedy, "Strategy versus Finance in Twentieth-Century Britain," in *Strategy and Diplomacy.*
25. The international monetary system of the late nineteenth century was highly centralized and dependent on British policy, despite the perception that the gold standard was a decentralized and automatic mechanism of adjustment.
26. Arthur Lewis calls the period 1873–1913 the British climacteric. It was a time when Britain's services trade, especially shipping and financial services, expanded faster than its trade in goods. This expansion did not offset a diminishing manufacturing base, low productivity, and an eventual decline even in foreign income. Arthur Lewis, *Growth and Fluctuations, 1870–1913* (Boston: George Allen and Unwin, 1978), p. 113.
27. Charles Lipson, *Standing Guard: Protecting Foreign Capital in the Nineteenth and Twentieth Centuries* (Berkeley: University of California Press, 1985), p. 9.
28. P. J. Cain and A. G. Hopkins, "Gentlemanly Capitalism and British Expansion Overseas I. The Old Colonial System, 1688–1850," *Economic History Review* 2d ser., 39, 4 (1986): 501–25; Lipson, *Standing Guard,* p. 15.
29. Lipson, *Standing Guard,* p. 46.
30. Confusion over how to define "true" insurance makes it difficult to determine precisely when it first emerged: "If the risk premiums associated with bottomry and respondentia loans are deemed valid consideration for insurance contracts, then the institution of insurance dates from the era of Ancient Greece. If the element of pooling, regardless of how limited in extent, is a test of insurance, then perhaps the institution should be dated from the Barcelona contracts of the Fourteenth Century. If the averaging notion must be present in substantial degree, the insurance business may be said to have its origins in the Sixteenth

Century with the marine contracts of Holland and England. Finally, if a sound actuarial basis is a prerequisite of insurance, the industry must seek its origins in the early part of the Eighteenth Century." By the late nineteenth century all these elements of modern-day insurance existed. Irving Pfeffer, *Insurance and Economic Theory* (Philadelphia: S. S. Huebner Foundation for Insurance Education, 1956), p. 50.

31. William M. Clarke, *The City in the World Economy* (London: Pelican Books, 1967), pp. 19–20.
32. See Avner Greif, Paul Milgrom, and Barry R. Weingast, "Coordination, Commitment, and Enforcement: The Case of the Merchant Guild," *Journal of Political Economy* 102, 4 (1994): 745–76; Paul Milgrom, Douglass North, and Barry Weingast, "The Role of Institutions in the Revival of Trade: The Law Merchant, Private Judges, and the Champagne Fairs," *Economy and Politics* 2 (March 1990): 1–23; Douglass C. North and Robert Paul Thomas, *The Rise of the Western World: A New Economic History* (Cambridge: Cambridge University Press, 1973).
33. William W. Baters, as quoted in Solomon Huebner, "The Development and Present Status of Marine Insurance in the United States," *Annals of the American Academy* 26 (September 1905, whole no. 90): 242.
34. For a history of insurance, see, among others, Barry Supple, *The Royal Exchange Assurance* (Cambridge: Cambridge University Press, 1970); D. E. W. Gibb, *Lloyd's of London: A Study in Individualism* (London: Macmillan, 1957).
35. Recounted in Harold Brown, *Hazard Unlimited,* 3d ed. (London: Lloyd's of London Press, 1987), p. 4.
36. Samuel Pipkin, "Insurance Legislation," paper presented to the Insurance Institute of Ireland, October 29, 1909, p. 1. Pipkin spoke virulently against legislation in general, not just insurance legislation.
37. At this time the only type of insurance covering political risks was marine insurance and, toward the latter half of the century, reinsurance. "The traditional form of marine policy names fifteen different perils and adventures that are borne and taken upon them by underwriters. And of these fifteen, eleven relate to war, piracy, and violence on the high seas." Gibb, *Lloyd's of London,* p. 220. Political risks insurance as a separate line of insurance did not yet exist, and neither did export credit insurance or investment guarantees.
38. Supple, *Royal Exchange Assurance,* p. 190.
39. House of Commons, Minutes of Evidence, July 24, 1903, Public Record Office (PRO), House of Commons (HC) 1/6830 118817, p. 182.
40. A. H. John, "Insurance Investment and the London Money Market of the Eighteenth Century," *Economica,* n.s., 20 (May 1953): 128.
41. Recall that insurance contracts are a promise to pay in the future; therefore, insurance customers are rationally interested in the likelihood that a particular insurer will remain in business for many years to come.
42. Testimony of Frederick William Martin, underwriter, Lloyd's of London, in House of Commons, Minutes of Evidence, July 24, 1903, p. 186.
43. Although neither the United States nor Spain signed this treaty, they were expected to uphold it. Privateering ended except by the southern states during

the U.S. Civil War. The treaty clearly defined the treatment of enemy ships: all enemy ships would be prizes of war, except ships of discovery; coastal fishing vessels; mail boats; hospital ships operating under the Hague Convention; ships protected by license, ransom bill, or days of grace; and cartel ships engaged in prisoner exchange. *Report of the Royal Commission on Supply of Food and Raw Materials in Time of War* (London: HMSO, 1905), p. 22.

44. *Report of the Royal Commission,* p. 26.

45. Frank Spooner, *Risks at Sea: Amsterdam Insurance and Maritime Europe, 1766–1780* (Cambridge: Cambridge University Press, 1983), p. 107.

46. Godfrey Hodgson, *Lloyd's of London* (New York: Viking, 1984), p. 57.

47. C. E. Golding and D. King-Page, *Lloyd's* (McGraw-Hill, New York: 1952), pp. 138–41. Lloyd's also used its information collection services to develop Lloyd's Shipping Index, which reported the latest movements of oceangoing ships. Lloyd's required subscribers to promise to use it only for their own business and not to allow outsiders to obtain copies. Golding and King-Page, *Lloyd's,* p. 146.

48. For more than a century, until the 1980s, Lloyd's successfully promoted and cherished its reputation, which has been one of its foremost assets in its operations abroad. For instance, after the great San Francisco earthquake of 1906, Lloyd's made its reputation in the United States when it told all its agents to accept without question any and all claims, even those not technically covered by the customer's policy. In 1965 the leaders of Lloyd's discovered to their horror that insurance remittances would be part of the sanctions on Rhodesia, forcing them for the first time to default on contractual obligations during peacetime. Edward Heath, leader of the Conservative opposition at the time, asked the chancellor of the exchequer to make an exception to the sanctions for this case; the exception was denied. In response, Lloyd's put all money that should have been paid to Rhodesian businesses and individuals in a special escrow account, to be paid out when all curbs were lifted. British insurers feared that American, European, and South African companies would take away Rhodesian business. As one insurer commented, "Americans don't play cricket." *New York Times,* December 31, 1965, p. 33.

49. The practice of unlimited liability has come under attack in the past decade. See Chapter 4.

50. "Lloyd's Business Increasing," *The Policy-Holder: An Insurance Journal,* December 20, 1922, p. 1149.

51. Brown, *Hazard Unlimited,* p. 50.

52. British history is replete with tales of coastal residents who deliberately misled ships onto rocky shores so that they could "salvage" the cargo for their own enrichment.

53. Golding and King-Page, *Lloyd's,* p. 157.

54. Its full title was the Association for the Protection of Commercial Interests as Respects Wrecked and Damaged Property. It functioned in association with Lloyd's agents while acting for all underwriters regardless of affiliation and was not primarily a profit-making organization. During World War II, it operated alongside and often as an agent of the British government. Golding and King-Page, *Lloyd's,* pp. 170–74.

55. Hodgson, *Lloyd's of London,* p. 66. Henry Hozier, secretary of Lloyd's from 1874 to 1906 and father-in-law to Winston Churchill, successfully built up the admirable worldwide agency system and network of signal stations belonging to Lloyd's.
56. Throughout the next half-century the system of syndicates and syndicates within syndicates would become increasingly byzantine and ultimately contribute to the disasters of the 1980s. See Chapter 4.
57. H. A. L. Cockerell, "Marine Insurance," in Cockerell and Edwin Green, *The British Insurance Business, 1547–1970: An Introduction and Guide to Historical Records in the United Kingdom* (New York: Holmes and Meier, 1976), p. 7.
58. Golding and King-Page, *Lloyd's,* p. 171.
59. Golding and King-Page, *Lloyd's,* p. 158. This form was on a "no cure—no pay" basis, meaning the salver received a fixed sum in the event of a successful salvage or else submitted to arbitration. Such rules of salvage are intended to encourage people to rescue ships in distress, while limiting the incentives for fraud.
60. Hodgson, *Lloyd's of London,* p. 13.
61. Golding and King-Page, *Lloyd's,* pp. 165–66, 169.
62. Huebner, "Marine Insurance," p. 256. An unexplored area of legal and political-economic history is a comparison of international insurance claims negotiations of the eighteenth century, international bond negotiations of the nineteenth and early twentieth centuries, and international debt negotiations of the late twentieth century.
63. William D. Winter, *Marine Insurance: Its Principles and Practice* (New York: McGraw-Hill, 1919), pp. 22–23.
64. Huebner, "Marine Insurance," p. 421.
65. Huebner, "Marine Insurance," p. 442.
66. Winter, *Marine Insurance,* p. 24.
67. From the point of view of the Americans, the London rating service was a destructive regime. Huebner, "Marine Insurance," p. 261.
68. King's Enemy Risks are defined as "the risks of capture, seizure, arrest, restraint, or detainment by the King's Enemies, and the consequences of hostilities or warlike operations by or against the King's Enemies whether there be a declaration of war or not; but excepting civil war, revolution, rebellion, insurrection, and civil strife arising therefrom, and piracy." PRO ZHC 1/8740 118767, p. 10.
69. See *Report of a Sub-committee of the Committee of Imperial Defence on the Insurance of British Shipping in Time of War,* August 1914, PRO ZHC 1/7858 118767.
70. See the account of Sir Norman Hill et al., "State Insurance against War Risks at Sea," in James T. Shotwell, ed., *Economic and Social History of the World War* (London: Humphrey Milford, Oxford University Press; New Haven: Yale University Press, 1927).
71. Gibb, *Lloyd's of London,* p. 221.
72. Testimony of Frederick William Martin, underwriter, Lloyd's of London, in House of Commons, Minutes of Evidence, July 24, 1903, p. 184.

73. Admiralty papers, PRO ADM 1/8913 120982.
74. *Report of a Sub-committee of the Committee of Imperial Defence,* p. 3. This report pointed out the collective action problem for insurers inherent in the mutual association structure. On the outbreak of war it would be difficult to convince all the members of a war risks association to make a contribution to the insurance pool, since not all members would use routes suddenly made dangerous by war (p. 4).
75. See the summary of experience with war risks insurance availability in *Report of a Sub-committee of the Committee of Imperial Defence,* pp. 2–3.
76. Gibb, *Lloyd's of London.*
77. Admiralty papers, PRO ADM 8913, p. 2.
78. War rates on shipping do not go into effect immediately on the outbreak of war; there is a lag time while ships still at sea return to port. Traditionally, no ships are attacked until after this grace period (though the Americans in the Spanish-American War ignored this custom). House of Commons, Minutes of Evidence, July 25, 1903, p. 180.
79. House of Commons, Minutes of Evidence, July 24, 1903, p. 181.
80. House of Commons, Minutes of Evidence, July 24, 1903, p. 183.
81. Testimony by Frederick William Martin, underwriter, Lloyd's of London, House of Commons, Minutes of Evidence, July 24, 1903, p. 185.
82. *Report of the Royal Commission on Supply of Food and Raw Materials in Time of War* (London: HMSO, 1905), pp. 1–2. The report stated that British shipping routes mainly were in the North and South Atlantic and the Mediterranean. Almost two-thirds of wheat and flour were shipped across the North Atlantic from 1898 to 1902, and from 1902 to 1904 about 21 percent crossed the North Atlantic, 26 percent the South Atlantic, and 45 percent the Mediterranean (p. 20).
83. An indemnity program requires no premium payment, whereas an insurance program does.
84. Report, George Balfour of Burleigh, chairman, 1904? PRO HC 1/6830 118817, p. 62.
85. Report, George Balfour of Burleigh, p. 55.
86. Report, George Balfour of Burleigh, p. 53.
87. The Naval Intelligence Department also proposed that shipowners be asked to enter into a formal agreement with the department concerning the protection of trade during war. It suggested forming an Expert Committee, chaired by the chairman of Lloyd's with a representative of Sun Alliance Insurance Co. and a shipowner/underwriter as members. Naval Intelligence Department, Confidential Memo on the Protection of Trade Manoevres, December 2, 1905.
88. Gibb, *Lloyd's of London,* p. 223; also *Report of the Committee on a National Guarantee for the War Risks of Shipping,* Admiralty papers, PRO ADM 1/8913 120982, p. 17.
89. The government codified the common practices of marine insurers shortly after the war in the Marine Insurance Act of 1906, which reaffirmed five basic principles: the customer must have an insurable interest in the property at risk and must provide full information "in utmost good faith," and the insurer must

identify the proximate cause of loss, indemnify the insured, and gain subrogation rights (i.e., after settling a claim for loss, the insurer owns the property and any further claims on it). Robert H. Brown and Peter B. Reed, *Marine Reinsurance* (London: Witherby, 1981), p. 10.

90. The Admiralty provided insurance to ships that might lose their private insurance by following naval direction during such maneuvers. The Admiralty encouraged the cooperation of commercial insurers in its efforts; though initially reluctant, most insurance companies eventually agreed to assist in implementing this program. The Treasury Department proved reluctant to insure shipping in cooperation with the commercial insurers, but the Admiralty insisted that it had no ability to deal with the complex risks with which the insurance companies were familiar. Confidential letter from Admiralty to underwriters, February 5, 1906; letter from Treasury to Admiralty, March 5, 1906; and letter from Admiralty to Treasury, March 7, 1906, PRO ADM 1001–7, Naval Trade Manoeuvres 1905–6.
91. Hill et al., "State Insurance," p. 16.
92. *Report by the Committee on a National Guarantee,* pp. 8, 9, 17.
93. Defence of Commerce, Proposed Peace Organization, September 16, 1908, p. 3, PRO ADM 116 1065B.
94. *Report by the Committee on a National Guarantee,* p. 19.
95. House of Commons, Minutes of Evidence, 15th day, July 24, 1903, PRO HC 1/6830 118817. These documents detail testimony by various private insurance underwriters.
96. Testimony by Frederick William Martin, House of Commons, Minutes of Evidence, July 24, 1903, p. 185.
97. Kennedy, *Strategy and Diplomacy,* p. 95.
98. Standing Committee of the Committee of Imperial Defence, Maintenance of Overseas Commerce in Time of War, Minute, November 22, 1912, PRO ADM 1/8913 120982, p. 2.
99. Gibb, *Lloyd's of London,* p. 224.
100. *Report of a Sub-committee of the Committee of Imperial Defence.*
101. *Report of a Sub-committee of the Committee of Imperial Defence,* August 1914, pp. 4–5.
102. *Report of a Sub-committee of the Committee of Imperial Defence,* pp. 11, 14.
103. Overseas Commerce in Time of War, memorandum by the Admiralty on the Report of a Sub-committee of the Committee of Imperial Defence on Local Transportation and Distribution of Supplies in Time of War, 1912, PRO ADM 1/8913.
104. Gibb, *Lloyd's of London,* p. 225.
105. Josiah Royce, "War and Insurance: An Address," delivered before the Philosophical Union of the University of California at its 25th Anniversary at Berkeley, California, August 27, 1914 (rpt; New York: AMS Press, 1979). All but the first four words of the quotation are italicized in the original.
106. Hill et al., "State Insurance," p. 46.

107. In 1914 an underwriter at Lloyd's pioneered air war risks insurance, and Lloyd's monopolized the business in the first few years of the war. The government began its own program in 1917. Gibb, *Lloyd's of London,* p. 227.
108. *Lloyd's List,* January 1, 1917, p. 7.
109. Hill et al., "State Insurance," p. 53.
110. Fernand Braudel, *The Perspective of the World,* vol. 3 of *Civilization and Capitalism, 15th-18th Century,* trans. Siân Reynolds (New York: Harper and Row, 1984), pp. 34–36.

Chapter 3. Testing the Limits of Private Protection.

1. Charles Lipson, *Standing Guard: Protecting Foreign Capital in the Nineteenth and Twentieth Centuries* (Berkeley: University of California Press, 1985), pp. xiv–xvi.
2. The regime itself, however, was not a "prohibition regime," to use Ethan Nadelman's term, because the prohibitions were only a limited part of the broader international risks insurance regime. See Ethan Nadelman, "Global Prohibition Regimes: The Evolution of Norms in International Society," *International Organization* 44 (Fall 1990): 479.
3. Robert J. A. Skidelsky, "Retreat from Leadership: The Evolution of British Economic Foreign Policy, 1870–1939," in Benjamin Rowland, ed., *Balance of Power or Hegemony: The Interwar Monetary System* (New York: New York University Press, 1976), pp. 147–94.
4. Paul Kennedy, *The Realities behind Diplomacy: Background Influences on British External Policy, 1865–1980* (London: George Allen and Unwin, 1981), pp. 223–24, 266–68.
5. Kennedy, *Realities behind Diplomacy,* pp. 223–24.
6. Skidelsky, "Retreat from Leadership," p. 161; Charles Kindleberger, *The World in Depression* (Berkeley: University of California Press, 1973 and 1987).
7. Paul Kennedy, *Strategy and Diplomacy, 1870–1945* (London: George Allen and Unwin, 1983), p. 94.
8. Kennedy, *Realities behind Diplomacy,* pp. 226, 253.
9. Phillip Darby, *Three Faces of Imperialism: British and American Approaches to Asia and Africa, 1870–1970* (New Haven: Yale University Press, 1987), p. 82.
10. Kennedy, *Realities behind Diplomacy,* p. 229.
11. Robert W. D. Boyce, "British Leadership in the International Economic System, 1925–31," in Gustav Schmidt, ed., *Konstellationen Internationaler Politik, 1924–34* (Bochum: Studienverlag Brockmeyer, 1983), p. 317.
12. Quoted in Kennedy, *Realities behind Diplomacy,* p. 256.
13. See Kindleberger, *World in Depression;* see also Boyce, "British Leadership," p. 317.
14. Stephen A. Schuker, *American "Reparations" to Germany, 1919–33: Implications for the Third World Debt Crisis,* Princeton Studies in International Finance, 61 (Princeton: Princeton Department of Economics, International Fi-

nance Section, July 1988). Schuker argues that, with Allied cooperation, Germany could have paid its reparations obligations. The Europeans recognized the benefits for them of a strong German economy but feared German expansionism. They all needed to reconstruct their economies after the devastation of the war but could not persuade the United States to share some of the burden of these costs by reducing or eliminating inter-allied debts. At the same time, Schuker argues investment in Germany by Americans indicated that the German economy had not been driven to chaos by the reparations burden, contrary to common perception today.

15. Darby, *Three Faces of Imperialism,* p. 120.
16. See Public Record Office (PRO) Index to Foreign Office Correspondence, 1920–23.
17. PRO Index to Foreign Office Correspondence, vol. 2, 1923, #1154.
18. For an excellent account of British exchange rate policy, see Alec Cairncross and Barry Eichengreen, *Sterling in Decline: The Devaluations of 1931, 1949, and 1967* (Oxford: Basil Blackwell, 1983).
19. Cairncross and Eichengreen, *Sterling in Decline,* p. 31.
20. Peter Alexis Gourevitch, *Breaking with Orthodoxy: Comparative Responses to International Economic Crises* (Ithaca: Cornell University Press, 1986). The limited way in which British government officials inserted themselves into insurance markets reflects the weak acceptance of the legitimacy of government intervention in the sphere of financial protection, in accordance with prevailing liberal principles at that time.
21. Overseas Trade (Credit and Insurance), Part IV of Imports and Exports Regulation, June 21, 1919, PRO Export Credit Guarantees papers (ECG) 5/1 119831, p. 11.
22. "The Export Credits Scheme," memo to the Board of Trade, March 1926, PRO Board of Trade papers (BT) 60/10/1 119458.
23. Judson of ECGD to Adams, Esq., PRO ECG 5/11.
24. The amount of business underwritten by Lloyd's of London cannot be determined easily. Lloyd's chose not to file accounting information with the government but to use an alternative available to it under the 1909 Assurance Company's Act: it put up a security deposit or guarantee, placed its premiums in a trust fund, and simply submitted a certificate indicating that its operations had been audited. The other insurance companies objected to the 1909 act partly on the basis of this alternative. One insurance journal noted, "We have always had a great regard for many Lloyd's Underwriters as individuals—but collectively, ever since the passing of the 1909 Assurance Company's Act, we have had a disagreement with them." From "Lloyd's Business Increasing," *The Policy-Holder: An Insurance Journal,* December 20, 1922, p. 1149.
25. Data on privately placed political risks insurance are extremely difficult to discover, because of the need to maintain business secrecy and the political sensitivity of some insurance contracts. After all, any firm that insures its business in a foreign country against political risks is implying that it has a lack of confidence in that country's government—which does not endear it to the local rulers.

26. For example, in a representative year—1924—the Index to Foreign Office Correspondence indicates queries concerning arms shipments for Manchuria (twice), from Austria for Greece (twice), for Turkey (twice), from Italian areas to Danzig and Stettin, from London to Rotterdam, from France to Serbia, and from Vladivostok to Odessa. At times, the insurers would simply warn the Foreign Office of certain transactions, such as Russian munitions passing through the Suez Canal. The letters themselves in most cases have been culled from the Public Record Office holdings. See the PRO Index to Foreign Office Correspondence for these listings.
27. The ECGD programs in the mid-1920s did not apply to Russia or to short-term credits in India, Ceylon, the Straits Settlements, or Hong Kong.
28. The Board of Trade estimated Russian debt at about £1 billion. Export Credit Guarantees Department, Minute of November 9, 1922, PRO ECG 5/3 119831.
29. "Russia and the Export Credits Scheme," part 2, memo, March 1926, PRO BT 60/10/1 119458.
30. "The Export Credits Scheme and Russia," amended memo as furnished to the president of the Board of Trade for debate, March 10, 1926, PRO BT 60/10/1 119458, pp. 1–3.
31. "Export Credits Scheme and Russia," pp. 4–5.
32. "Russia and the Export Credits Scheme," memorandum draft for Cabinet, March 1926, PRO BT 60/10/1 119458. The same memo pointed out the possibility of negotiating with Estonia and then reexporting from there to Russia.
33. Derek Aldcroft, *From Versailles to Wall Street* (London: Penguin Books, 1987), esp. chap. 9.
34. Aldcroft, *From Versailles to Wall Street,* esp. chap. 11.
35. Cairncross and Eichengreen, *Sterling in Decline,* pp. 41–42.
36. "Russia and the Export Credits Scheme," memorandum draft for Cabinet, p. 2.
37. "John Hetherington and Sons," *The Times,* September 17, 1925.
38. "Russia and the Export Credits Scheme," part 2, memo, March 1926. This memo noted that much more trade is "said" to have been done by U.S. firms.
39. F. H. Nixon, Department of Overseas Trade, to the Export Credit Guarantees Department, September 25, 1925, PRO BT 60/10/1.
40. "Export Credits Scheme and Russia," p. 7. At the same time as Russia sent a trade mission to London, it was negotiating with the Germans. The Germans arranged special credits for the Russians, with the German government guaranteeing part of the risk. Four private insurance companies participated in the negotiations, though German banks apparently were reluctant to join them (p. 6).
41. Resolution passed at Demonstration of Workers in Birkenhead, June 21, 1925, PRO BT 60/10/1 119458.
42. Minutes of the Board of Trade, September 28, 1925, referencing Russian orders.
43. PRO Index to Foreign Office Correspondence, vol. 2, 1925, #943.
44. One memo quoted a rate of 24 percent per year on Russian three-month bills, which is such a high rate it is surprising anyone took it. "Export Credits Scheme and Russia," p. 4.

45. Kennedy, *Realities behind Diplomacy,* pp. 246–47.
46. See Cairncross and Eichengreen, *Sterling in Decline,* pp. 72–73.
47. In 1931 multilateral clearing broke down. Great Britain established the sterling bloc, which included the Commonwealth, Argentina, Sweden, Norway, and Denmark.
48. ECGD agreements on Soviet business continued to be controversial well into the 1930s, particularly because of the opposition engendered by the existence of still-unpaid prerevolutionary Russian obligations.
49. PRO ECG 5/13.
50. PRO ECG 5/9.
51. A. J. H. Latham, *The Depression and the Developing World, 1914–1939* (London: Croom Helm, 1981). Latham argues India was the key to the reorientation of multilateral settlements, since the British trade deficit with the United States was covered by its surplus with India. By 1928, however, Britain's surplus with India fell far short of balancing its deficit with the United States, and thus it was crucial for the British government to stimulate more exports to India. Nevertheless, key European decision makers did not perceive Asia (or Africa), apart from the Far East, as affecting the global system significantly, as discussed by Darby, *Three Faces of Imperialism.*
52. William R. Keylor, *The Twentieth Century World: An International History,* 2d ed. (New York: Oxford University Press, 1992), p. 243.
53. "Export Guarantees Bill and Financial Resolution, Brief for Minister," Export Credit Guarantees Department, 1937/38? PRO ECG 5/17 486, pp. 15–17.
54. The Berne Union ceased to exist during World War II but was reestablished afterward; the ICIA also shut down during the war.
55. "War and Civil Risks," *The Policy-Holder: An Insurance Journal,* January 27, 1937, p. 99.
56. PRO Index to Foreign Office Correspondence, vol. 2, 1936, #332.
57. PRO Index to Foreign Office Correspondence, vol. 2, 1933–37, #120987.
58. "War and Civil Risks," p. 99.
59. PRO Index to Foreign Office Correspondence, vol. 2, 1936, #335.
60. PRO Index to Foreign Office Correspondence, vol. 2, 1933–37, #120987.
61. PRO Index to Foreign Office Correspondence, vol. 2, 1933–37, #120987.
62. Spanish insurance claims turned out to be both numerous and varied, including, for instance, claims filed by the British vice-consul and pro-consul for their personal losses. Lloyd's actually refused to renew an insurance policy on the villa of the consul in Malaga against the risk of war and riots. Even a load of codfish, seized by the Spanish government at Valencia, turned up in complaints about the settlement of war risks insurance claims (PRO Index to Foreign Office Correspondence, vol. 2, 1933–37, #120987). In one case, a British insurer suggested that the owners of a captured Soviet vessel pay the Nationalists to return the ship. The underwriters would then recompense the owners, hoping they could avoid declaring the ship a total loss, which would cost immeasurably more (PRO Index to Foreign Office Correspondence, vol. 2, 1923–43, #121006).

63. Export Credit Guarantees, "Secretary's Report to the 15th Ordinary Meeting of the International Credit Insurance Association on the period from April to September 1938," PRO ECG 5/30 120688, p. 3.
64. Transfer risk is the possibility that one will be blocked from taking money out of a country.
65. Review of Business, April 6, 1937, PRO ECG 5/21.
66. H. Karrer/International Credit Insurance Association, "Report on Policy Clauses Designed to Exclude Catastrophic Risks, Summary of Conclusions," November 1938, PRO ECG 5/30 120688.
67. Karrer, "Report on Policy Clauses."
68. Gibb, *Lloyd's of London,* p. 232.
69. "War and Civil Risks," p. 99.
70. The agreement excluded the United States and Canada, which at the time were out of bombing range. In addition, American law forbade companies from concluding foreign agreements.
71. Board of Trade, "War Risk Insurance," 1937, PRO BT 58/304 119531, p. 1.
72. Lloyd's underwriters could sell marine risks insurance without the war and civil war exclusion clause only for "excepted classes" of business as determined by the Lloyd's War Board. Such exceptions generally include personal accident insurance during war (in great demand during the Vietnam War as the massive media presence required insurance against personal injury), insurance on goods being transported by sea or air, and aircraft hulls—with a five-powers termination clause if war breaks out among the great powers. A. A. Cassidy, "Underwriting Political Risks," *C. I. I. Journal* 6 (April 1982): 86.
73. "War and Civil Risks." According to *The Policy-Holder,* a professional journal, the risk of war and civil war did not belong in the domain of private insurance.
74. Board of Trade, "War Risk Insurance," pp. 1–2.
75. Secretary Goldring of Property Owners Protection Association to the Board of Trade, June 24, 1937, PRO BT 58/304 119531.
76. Karrer, "Report on Policy Clauses," p. 6.
77. Darby, *Three Faces of Imperialism,* pp. 125, 133.
78. Kennedy, *Realities behind Diplomacy,* pp. 235–36.
79. The participants also debated whether an independent export credit agency, or simply a department within the Board of Trade, should be established. 1936, PRO Foreign Office papers (FO) 248/1352 387.
80. Minute, Export Credit Guarantees Department, September 26, 1938, PRO ECG 5/29 120569.
81. Minute, Export Credit Guarantees Department, September 26, 1938.
82. "Export Guarantees Bill . . . Brief for Minister," p. 17.
83. Minute, Export Credit Guarantees Department, September 26, 1938.
84. Minute, Export Credit Guarantees Department, September 26, 1938, p. 5.
85. "Export Guarantees Bill and Financial Resolution, Brief for Minister," Export Credit Guarantees Department, 1937/38? PRO ECG 5/17 486.
86. Export Credit Guarantees, "Secretary's Report."
87. "City Notes," *The Times,* August 3, 1937.

88. R. Michael Allen and W. Kip Viscusi, "Insuring the Expropriation Risks of Multinational Firms," *Stanford Journal of International Studies* 11 (Spring 1976): 153–68.
89. Allen and Viscusi, "Insuring the Expropriation Risks."
90. "Export Credit Guarantees," *Stock Exchange Gazette,* July 31, 1937.
91. R. S. Hudson to secretary of state for foreign affairs, April 26, 1938, PRO ECG 5/29 120659.
92. Karrer, "Report on Policy Clauses."
93. Gibb, *Lloyd's of London,* pp. 228–29. In order to maintain its business in the United States during the war, Lloyd's underwriters also arranged to establish a trust fund in American hands to hold premiums and pay claims and expenses; this scheme would credibly assure American business that the British government could not make claims on those dollar balances and that British insurance could be relied on even during wartime. Gibb, *Lloyd's of London,* pp. 236–37.
94. During the war the war risks insurance associations and the Ministry of War Transport concluded many agreements to cooperate in continuing to provide insurance support for merchant shipping.
95. Julian Barnes refers cynically to the profits Lloyd's made on "death and spare parts" policies offered during the bombing raids on London. Julian Barnes, "The Deficit Millionaires," *New Yorker,* September 20, 1993, p. 78.
96. Hardy Glass, "Pathways in International Insurance and Development Trends in Europe," in Hardy Glass, compiler, *International Insurance: A Tribute to Professor Alfred Manes* (New York: International Insurance Monitor, 1960), pp. 76–77. The same author also wrote "Astrological Considerations in the Evaluation of Insurance Risks" (1942).
97. Karrer, "Report on Policy Clauses," p. 7. In poverty-stricken countries in which the difference in wealth between the minority and majority of the population is wide and in which governing institutions are weak, a lost harvest may indeed be more catastrophic than the violent overthrow of those in power.
98. Karrer, "Report on Policy Clauses," p. 7.
99. PRO Index to Foreign Office Correspondence, vol. 2, 1923–43, #121006. A more recent parallel exists, in reverse. Refugee Palestinians driven out of Lebanon by the Israeli invasion in 1982 planned to hire a ship to sail back in triumph. Informed of this, the Israelis directly contacted insurers in London to inform them that any such ship might be bombed. The insurance underwriters, in turn, discouraged shipowners from even considering leasing a ship to the Palestinians, by denying insurance entirely or raising the premium significantly. In any case, the ship in question was bombed before leaving harbor in Cyprus. CBS Evening News, February 15, 1988.

Chapter 4. Redefining Risk and Responsibility.

1. The literature on U.S. decline blossomed in the 1980s but has since faded somewhat, particularly the variants associated with hegemonic stability theory. The historical comparisons of the United States and Great Britain remain valid,

however, in the similarity of the economic and political challenges to their dominance in world affairs. See Paul Kennedy, *The Rise and Fall of the Great Powers* (New York: Random House, 1987); Robert O. Keohane, *After Hegemony: Cooperation and Discord in the World Political Economy* (Princeton: Princeton University Press, 1984); Charles Kindleberger, "Dominance and Leadership in the International Economy: Exploitation, Public Goods, and Free Rides," *International Studies Quarterly* 25 (June 1981): 242–54; Mancur Olson, *The Rise and Decline of Nations: The Political Economy of Growth, Stagflation, and Social Rigidities* (New Haven: Yale University Press, 1982); Bruce Russett, "The Mysterious Case of Vanishing Hegemony; or, Is Mark Twain Really Dead?" *International Organization* 39 (Spring 1985): 207–31; Duncan Snidal, "The Limits of Hegemonic Stability Theory," *International Organization* 39 (Autumn 1985): 579–614; Arthur Stein, "The Hegemon's Dilemma: Great Britain, the United States, and the International Economic Order," *International Organization* 38 (Winter 1984): 355–86; Joseph Nye, *Bound to Lead: The Changing Nature of American Power* (New York: Basic Books, 1990); Henry Nau, *The Myth of America's Decline: Leading the World Economy into the 1990s* (Oxford: Oxford University Press, 1990); Richard Rosecrance, *America's Economic Resurgence: A Bold New Strategy* (New York: Harper and Row, 1990).

2. Charles Lipson, *Standing Guard: Protecting Foreign Capital in the Nineteenth and Twentieth Centuries* (Berkeley: University of California Press, 1985).
3. Helen Hughes, "Perspective: The Risks of Lending in Developing Countries," in Richard J. Herring, ed., *Managing International Risk* (Cambridge: Cambridge University Press, 1983), p. 168. For an extended analysis of the expansion of state guarantees and insurance, and their role in supporting the international property rights regime, see Lipson, *Standing Guard.*
4. After World War II, the U.S. government initiated a program to promote investment in Europe by providing insurance against inconvertibility. In the 1950s, to stimulate private investment in the developing world, the U.S. government expanded similar programs administered by the Agency for International Development to cover the risks of expropriation and revolution. These programs would be consolidated in the Overseas Private Investment Corporation, an independent agency founded in 1969. In addition, the U.S. Export-Import Bank began to offer political risk cover in 1960. The next year, President John Kennedy and Treasury Secretary C. Douglas Dillon announced that the United States and fifty-seven insurance companies would form the Federal Credit Insurance Administration (FCIA) to work with the Export-Import Bank to sell export credit and political risks insurance on short-term export projects.
5. Other government agencies provided political risk assistance on a selective basis. For example, the U.S. Maritime Board has supplied war risks insurance on shipping in selected areas, and the U.S. Department of Transportation has issued aviation war insurance for civilian aircraft when commercial insurance was unavailable or too expensive (*New York Times,* March 1, 1957, December 3, 1959, and August 3, 1976).
6. Stacy Shapiro, "London Political Risk Market Tightens," *Business Insurance,* October 15, 1984, pp. 47–48.

7. Stephen Kobrin, *Description and Analysis of the U.S. Market for Political Risk Insurance For Overseas Investments in Developing Countries* (OPIC Contract 85-C-015, April 24, 1986), p. 5.
8. The Interamerican Federation of Insurance Companies (FIDES), consisting of fifteen Latin American companies plus a U.S. and Spanish representative, was founded in 1947 to promote, among other things, the ethical, technical, and legal rules of insurance and reinsurance and the exchange of information and experience among members. The Commission Européenne d'Assurance performs similar functions in Europe. Mauricio Kitaigorodzki, "Buenos Aires: World Insurance Forum," *Best's Review/Property-Casualty Edition,* December 1987, p. 96.
9. UNCTAD's efforts to expand the local insurance capability of developing countries have had limited success, especially in reinsurance, since most countries simply lack the financial resources to cover large risks. UNCTAD, "Report of the Committee on Invisibles and Financing Related to Trade of the Second Part of its Twelfth Session," UNCTAD, May 14, 1987, TD/B/C.3 (XII)/Misc. 4; Raymond J. Krommenacker, "L'Assurance-réassurance de droit privé dans les relations entre pays développés et pays en voie de développement et l'action des organisations internationales: La Conférence des Nations Unies pour le Commerce et le Développement," *Mémoire* (Geneva: Institut Universitaire de Hautes Etudes Internationales, 1972); Donald L. MacDonald, *Risk Control in the Overseas Operations of American Corporations,* Michigan International Business Studies, 15 (Ann Arbor: University of Michigan, no date).
10. *Governors' Journal,* International Insurance Seminars, May 1986. The recent Uruguay Round of trade negotiations under the General Agreement on Tariffs and Trade (GATT) set aside for future negotiation under the World Trade Organization any final resolution of insurance trade issues.
11. The national investment guarantee schemes in particular remained underused until the 1980s.
12. The U.S. space shuttle launch in 1983, for example, had $1 billion in insurance cover. Alan Cameron and Roy Farndon, *Scenes from Sea and City: Lloyd's List, 1734–84* (London: Lloyd's List/Lloyd's of London Press, 1984), p. 113.
13. Earlier the main political risk for international transactions had been the wave of nationalizations and expropriations in 1960s postcolonial states. Corporate leaders at that time took for granted a greater ability on the part of their home governments to enforce (sometimes militarily) a political and financial resolution that was favorable to their interests. Outright nationalization and expropriation of foreign assets diminished over time, evolving into "creeping expropriation" and eventually trailing off and leading to new forms of investment such as joint ventures and strategic alliances. Charles Oman, *New Forms of Investment in Developing Country Industries: Mining, Petrochemicals, Automobiles, Textiles, Food* (Paris: OECD, 1989).
14. Interestingly, a political analyst at Gulf Oil presciently warned of the shah's probable fall months before it happened; the company was able to plan ahead for the loss of Iranian oil. Louis Kraar, "The Multinationals Get Smarter about Political Risks," *Fortune,* March 24, 1980, pp. 86–100.

15. Stacy Shapiro, "Study Political Risks in Every Country, Risk Manager Says," *Business Insurance,* November 14, 1983, p. 17. For a particularly interesting view of U.S. commitments to protect commercial projects in Iran, see the collection of U.S. intelligence documents captured from the Tehran embassy by Iranian revolutionary students and painstakingly reconstructed from shredded fragments: "Muslim Students Following the Line of the Imam—Documents from the U.S. Espionage Den," U.S. National Archives.
16. Shapiro, "Study Political Risks"; John Salinger, head of the political risk division of AIG, in Robert Schulman, "A World in Flux Means Steady Work for Risk Analysts," *New York Times,* November 4, 1990, p. 12. AT&T lost $50 million in uninsured investments in Iran; afterwards it made a point of buying political risks insurance. Michael Isikoff, "Crises Spur Growth of Political Insurance," *Washington Post,* November 18, 1984, pp. F3–4.
17. Anthony Palmer, "Oil Price Collapse a Key Factor," *Lloyd's List,* May 27, 1986, p. 5.
18. Stephen Merrett, "Trends," *Underwriters Post,* July 1981, p. 53.
19. David W. Rossiter, "Political Risk and the United States," paper presented at the Conference on Political Risk Management, New York, June 25, 1985, p. 11.
20. For analyses of international finance, see Philip G. Cerny, ed., *Finance and World Politics: Markets, Regimes, and States in the Post-hegemonic Era* (Aldershott, England: Edward Elgar, 1993); Eric Helleiner, *States and the Reemergence of Global Finance: From Bretton Woods to the 1990s* (Ithaca: Cornell University Press, 1994); Jeffry Frieden, *Banking on the World: The Politics of International Finance* (New York: Basil Blackwell, 1989); Susan Strange, *Casino Capitalism* (Oxford: Basil Blackwell, 1986); Tony Porter, *States, Markets, and Regimes in Global Finance* (New York: St. Martin's Press, 1993); Stephan Haggard, Chung H. Lee, and Sylvia Maxfield, eds., *The Politics of Finance in Developing Countries* (Ithaca: Cornell University Press, 1993).
21. Frieden, *Banking on the World,* p. 85.
22. Other insurers did not agree. After the kidnapping of Charles Lindbergh's son, Lloyd's underwriters pioneered in selling insurance against kidnap and ransom. The business expanded rapidly in the 1960s in response to a series of kidnappings in South America and even the United States. A. A. Cassidy, "Underwriting Political Risks," *C.I.I. Journal* 6 (April 1982): 90.
23. Philip Moore, "All Down to Politics," *Policy Market,* July 1986, pp. 12–14.
24. "The New York Colossus," *Business Week,* July 23, 1984, p. 98. The importance of particular cities to regional and even global growth and development has been explored in the following innovative works: Jane Jacobs, *Cities and the Wealth of Nations* (New York: Vintage, 1985); Saskia Sassen, *The Global City: New York, London, Tokyo* (Princeton: Princeton University Press, 1991); Kenichi Ohmae, *The End of the Nation-State: The Rise of Regional Economics* (New York: Free Press, 1995).
25. The U.S. insurance industry is exempt from the antitrust laws under the McCarran-Ferguson Act of 1944 in the belief that some collusion would prevent socially harmful insurer insolvencies; instead, the separate states regulate the insurers. John F. Dobbyn, *Insurance Law in a Nutshell* (St. Paul, Minn.:

West, 1981). Insurers successfully argued that they needed to pool their loss data on a national basis in order to set rates fairly and that strong state regulation would be sufficient to restrain exploitation of consumers. The Insurance Services Office collected data on loss experience and payouts on claims from all insurers and used it to establish rating guidelines. Consumers long have complained about the secrecy of the data, and banks, financial holding companies, and other potential competitors of the insurance companies have launched a campaign against this exemption. During the mid-1980s, when insurers and reinsurers refused to cover some risks, such as for asbestos and hazardous waste, eight state attorneys general launched an antitrust suit against four national insurers (later expanded to nineteen states and thirty-two insurance industry representatives), claiming conspiracy to deny coverage. As of 1996 the insurers have resisted wholesale deregulation, but the end of the current system may be near.

26. John D. Hibbard, *CIGNA Worldwide,* Harvard Business School Case 9–589–098 (Cambridge: Harvard College, 1989; revised July 1, 1991), p. 6.
27. The use of brokers to place insurance business varies by country; the British insurance industry is dominated by broker-placed business, whereas other European markets are significantly less dependent on it. Hibbard, *CIGNA Worldwide.*
28. Additionally, as noted above, a large number of American private insurers organized the FCIA, which worked with the U.S. Export-Import Bank to provide political risks and export credit insurance.
29. The merged companies are now called CWW, or CIGNA Worldwide, which is one of the largest United States–based international insurers. Hibbard, *CIGNA Worldwide,* 1991, p. 7.
30. AIG was created in Shanghai in 1909, but it is now headquartered in the United States.
31. Today Lloyd's is one of the biggest sources of insurance on oil, marine, and jumbo risks; is still a leader in new coverage such as for satellites and war risks; and is a major player in reinsurance.
32. OPIC, discussed in more detail below, suffered scandalous losses in the early 1970s on the projects it had guaranteed in Chile, projects that were nationalized by Salvador Allende. The program came close to being ended at that time.
33. Note that OPIC turned primarily to London insurers for assistance. U.S. insurers and reinsurers refused to participate at first, because of their lack of experience and resources; later some were willing to join with Lloyd's in this venture. Alan C. Brennglass, *The Overseas Private Investment Corporation: A Study in Political Risk* (New York: Praeger, 1983). The Lloyd's-led group agreed to cover $250 million of the outstanding $2.4 billion of U.S. expropriation guarantees. "Agency Will Insure U.S. Expropriations," *New York Times,* December 17, 1971, p. 61.
34. OPIC executives did not renew the contract, deciding it was an unnecessary expense. Robert Svensk, "The Role of Private Sector Insurance," in Fariborz Ghadar, Stephen Kobrin, and Theodore H. Moran, eds., *Managing International Political Risk: Strategies and Techniques* (Washington, D.C.: Ghadar and Associates, 1983).

35. Henri Loubergé and Pierre Maurer, "Private Initiative and Public Intervention on the Market for Export Credit Insurance," *Geneva Papers on Risk and Insurance* 10 (April 1985): 100–111.
36. Isikoff, "Crises Spur Growth."
37. Loubergé and Maurer, "Private Initiative," p. 108.
38. MacDonald, *Risk Control.*
39. Lee Coppack, "Insurers under Pressure over Political Risks," *Lloyd's List,* December 24, 1982.
40. Contract frustration insurance covers the cancellation or repudiation of contracts due to political tensions or government interference. Kidnap and ransom insurance covers risks of kidnapping, extortion, and hostage takings; corporations now routinely seek such insurance for their executives abroad. The insurers generally work closely with security and detective firms, such as Control Risks or Kroll Associates, which provide advice on maintaining personal security, negotiate with kidnappers, and conduct investigations. By teaching those insured how to take precautions, the insurers intend to reduce the chance of loss—as in other attempts to control opportunistic behavior. The security firms draw on the expertise of former members of police and intelligence agencies and military forces, including the SAS, FBI, CIA, and even KGB. Anthony Faiola, "Making Executives' Security Their Business," *Washington Post,* Business Section, March 20, 1995, p. 7; L. J. Davis, "International Gumshoe," *New York Times Magazine,* August 30, 1992, pp. 46–52.
41. Kobrin, *Description and Analysis,* pp. 7–8.
42. The chairman of Mutual Marine Office Ltd., in trying to drum up support for land war risks, said, "It should be fun, and it could be rewarding." "Cover Proposed for Land War Risks," *Business Insurance,* October 15, 1984, p. 48.
43. Kobrin, *Description and Analysis,* p. 17. Other firms insist on keeping political risk products separate from their other insurance business.
44. Stacy Shapiro, "Insurers Consider Land War Risks," *Business Insurance,* November 12, 1984, p. 96.
45. This term was coined by Susan Strange, *Casino Capitalism.*
46. More than a decade earlier, in 1969, the Cromer Report detailed the conflicts of interest among the outside names who provided the capital for Lloyd's, the active agents who actually did the underwriting, and the brokers who brought the business to the underwriters. Lloyd's did not make the report public and did not implement any reforms.
47. "Self Regulation at Lloyd's," report of the Fisher working party, May 1980 (no mark), p. 3.
48. "Lloyd's Mess," *The Economist,* July 27, 1991, pp. 14–19.
49. Reportedly said by Ian Posgate, a leading underwriter and subject of numerous investigations who later was banned from the business; Julian Barnes, "The Deficit Millionaires," *New Yorker,* September 20, 1993, p. 85.
50. Because of their unlimited liability, individuals who were members of those underwriting syndicates that suffered unprecedented losses had to cover those losses out of their own pockets (the "deficit millionaires," as Barnes called them [see n. 49]), leading to bankruptcy and even suicide; mostly it has led to a huge

amount of litigation. The tentacles of this problem reached out to affect one recent U.S. Supreme Court nominee, Stephen Breyer, who gave up his membership in Lloyd's when it became both a source of financial loss and a politically contentious issue in his confirmation hearings.

51. Storms in Europe, hurricanes and earthquakes in the United States, the explosion of the Piper Alpha oil rig, and the oil spill of the *Exxon Valdez* all contributed to massive claims on Lloyd's underwriters. In addition, like insurers everywhere, many Lloyd's underwriters began facing tremendous losses from environmental pollution claims.

52. William Pitt, "An Outsider's Insider Tackles the Mess at Lloyd's," *Institutional Investor* 27 (February 1993): 143–45.

53. For popular accounts of recent scandals and slights to the august institution of Lloyd's, see Godfrey Hodgson, *Lloyd's of London* (New York: Viking, 1984); Adam Raphael, *Ultimate Risk* (New York: Four Walls Eight Windows, 1995); Elizabeth Luessenhop and Martin Mayer, *Risky Business* (New York: Scribner, 1995); and the amusing Barnes, "Deficit Millionaires." Some people have commented snidely that the supermodern Lloyd's headquarters building, reminiscent of a beached and only half-finished ocean liner, is symbolic of the institution's decline.

54. *The Economist,* July 4, 1992, pp. 67–68. One major reform that will have profound effects on the traditional structure of Lloyd's is the extension of membership to corporate investors (as opposed to individuals). See *The Economist,* September 18, 1993, pp. 83–84. Lloyd's plans to settle most claims and spin off its loss-making business into a separate company in 1997.

55. Among those considering entering this business were certain banks, including Citibank, which explored the possibility of offering political risks insurance in combination with its credit transactions. Kobrin, *Description and Analysis,* p. 9.

56. As a report in *The Economist* stated, "The stupidity of cash-flow underwriting and its threat to the industry is clear to all and sundry." "Slow: Danger Ahead," September 25, 1982, p. 6. The underwriting cycle, discussed in Chap. 1, is the business cycle for insurers. High profitability and low barriers to entry entice new entrants to the market, leading to overcapacity, competition, and price cutting; high losses eventually lead to a shakeout, as losers leave the business and prices can be raised again.

57. The UNCTAD in the late 1980s grew concerned that many foreign reinsurers active in developing countries were inexperienced, unreliable, and viewed reinsurance underwriting "merely as a vehicle for developing investment funds at a time characterized by extraordinary high interest rates." Developing country insurance markets relied heavily on outside reinsurers and would be quite vulnerable to any disruptions or instabilities in the market. United Nations Conference on Trade and Development, "Invisibles: Insurance, Reinsurance Security," study by the UNCTAD Secretariat, TD/B/C.3/221 February 3, 1987, p. 3.

58. "Slow: Danger Ahead," p. 6.

59. Steve Taravella, "Political Risk Cover Taking Off in U.S. Market," *Business Insurance,* October 15, 1984, p. 44.

60. Comment by Joe Tavares, manager of political risk at CIGNA Worldwide, as quoted in Taravella, "Political Risk Cover," p. 44.
61. Brian D. Freund, "Why We Are Headed for Another Insurance Crisis," *Global Trade* 108 (October 1988): 31–33.
62. Five or six Lloyd's underwriters withdrew from covering political risk, leaving Merrett Syndicates and Robertson and Hiscox as the sole Lloyd's political risks insurers. Stacy Shapiro, "London Political Risk Market Tightens," *Business Insurance,* October 15, 1984, pp. 47–48.
63. Lloyd's has been particularly hard hit by its deep involvement in the U.S. market for pollution and environmental accident insurance. U.S. courts have interpreted liability very broadly, and Lloyd's has paid out billions of dollars on claims for policies originally written decades ago. This situation poses a public policy problem, as ultimately no insurer may be willing to provide these coverages at reasonable prices—or at all. See Mark J. Spalding, "Is a Threat to Lloyd's of London also a Threat to the Environment?" *Journal of Environment and Development* 2 (Summer 1993): 111–28.
64. Antony M. Baker, "Liberalization of Trade in Services—The World Insurance Industry," in Orio Giarini, ed., *The Emerging Services Economy* (Oxford: Pergamon Press, 1987), p. 199.
65. John W. Milligan, "Coping with the Rigors of a Tough Market," *Institutional Investor,* April 1985, pp. 159–67.
66. Michele Milone, "Political Risk and Lloyd's: Still a Pair," *National Underwriter* (Property-Casualty Edition), September 28, 1987, pp. 40–41.
67. The number of reinsurers expanded considerably during the 1980s, for several reasons: reinsurance is less regulated domestically than direct insurance and thus can operate where direct insurers cannot; captive insurers (a form of self-insurance) rely on reinsurance for their largest risks; and transactions have grown in size and technological complexity, leading to increased demand. Baker, "Liberalization of Trade in Services," p. 202.
68. Most reinsurance contracts are placed by international brokers, such as Kemper and Prudential, which often are viewed by reinsurers as being much too influential in shaping the industry.
69. Interview, UNCTAD, March 1987.
70. Taravella, "Political Risk Cover," p. 46.
71. Kobrin, *Description and Analysis,* p. 12. UNCTAD raised concerns about reinsurance security and its impact on developing countries throughout this period. Developing country representatives complained of discriminatory terms granted by Western reinsurers to business in developing states and believed that reinsurers struggling with losses in the OECD countries were unfairly raising rates in the non-OECD countries in response. See UNCTAD, "Report of the Committee on Invisibles."
72. Kobrin, *Description and Analysis,* p. 15. When news leaked about CIGNA's unusual policy, banks questioned other political risk underwriters about their willingness to underwrite inconvertibility risks; most declined, because of concerns about insurability and lack of capacity. Shapiro, "London Political Risk Market Tightens."

73. Interview, Association of British Insurers, August 1987.
74. William Glaberson, "How Risk Rattled the Street," *New York Times,* November 1, 1987, sec. 3, p. 1. The instability of modern financial markets, including instruments for managing risk, would be demonstrated forcefully in the crisis of 1987.
75. The best-known political risk consultancy is probably Kissinger Associates, founded by former U.S. secretary of state Henry Kissinger. Business Risk International, Inc., a division of the Economist Group, also has high visibility in this area. Many observers have been skeptical of the value of these analyses, partly because of the exclusion of political risk analysts from the strategic planning process within most firms, limiting their influence on corporate decision making. John T. Reid, "Perspective: Managing Country Risk for a Manufacturing Corporation," in Herring, *Managing International Risk,* pp. 184–90.
76. Theodore Moran estimates that broad social revolution accounts for less than half of all political losses. "International Political Risk Assessment, Corporate Planning, and Strategies to Offset Political Risk," in Ghadar et al., *Managing International Political Risk,* pp. 158–66.
77. Richard Stern, of OPIC, in 1983 described an investor's rights as being determined by, among other things, a host country's constitution, statutes, decrees, and regulations; any joint venture agreements concluded; articles of incorporation and bylaws of the foreign firm; management and technical assistance agreements; supply contracts; and agreements with lenders. Hughes, "Perspective," p. 172.
78. Richard Stern, "Comments," in Ghadar et al., *Managing International Political Risk,* p. 93.
79. Hughes, "Perspective." Some of the more obscure financial techniques have become front-page news with the recent collapse of Barings Bank in Britain and the bankruptcy of Orange County, California, after they lost millions of dollars on derivatives.
80. Loubergé and Maurer, "Private Initiative."
81. For two assessments of these trends a decade apart, see Vince McCullough, "At Risk: A Survey of International Insurance," *The Economist,* September 25, 1982, pp. 1–23; and "Alternative Insurance: Auto-Cover," *The Economist,* September 26, 1992, pp. 94–95; see also Baker, "Liberalization of Trade in Services."
82. Baker, "Liberalization of Trade in Services," p. 199.
83. This statement refers to specialized political risks insurance and not to the broader category of international risks, including export credit insurance, marine insurance, and investment guarantees.
84. PanFinancial was formed by Skandia Insurance of Sweden, Yasuda Fire and Marine Insurance of Tokyo, and Continental Insurance of the United States.
85. Elizabeth Kessler, "Political Risk Insurance and the Overseas Private Investment Corporation: What Happened to the Private Sector?" *New York Law School Journal of International and Comparative Law* 13, 2 (1992): 214.
86. Kessler, "Political Risk Insurance," p. 215. Data on political risks insurance are notoriously suspect, since such information is considered highly sensitive

and is not publicly collected. As one analyst notes, the field of political risks insurance is hampered by a lack of real data, and opinions about the development and evolution of the market often conflict. Kobrin, *Description and Analysis.*

87. See Philip G. Cerny, *The Changing Architecture of Politics: Structure, Agency, and the Future of the State* (London: Sage, 1990), for a more complete analysis of what he terms the "competition state."

88. Paul Krugman, "Competitiveness: A Dangerous Obsession," *Foreign Affairs* 73 (March 1994): 28–44.

89. Developing country governments often restrict foreign direct investment through such regulatory requirements as prior government approval and registration of the investment, limits on profit or capital remittances, exchange controls, limits on business expansion and transfers of ownership, and requirements for partial local ownership.

90. Thomas L. Brewer, "Trends in International Business, Thought, and Literature: The Past and Future of Political Analysis for International Business," *International Executive* 35 (November/December 1993): 539–48.

91. By the early 1980s numerous scholars and policy makers commented on the "decline" of the United States, stimulating a vigorous debate over whether this portrayal was accurate. By the mid-1990s this debate largely withered away, as profound restructuring of U.S. industry combined with a lower dollar value to stimulate an export boom and a growing economy, even as major competitors such as Japan suffered deep recession. For the debate between "declinists" and their critics, see Kennedy, *Rise and Fall of the Great Powers;* Olson, *Rise and Decline of Nations;* Nye, *Bound to Lead;* Nau, *Myth of America's Decline;* Rosecrance, *America's Economic Resurgence.*

92. The international property rights regime described by Lipson in *Standing Guard* in 1985 became even more institutionalized over the course of the next decade, as political leaders in almost every corner of the world espoused free markets and capital mobility.

93. Robert Svensk, "Whatever Happened to New Products?" paper presented at the Risks Insurance Management Society annual meeting, 1986, Toronto.

94. H. H. Hashek, "Export Credit Insurance and the Debt Crisis," *Geneva Papers on Risk and Insurance* 11 (October 1986): 285–91.

95. Richard Feinberg, *Subsidizing Success: The Export-Import Bank in the U.S. Economy* (Cambridge: Cambridge University Press, 1982), p. 110.

96. For example, the German Hermes is a private company that administers the government program, and the French CoFACE is a public company in which private investors hold shares.

97. The positive role of insurance in supporting larger policy goals was forcefully advocated by Adlai E. Stevenson and Alton Frye in response to changes in the Soviet Union in "Trading with the Communists," *Foreign Affairs* 68 (Spring 1989): 53–71.

98. Feinberg, *Subsidizing Success.* In *Standing Guard,* Lipson examines changes in what he terms the foreign property rights regime and analyzes the role of government investment guarantees in establishing and enforcing many of the

elements of that regime. Property rights and investment guarantees are closely linked, and one could argue that the insurance regime reinforces and overlaps with the foreign property rights regime, particularly since political risks insurance specifically remedies the failure of existing property rights protection. Lipson focuses on host/home country interactions, however, whereas the insurance regime is dominated by the dynamics between the commercial insurers and government agencies.

99. Bruce Fitzgerald and Terry Monson, "Export Credit and Insurance for Export Promotion," *Finance and Development* 25 (December 1988): 53.

100. Feinberg, *Subsidizing Success.* Lipson, in *Standing Guard,* notes that when OPIC came under severe attack at its reauthorization hearings in 1974, the corporate community overwhelmingly supported it, in opposition to the AFL-CIO, which has consistently opposed it on the grounds that it helps corporations export jobs (pp. 246–47).

101. Lipson, *Standing Guard;* see also Thomas L. Brewer, *Foreign Direct Investment Dispute Settlement Procedures,* Georgetown University School of Business Administration Working Paper Series (Washington, D.C., May 1994).

102. Hashek, "Export Credit Insurance."

103. David P. Baron, *The Export-Import Bank: An Economic Analysis* (New York: Academic Press, 1983).

104. See Cerny on the "competition state," in *Changing Architecture of Politics.*

105. John Ray, "The OECD 'Consensus' on Export Credits," *World Economy* 9 (September 1986): 295–309; David Blair, *Trade Negotiations in the OECD: Structures, Institutions, and States* (London: Kegan Paul International, 1993); Monika Sie Dhian Ho and Klaas Werkhorst, "Disciplining State Aids to Exports: The Case of Officially Supported Export Credit Insurance," manuscript, April 1994.

106. The effects of subsidized export credit insurance on markets are more difficult to track than the effects of subsidized export credit. Export credit insurance contracts may designate any of a number of participants to a transaction as benefiting from the insurance—the buyer, seller, bank, or other intermediaries interested in seeing the transaction completed. Thus, any effects on trade and investment flows may be widely dispersed and not consistent in direction.

107. The literature on the debt crisis is immense and overlaps with the literature on international finance already mentioned. Among works not already cited see Charles Lipson, "Bankers' Dilemmas: Private Cooperation in Rescheduling Sovereign Debts," in Kenneth Oye, ed., *Cooperation under Anarchy* (Princeton: Princeton University Press, 1986), pp. 200–225; Jeffry Frieden, *Debt, Development, and Democracy: Modern Political Economy and Latin America, 1965–1985* (Princeton: Princeton University Press, 1991); Charles Lipson, "The International Organization of Third World Debt," *International Organization* 35 (Autumn 1981): 603–31; Carlos Diaz Alejandro, "Latin American Debt," *Brookings Papers on Economic Activity* 2 (1984): 335–89; Barry Eichengreen and Peter Lindert, eds., *The International Debt Crisis in Historical Perspective* (Cambridge: MIT Press, 1989).

108. Hughes, "Perspective," p. 172.

109. Richard N. Cooper, "Managing Risks to the International System," in Herring, *Managing International Risks,* p. 37.

110. Lipson, "Bankers' Dilemmas."

111. "Citicorp Covers Its Assets," *Dun's Business Month,* October 1984, p. 54. The policy covered prolonged delays in loan repayments due to the debtor's inability or refusal to pay in dollars. Citicorp may have initiated this policy in an effort to allay the concerns of bank regulators over the adequacy of its reserves and the scale of its risks.

112. Miles Wright, "Older and Wiser," *ReActions,* June 1984, pp. 37–38.

113. Taravella, "Political Risk Cover," p. 46. Almost ten years later, in 1992, the ExImbank canceled its contract with the FCIA because of possible conflicts of interest; the bank now administers the insurance program itself. Keith Bradsher, "The Businessman at Ex-Im," *New York Times,* August 23, 1992, p. F7.

114. In an excellent analysis of the U.S. ExImbank in 1982, Feinberg, in *Subsidizing Success,* notes the influence of large customers on the ExImbank, its close integration with the banking community, its overlaps with private banking behavior, its willingness to forgo profits to support the profitability of its customers, its utility for pursuing national goals, and the ways in which foreign competition drives its programs (xiii). Later in the decade the competitiveness issue and support for the financial community would become even more important, but the other characteristics would change. What would not change is the public questions about who benefited from ExImbank programs.

115. "Taking Lenders to the Cleaners," *The Economist,* August 1, 1987, p. 72. These deficits came from both credit and insurance operations. The insurance programs of the U.S. agency had grown larger than its lending programs by 1985, the opposite of its traditional mix of business.

116. Nevertheless, a 1984 report to the British minister of trade on the ECGD stated that "the Department's wish to ensure that its underwriting portfolio is well spread, not unnaturally, inhibits it from encouraging the private sector to take as large a share of total exporting risks as the latter appears capable of absorbing." *Report of the Committee to Consider the Structure, Functions, and Status of the Export Credit Guarantees Department (ECGD)* (London: HMSO, March 1984), p. 13.

117. Bengt H. Kjellgren, vice-president of Citibank and chairman of the National Foreign Trade Council Export Finance Committee, "Government Export Credit Protection: A Strong but Leaky Umbrella," speech at Conference on Multinational Risk Management, New York, June 25, 1985.

118. "Taking Lenders to the Cleaners."

119. Eduard Brau, K. Burke Dillon, Chanpan Puckahtikom, and Miranda Xafa, *Export Credits: Developments and Prospects: World Economic and Financial Surveys* (Washington, D.C.: International Monetary Fund, July 1986), p. 2. The first phase of the debt crisis was treated as a temporary liquidity crisis; by 1985 the Baker Plan signaled the first official acknowledgment of more profound structural difficulties, which required stronger efforts to renew capital flows to

debtor states. The Baker Plan encouraged further bank lending but provided no real incentives, and failed in its goals. Four years later the Brady Plan finally stated the official realization that not all debt would be repaid.

120. Brau et al., *Export Credits.*

121. Frank A. Southard, in his "Address to Philadelphia World Insurance Congress, April 25-28, 1982," used a very restrictive definition of political risk in making this claim. *World Insurance Outlook: Summary Proceedings* (Philadelphia: Corporation for the Philadelphia World Insurance Congress, 1982), pp. 234–39.

122. "Taking Lenders to the Cleaners."

123. In 1990 the Export-Import Bank had to establish a reserve of $4.8 billion to cover possible losses on 40 percent of its outstanding loans and loan guarantees. John M. Berry, "$4.8 Billion Reserve Set by Ex-Im Bank," *Washington Post,* January 5, 1990, pp. G1–3. The potential losses are on projects ranging in location from developing countries to eastern Europe and include losses from pre-Castro Cuba and pre-Communist China.

124. The British ECGD combines both functions; its investment guarantees, like the U.S. ones, are directed to projects in developing countries.

125. Kessler, "Political Risk Insurance," p. 210.

126. Although quasi-independent, the board of directors of OPIC includes representatives from the Departments of Agriculture, Interior, and Treasury; the U.S. Agency for International Development; and the Office of the U.S. Trade Representative, as well as representatives from the private sector.

127. Although OPIC has been quite profitable in recent years, its heavy losses in Latin America in the early 1970s prompted its managers to try reinsuring its portfolio in the private market, as described above.

128. Kessler, "Political Risk Insurance," p. 211.

129. The definition of a low-income country was expanded to permit Israel to obtain investment guarantees; its high per capita income normally places it outside the developing country category.

130. This possibility is pointed out by R. Michael Allen and W. Kip Viscusi, "Insuring the Expropriation Risks of Multinational Firms," *Stanford Journal of International Studies* 11 (Spring 1976): 158. Unfortunately, they do not name actual cases where this occurred.

131. One place OPIC and the ExImbank cannot operate is at home. In 1985 a Senate bill proposed that the government cover all kinds of political risks facing U.S. businesses, including those due to the actions of the U.S. government itself. The ups and downs of the U.S.-Soviet relationship, for instance, including the sudden withdrawal of permits for exports to the USSR, had played havoc with the plans of some firms, which sought relief through this unusual avenue; the bill never passed. See U.S. Senate, Committee on Banking, Housing and Urban Affairs, Subcommittee on International Finance and Monetary Policy, Hearing, *The Political Risk Insurance Act of 1983,* #S-1568, July 27, 1983 (Washington, D.C.: Government Printing Office, 1983).

132. Recall that the British Foreign Office historically relied on Lloyd's agents in foreign ports for information on local conditions. Today Lloyd's and other

insurance firms conduct massive information-gathering services in tandem with their underwriting business.

133. World Bank, *Multilateral Investment Guarantee Agency (MIGA),* report prepared by Legal Department, December 1985.

134. Discussions for the MIGA began in 1981, before the debt crisis; it might have failed, however, as did earlier efforts, without such a financial crisis.

135. MIGA, *Annual Report 1990,* p. 3. Noting that investment disputes often become politicized, a World Bank special report on the MIGA in 1986 stated, "MIGA seeks to remove these disputes from the political arena and ensure that they will be resolved only on the basis of legal and economic criteria." "The Multilateral Investment Guarantee Agency (MIGA)," *World Bank News,* July 1986, p. 8.

136. Originally, the World Bank itself had been envisioned as an investment guarantee agency. For forty years various attempts have been made to establish a full-fledged multilateral investment guarantee agency. The sticking point has always been in the definition of foreign property rights and the procedure for settlement of disputes. The MIGA is envisaged as providing more than guarantees: it is a forum for policy coordination on investment issues; it views host governments as direct participants by promoting capital flows among developing countries, providing host governments with safeguards over investments, and giving home and host countries equal voting power; and it is envisioned as relatively independent of the World Bank. Ibrahim Shihata, a major force behind the MIGA and previously involved in the regional Arab Investment Guarantee Agency, has written extensively on this topic: see Shihata, "The Role of the ICSID and the Projected Multilateral Investment Guarantee Agency (MIGA)," *Aussenwirtschaft* 41 (1986): 105–22; "Towards Greater Depoliticization of Investment Disputes," *ICSID Review* 1 (Spring 1986): 1–25; and *MIGA and Foreign Investment: Origins, Operations, Policies, and Basic Documents of the MIGA* (Boston: Kluwer Academic, 1988); see also Manfred Holthus, Dietrich Kebschull, and Karl Wolfgang Menck, *Multilateral Investment Insurance and Private Investment in the Third World* (Hamburg: Verlag Weltarchiv, 1984).

137. In fact, World Bank representatives prepared to go forward on the MIGA without the United States as a charter member, given the budget crisis of that time that limited the ability of American officials to make new financial commitments. Meeting, U.S. Council for International Business, May 9, 1986.

138. A. W. Clausen, *The Development Challenges of the Eighties—A. W. Clausen at the World Bank: Major Policy Addresses, 1981–86* (Washington D.C.: World Bank, 1986), p. 377.

139. "Taking up the Running: A Survey of the World Bank," *The Economist,* supplement, September 27, 1986, p. 50.

140. Apparently, German representatives in early debates over the design of the MIGA wanted it to negotiate treaties with host governments on establishment rights, designing a "model treaty" with fairly stringent conditions. This suggestion was not explicitly incorporated into the final agreement, although perhaps the wave of liberal investment policy reforms in developing countries by the end of the 1980s achieved the same goals.

141. One of the early reports prepared by World Bank staff pointed out that developing country investments tended to have higher returns than those in developed countries, and yet their share of direct investment capital stagnated. In other words, investors preferred less attractive investments in developed countries over more profitable investments in developing countries. This paradox could be explained by risk aversion, and thus investment guarantees were expected to promote additional investments. "Multilateral Investment Guarantees: Questions and Answers," World Bank staff paper, March 21, 1986.
142. Reid, "Perspective," p. 185.
143. Peter Gartland, *Reinsurance—Future Shock: Survival at the Sharp End of the Insurance Business* (London: Institute for International Research, 1980).
144. For example, during the conflict in Vietnam, marine insurance war risk rates tracked the level of tension in the area. The U.S. government predicted it would save millions of dollars when five liner conferences and eleven carriers agreed in 1966 to halve the war risk compensation charges they assessed the government to cover their increased insurance rates. "Transport Notes: Risk Charges Cut," *New York Times,* August 2, 1966, p. 66.
145. "Insurance Rates Increased on Cargo to Middle East," *New York Times,* September 18, 1970, p. 9.
146. Victor Dover, "International Aspects of Marine Insurance," in Hardy F. Glass, compiler, *International Insurance: A Tribute to Professor Alfred Manes* (New York: International Insurance Monitor, 1960), pp. 36–38.
147. Stacy Shapiro, "Attempt to Lower Hull Risk War Rates Worries Insurers," *Business Insurance,* October 14, 1985, p. 30; Tyler Marshall, "For Persian Gulf Tankers, It's Back to Business," *New York Times,* April 23, 1988, p. 12.
148. "Gulf Insurance Premiums Skyrocket," *Flight International* 139 (January 16, 1991): 9; "Gulf Rates," *Aviation Week and Space Technology* 136 (January 14, 1991): 41.
149. As described by Loay M. Al-Naqib, an Arab insurer, Islamic teachings do not explicitly deal with insurance; Muslims are divided in their opinions on whether insurance comes under the prohibition against usury and gambling. The Islamic alternative to commercial insurance is mutual or cooperative insurance organizations. "Political Risk Coverage Important in Arab Region," *Best's Review/Property-Casualty Edition,* September 1986, p. 109.
150. During the Falklands conflict Lloyd's underwriters insured both sides; when the U.K. government objected, they handed off their Argentinian business to Lloyd's underwriters in Germany.
151. "Today's Pirates Pose Double Trouble," *Parade Magazine,* April 3, 1994, p. 16.
152. Gartland, *Reinsurance,* p. 2.
153. Many governments provide insurance against political risks for merchant navies and air transportation, viewing them as vital to national interests.
154. *U.S. Export-Import Bank Annual Reports,* "Authorizations Summary," various years.
155. "Insurance Services Group Sale Confirmed," *Euromoney, Trade Finance, and Banker International,* December 31, 1991, p. 20.

156. The MIGA provided guarantees of $132,310,000 in 1990 and tripled this amount in the next five years. *MIGA Annual Report* (various years).
157. Kessler, "Political Risk Insurance," p. 214.
158. Kobrin, *Description and Assessment,* p. 5. Kobrin argues that even the imprecise estimates we have demonstrate that the private market for political risks, however defined, is relatively small.
159. For some of the strategies designed to reduce the likelihood of nationalization, see Theodore H. Moran, "Transnational Strategies of Protection and Defense of Multinational Corporations," *International Organization* 27 (Spring 1973): 273–87.
160. Charles Oman, *New Forms of International Investment in Developing Countries* (Paris: OECD, 1984); Group of Thirty, *Foreign Direct Investment, 1973–87* (New York: Group of Thirty, 1984).
161. See "Managing Risk," special report, *Business Week,* October 31, 1994, pp. 86–104; "Too Hot to Handle? A Survey of Corporate Risk Management," *The Economist,* special supplement, February 10, 1996, pp. 1–22.
162. Baker, "Liberalization of Trade in Services," p. 201.
163. Cameron and Farndon, *Scenes from Sea and City,* p. 113.
164. Kessler strongly argues that there is insufficient private sector political risks insurance because of the fluctuations in capacity and the relative unprofitability of political risks business compared with alternative lines of insurance. Kessler, "Political Risks Insurance."
165. Kessler, "Political Risk Insurance."
166. Kobrin, *Description and Analysis.*
167. *Report of the Committee to Consider the Export Credit Guarantees Department,* p. 7.
168. In 1991 the British government privatized the ECGD's short-term risks business in the belief that commercial insurers were better equipped to handle it. The government agreed to reinsure British business of the new firm for three years while encouraging it to seek private reinsurance. A few years afterward many exporters complained of the lack of short-term export credit insurance capacity, and critics observed that the new firm had been unable to buy private reinsurance and remained dependent on the government. "Exposed! Political Risk Cover," *Corporate Cover,* June 1, 1993, p. 1.
169. Lipson, "Bankers' Dilemmas," p. 204.
170. Julian G. Y. Radcliffe, "Coverage of Political Risk by the Private Insurance Industry," *Aussenwirtschaft* 41 (1986): 135.
171. See Kobrin, *Description and Analysis,* for an excellent comparison of the strengths and weaknesses of the private and public sector political risks insurers.
172. Philip Moore, "All Down to Politics," *Policy Market,* July 1986, pp. 12–14. Even domestic risks can be difficult to cover. For instance, the U.K. government has been under pressure to devise a public or public-private enterprise to insure commercial buildings against terrorist attack, but government and industry representatives are adamant about wanting nothing to do with assuming the financial risk of IRA terrorism. "Bombed Out: Terrorist Insurance," *The Economist,* December 12, 1992, p. 89.

Chapter 5. The Infrastructure of Global Capitalism.

1. Indirectly, the insurers have been forced to change by the litigation and expanded definitions of liability forced on them by the court system in the United States. This trend has not yet directly affected international risks insurance, however.
2. Philip G. Cerny, "Financial Market Deregulation and the Competition State," Conference Group on Political Economy, Washington, D.C., August 31, 1988. David Baldwin, approving of this role for government, comments, "Economic statecraft in the form of allowing and possibly even promoting private international trade . . . is by far the most effective—and cost-effective—way for one country to acquire the goods and services of another. No other technique of statecraft even begins to approach international trade for effectiveness in promoting this important foreign policy goal." David A. Baldwin, *Economic Statecraft* (Princeton: Princeton University Press, 1985), p. 116. Cerny's basic proposition about states becoming entrepreneurial market actors contrasts with the argument holding that states are simply like firms that produce primarily public goods, including protection. For the latter position, see Richard D. Auster and Morris Silver, *The State as a Firm: Economic Forces in Political Development* (Boston: Martinus Nijhoff, 1979); Lane, *Profits from Power.*
3. Bruce Fitzgerald and Terry Monson, "Export Credit and Insurance for Export Promotion," *Finance and Development* 25 (December 1988): 53–55.
4. R. Michael Allen and W. Kip Viscusi, "Insuring the Expropriation Risks of Multinational Firms," *Stanford Journal of International Studies* 11 (Spring 1976): 164.
5. Yair Aharoni argues that the government is now expected to reduce risks in all phases of life, changing the welfare state into an insurance state. He was speaking here of the domestic context only, but the same process may be occurring in the international arena. Of course, government downsizing in the 1990s may well be reversing this trend. Aharoni, *The No-Risk Society* (Chatham, N.J.: Chatham House, 1981).
6. MIGA, *Annual Report 1990,* p. 12.
7. By law, however, the ExImbank cannot support any projects that harm U.S. production and employment.
8. "New Eximbank Chairman Looks to Expand Lending," *Washington Post,* July 24, 1994, pp. H1–6.
9. Peter Behr, "Raising the Stakes at the Export-Import Bank," *Washington Post,* July 24, 1994, p. H1.
10. Adlai E. Stevenson and Alton Frye, "Trading with the Communists," *Foreign Affairs* 68 (Spring 1989): 53–71.
11. "Business and Finance," *The Economist,* October 2, 1993, p. 7.
12. Patricia Davis, "Checkbook Diplomacy: The Normalization of German-Polish Relations," manuscript, 1996.
13. "Bonn Approves DM 2.3 Billion in Export Guarantees for CIS States," *This Week in Germany,* February 2, 1996, p. 4.
14. As Susan Strange comments, MIGA programs do not help investment in health, education, or social security, nor do they assist small business and small

farmers. *The Retreat of the State: The Diffusion of Power in the World Economy* (New York: Cambridge University Press, 1996).

15. An excellent analysis of the founding of the EBRD can be found in Steven Weber, "Origins of the European Bank for Reconstruction and Development," *International Organization* 48 (Winter 1994): 1–38. Weber does not directly address the role of the EBRD in risk reduction, insurance, and guarantees but focuses on the institution-building process.
16. "Sisters in the Wood: A Survey of the IMF and the World Bank," *The Economist,* October 12, 1991, pp. 1–48. The EBRD also has been criticized for the profligate spending and personal aggrandizement of its first leader, Jacques Attali.
17. "Magazine Cites Parker as Innovative," *National Underwriter,* March 4, 1991, p. 39.
18. Mercedes Perez, "Insuring a Brave New Europe," *Best's Review/Property-Casualty Edition,* July 1990, p. 150.
19. "Industry Officials Analyze Insurance for U.S. Investments in Former USSR," *Post-Soviet Business Monitor,* May 31, 1993, p. 4.
20. Reported by Andrea Durbin, Friends of the Earth-U.S., in "Discussion Paper on the World Bank Group's Role in Private Sector Lending," 1995, p. 2.
21. Attributed to Neal Soss, economist and a partner in an investment management firm, in Steven Pearlstein and John M. Berry, "Mexico Aid Plan Contains Major Changes," *Washington Post,* February 1, 1995, p. A7.
22. Paul Lewis, "Socializing Risk to Foster Free Markets," *New York Times,* February 12, 1995, p. F13.
23. Michel Camdessus, "Coping with the Challenges of Globalization," *IMF Survey,* October 23, 1995, p. 316.
24. Mark Hertsgaard, "Who's Afraid of Global Warming?" *Washington Post,* January 21, 1996, p. C1.
25. See also Jeremy Leggett, ed., *Climate Change and the Financial Sector* (Munich: Gerlag Akademie Verlag, 1996); Mark J. Spalding, "Is a Threat to Lloyd's of London Also a Threat to the Environment?" *Journal of Environment and Development* 2 (Summer 1993): 111–28.
26. Spalding, "Threat to Lloyd's," p. 114.
27. Spalding, "Threat to Lloyd's," p. 121.
28. For lack of space, this discussion has left aside the prominent role played by the insurance industry in the liberalization of trade in services. For details, see John D. Hibbard, *CIGNA Worldwide,* Harvard Business School Case #9-589-098 (Cambridge: Harvard College, 1989; revised July 1, 1991); Organization for Economic Cooperation and Development, *International Trade in Services: Insurance—Identification and Obstacles* (Paris: OECD, 1983); Bruce Stokes, "Getting Services on the Agenda," *National Journal,* August 30, 1986, p. 2060.
29. Richard Rosecrance, *The Rise of the Trading State: Commerce and Conquest in the Modern World* (New York: Basic Books, 1986).
30. Roberto Mangabeira Unger, *Plasticity into Power: Comparative Historical Studies on the Institutional Conditions of Economic and Military Success* (Cambridge: Cambridge University Press, 1987), p. 125. See also Frederic Lane,

Profits from Power: Readings in Protection Rent and Violence-Controlling Enterprises (Albany: State University of New York Press, 1979).

31. See Virginia Haufler, "Learning to Cope: Risk Management in History," paper presented at the Washington International Theory Seminar, Washington, D.C., May 5, 1995.
32. Charles Lindblom, *Politics and Markets: The World's Political-Economic Systems* (New York: Basic Books, 1977).
33. For an exploration of business diplomacy, see John Stopford and Susan Strange, *Rival States, Rival Firms: Competition for World Market Shares* (New York: Cambridge University Press, 1991).
34. See Virginia Haufler, "Crossing the Boundary between Public and Private," in Volker Rittberger, ed., *Regime Theory and International Relations* (Oxford: Oxford University Press, Clarendon Press, 1993), pp. 94–111.
35. The classic work on this topic is Robert Keohane and Joseph Nye, Jr., *Power and Interdependence,* 2d ed. (Glenview, Ill.: Scott, Foresman, 1989).
36. Ulrich Pfister and Christian Suter, "International Financial Relations as Part of the World-System," *International Studies Quarterly* 31 (September 1987): 251.
37. "A Question of Balance: A Survey of American Insurance," *The Economist,* October 27, 1990, p. 6.
38. Raymond Barre, "The State and the Demand for Security in Contemporary Societies," *Geneva Papers on Risk and Insurance* 8 (April 1983): 88–94.
39. Unger, *Plasticity into Power.* Susan Strange has commented that wherever the insurance business is left to the market (speaking of insurance broadly, including social insurance), then the rich can choose whether to translate their risks into an insurance cost instead. Strange, *Retreat of the State.*
40. Unger, *Plasticity into Power,* p. 148.
41. Karl Polanyi, *The Great Transformation: The Political and Economic Origins of Our Time* (Boston: Beacon Press, 1957), p. 15.

Selected Bibliography

The notes to the text provide complete information on every source used in this work. This selective bibliography contains the main theoretical and substantive sources and does not include most government documents, conference papers, or newspapers and magazine articles. I have arranged it in three broad categories: insurance and risk, business, and politics and general history. There are many sources that could be placed in more than one category, however; in such cases, my decision was based on how I used the source.

Insurance and Risk: Theory, Policy, and Institutional History

Abraham, Kenneth S. *Distributing Risk: Insurance, Legal Theory, and Public Policy.* New Haven: Yale University Press, 1986.

Aharoni, Yair. *The No-Risk Society.* Chatham, N.J.: Chatham House, 1981.

Allen, R. Michael, and W. Kip Viscusi. "Insuring the Expropriation Risks of Multinational Firms." *Stanford Journal of International Studies* 11 (Spring 1976): 153–68.

Andreole, Stephen, and Gerald W. Hopple. *Revolution and Political Instability: Applied Research Methods.* New York: St. Martin's Press, 1984.

Aronson, Jonathan David. "Banking and Insurance." In Susan Strange and Roger Tooze, eds., *The International Politics of Surplus Capacity: Competition for Market Shares in the World Recession*, pp. 111–24. London: George Allen and Unwin, 1981.

Arrow, Kenneth. *Essays in the Theory of Risk-Bearing.* New York: North-Holland, 1974.

——. "Insurance, Risk, and Resource Allocation." In *Collected Papers of Kenneth J. Arrow: The Economics of Information,* pp. 77–86. Cambridge: Harvard University Press, Belknap Press, 1984.

Baker, Antony M. "Liberalization of Trade in Service—The World Insurance Industry." In Orio Giarini, ed., *The Emerging Service Economy,* pp. 193–212. Oxford: Pergamon Press, 1987.

Barnes, Julian. "The Deficit Millionaires." *New Yorker,* September 20, 1993, pp. 73–93.

Baron, David P. *The Export-Import Bank: An Economic Analysis.* New York: Academic Press, 1983.

Barre, Raymond. "The State and the Demand for Security in Contemporary Societies." *Geneva Papers on Risk and Insurance* 8 (April 1983): 88–94.

Becker, Gary, and Isaac Ehrlich. "Market Insurance, Self-Insurance, and Self-Protection." *Journal of Political Economy* 80 (July/August 1972): 623–48.

Brandon, Lawrence G. *Sound a Clear Call: Unveiling the Future of the Insurance Industry.* Malvern, Pa.: CPCU-Harry J. Loman Foundation, 1984.

Brau, Eduard, K. Burke Dillon, Chanpan Puckahtikom, and Miranda Xafa. *Export Credits: Developments and Prospects, World Economic and Financial Surveys.* Washington, D.C.: International Monetary Fund, July 1986.

Brennglass, Alan C. *The Overseas Private Investment Corporation: A Study in Political Risk.* New York: Praeger, 1983.

Brewer, Thomas L. "Trends in International Business, Thought, and Literature: The Past and Future of Political Analysis for International Business." *International Executive* 35 (November/December 1993): 539–48.

——, ed. *Political Risks and International Business.* New York: Praeger, 1985.

Brown, Harold. *Hazard Unlimited.* 3d ed. London: Lloyd's of London Press, 1987.

Brown, Robert H., and Peter B. Reed. *Marine Reinsurance.* London: Witherby, 1981.

Bunn, D. W., and M. M. Mustafaoglu. "Forecasting Political Risk." *Management Science* 24 (November 1978): 1557–67.

Cameron, Alan, and Roy Farndon. *Scenes from Sea and City: Lloyd's List, 1734–84.* London: Lloyd's List/Lloyd's of London Press, 1984.

Carter, Robert L., and Gerard M. Dickinson. *Barriers to Trade in Insurance,* Thames Essay 10. London: Trade Policy Research Centre, 1979.

Cockerell, H. A. L. *Sixty Years of the Chartered Insurance Institute, 1897–1957.* London: Chartered Insurance Institute, 1957.

Cockerell, H. A. L., and Edwin Green. *The British Insurance Business, 1547–1970: An Introduction and Guide to Historical Records in the United Kingdom.* New York: Holmes and Meier, 1976.

Cooper, George E., Jr. "Political Risk and Methods of Reducing It: The Case of Trading Companies." In Fariborz Ghadar, Stephen Kobrin, and Theodore H. Moran, eds., *Managing International Political Risk: Strategies and Techniques,* pp. 32–38. Washington, D.C.: Ghadar and Associates, 1983.

Cooper, Richard N. "Managing Risks to the International System." In Richard J.

Herring, ed., *Managing International Risk,* pp. 23–52. Cambridge: Cambridge University Press, 1983.

Davison, Ian Hay. *A View of the Room: Lloyd's: Change and Disclosure.* New York: St. Martin's Press, 1987.

d'Estaing, Giscard. *Financement et garanties du commerce international.* Paris: Presses Universitaires de France, 1977.

Dickson, P. G. M. *The Sun Insurance Office, 1710–1960.* London: Oxford University Press, 1960.

Dobbyn, John F. *Insurance in a Nutshell.* St. Paul, Minn.: West, 1981.

Doman, Leon H. *Supra-national Regulation of Insurance: The Effects of International Treaties and Agreements on Insurance and Reinsurance.* New York: Worldwide Research Corp., 1966.

Dover, Victor. "International Aspects of Marine Insurance." In Hardy F. Glass, compiler, *International Insurance: A Tribute to Professor Alfred Manes,* pp. 23–43. New York: International Insurance Monitor, 1960.

Drew, Bernard. *The London Assurance: A Chronicle.* Oxford: Kemp Hall Press for London Assurance, 1928.

Dunning, John H. *Insurance in the Economy,* Occasional Paper 34. London: Institute of Economic Affairs, 1971.

Fitzgerald, Bruce, and Terry Monson. "Export Credit and Insurance for Export Promotion." *Finance and Development* 25 (December 1988): 53–55.

Gartland, Peter. *Reinsurance—Future Shock: Survival at the Sharp End of the Insurance Business.* London: Institute for International Research, 1980.

Ghadar, Fariborz, Stephen Kobrin, and Theodore H. Moran, eds. *Managing International Political Risk: Strategies and Techniques.* Washington, D.C.: Ghadar and Associates, 1983.

Giarini, Orio, ed. *The Emerging Service Economy.* Oxford: Pergamon Press, 1987.

Gibb, D. E. W. *Lloyd's of London: A Study in Individualism.* London: Macmillan, 1957.

Glass, Hardy F. "Pathways in International Insurance and Development Trends in Europe." In Hardy F. Glass, compiler, *International Insurance: A Tribute to Professor Alfred Manes,* pp. 75–126. New York: International Insurance Monitor, 1960.

Golding, Cecil E., and D. King-Page. *Lloyd's.* New York: McGraw-Hill, 1952.

Hashek, H. H. "Export Credit Insurance and the Debt Crisis." *Geneva Papers on Risk and Insurance* 11 (October 1986): 285–91.

Haufler, Virginia. "Learning to Cope: Risk Management in History." Paper presented at the Washington International Theory Seminar, Washington, D.C., May 5, 1995.

Heimer, Carol. *Reactive Risk and Rational Action: Managing Moral Hazard in Insurance Contracts.* Berkeley: University of California Press, 1985.

Hekman, Christine R. "Evaluation of Risk in International Portfolios." In Carl Beidleman, ed., *The Handbook of International Investing,* pp. 249–72. Chicago: Probus Publishing, 1987.

Henry, Donald Putnam. *The Financial Cost of Export Credit Guarantee Programs.* Report prepared for the Office of the Under Secretary of Defense for Policy, R-3491-USDP. Santa Monica, Calif.: RAND Corporation, June 1987.

Herring, Richard J., ed. *Managing International Risk: Essays Commissioned in Honor of the Centenary of the Wharton School, University of Pennsylvania.* Cambridge: Cambridge University Press, 1983.

Hill, Sir Norman. "State Insurance against War Risks at Sea." In Sir Norman Hill, S. G. Warner, Sidney Preston, A. E. Sich, Sir A. W. Watson, Sir William Beveridge, Sir William Schooling, *War and Insurance.* In James T. Shotwell, series ed., *Economic and Social History of the World War,* pp. 11–53. London: Humphrey Milford, Oxford University Press, 1927.

Hodgson, Godfrey. *Lloyd's of London: A Reputation at Risk.* London: Allen Lane, 1984. Rev. ed. New York: Penguin Books, 1986.

Holthus, Manfred, Dietrich Kebschull, and Karl Wolfgang Menck. *Multilateral Investment Insurance and Private Investment in the Third World.* Hamburg: Verlag Weltarchiv, 1984.

Huebner, Solomon. "The Development and Present Status of Marine Insurance in the United States." *Annals of the American Academy* 26 (September 1905, whole no. 90): 241–71.

Hughes, Helen. "Perspective: The Risks of Lending to Developing Countries." In Richard J. Herring, ed., *Managing International Risk,* pp. 168–76. Cambridge: Cambridge University Press, 1983.

Jodice, David A., compiler. *Political Risk Assessment: An Annotated Bibliography.* Westport, Conn.: Greenwood Press, 1985.

John, A. H. "Insurance Investment and the London Money Market of the Eighteenth Century," *Economica,* n.s., 20 (May 1953): 137–58.

Jones, Charles. "Insurance Companies." In D. C. M. Platt, ed., *Business Imperialism, 1840–1930,* pp. 53–76. Oxford: Oxford University Press, Clarendon Press, 1977.

Kahneman, Daniel, and Amos Tversky. "Prospect Theory: An Analysis of Decision under Risk." *Econometrica* 47 (March 1979): 263–91.

Kessler, Elizabeth. "Political Risk Insurance and the Overseas Private Investment Corporation: What Happened to the Private Sector?" *New York Law School Journal of International and Comparative Law* 13, 2(1992): 203–27.

Knight, Frank. *Risk, Uncertainty, and Profit.* Boston: Houghton Mifflin, 1921.

Kobrin, Stephen J. *Description and Analysis of the U.S. Market for Political Risk Insurance for Overseas Investments in Developing Countries.* OPIC Contract 85-C-015, April 24, 1986.

Krommenacker, Raymond J. "L'Assurance-réassurance de droit privé dans les relations entre pays développés et pays en voie de développement et l'action des organisations internationales: La Conférence des Nations Unies pour le Commerce et le Développement." *Mémoire.* Geneva: Institut Universitaire de Hautes Etudes Internationales, 1972.

Laffont, Jean-Jacques. *The Economics of Uncertainty and Information.* Trans. John P. Bonin and Helene Bonin. Cambridge: MIT Press, 1989.

Loubergé, Henri, and Pierre Maurer. *Financement et assurance des Crédits à l'exportation—Aspects théoriques et pratiques en vigueur dans les pays Europeéns*. Geneva: Editions Droz, 1985.

——. "Private Initiative and Public Intervention on the Market for Export Credit Insurance." *Geneva Papers on Risk and Insurance* 10 (April 1985): 100–11.

Luessenhop, Elizabeth, and Martin Mayer. *Risky Business*. New York: Scribner, 1995.

MacDonald, Donald L. *Risk Control in the Overseas Operations of American Corporations*, Michigan International Business Studies, 15. Ann Arbor: University of Michigan, no date.

Martin, Frederick. *The History of Lloyd's and of Marine Insurance in Great Britain*. London: Macmillan, 1876.

Mayers, David, and Clifford W. Smith, Jr. *Toward a Positive Theory of Insurance*, Monograph Series in Finance and Economics, 1. New York: Salomon Brothers Center for the Study of Financial Institutions, 1982.

Moore, Peter G. *The Business of Risk*. Cambridge: Cambridge University Press, 1983.

Moran, Theodore H. "International Political Risk Assessment, Corporate Planning, and Strategies to Offset Political Risk." In Fariborz Ghadar, Stephen Kobrin, and Theodore H. Moran, eds., *Managing International Political Risk: Strategies and Techniques*, pp. 158–66. Washington, D.C.: Ghadar and Associates, 1983.

Organization for Economic Cooperation and Development. *International Trade in Services: Insurance—Identification and Obstacles*. Paris: OECD, 1983.

Pfeffer, Irving. *Insurance and Economic Theory*. Philadelphia: S. S. Huebner Foundation for Insurance Education, 1956.

Post, James E. *Risk and Response: Management and Social Change in the American Insurance Industry*. Lexington, Mass.: Lexington Books, 1976.

Radcliffe, Julian G. Y. "Coverage of Political Risk by the Private Insurance Industry." *Aussenwirtschaft* 41(1986): 135–39.

——. "The Principles of Managing Political Risks and the Use of Insurance." In Fariborz Ghadar, Stephen Kobrin, and Theodore Moran, eds., *Managing International Political Risk: Strategies and Techniques*, pp. 98–113. Washington, D.C.: Ghadar and Associates, 1983.

Raphael, Adam. *Ultimate Risk*. New York: Four Walls Eight Windows, 1995.

Reid, John T. "Perspective: Managing Country Risk for a Manufacturing Corporation." In Richard Herring, ed., *Managing International Risk*, 184–90. Cambridge: Cambridge University Press, 1983.

Royce, Josiah. "War and Insurance: An Address." Delivered before the Philosophical Union of the University of California at its 25th Anniversary at Berkeley, California, August 27, 1914. Reprint. New York: AMS Press, 1979.

Shepherd, A. F. *Links with the Past: A Brief Chronicle of the Public Service of a Notable Institution*. London: Eagle and British Dominions Insurance Co., 1918.

Shihata, Ibrahim. "Arab Investment Guarantee Corporation: A Regional Investment Insurance Project." *Journal of World Trade Law* 6, 2(1972): 185–202.

——. *MIGA and Foreign Investment: Origins, Operations, Policies, and Basic Documents of the MIGA*. Boston: Kluwer Academic, 1988.

——. "The Role of the ICSID and the Projected Multilateral Investment Guarantee Agency (MIGA)." *Aussenwirtschaft* 41 (1986): 105–22.

Shubik, Martin. "Political Risk: Analyses, Process, and Purpose." In Richard J. Herring, ed., *Managing International Risk*, pp. 109–38. Cambridge: Cambridge University Press, 1983.

——, ed. *Risk, Organizations, and Society*. Boston: Kluwer Academic, 1991.

Siebert, Horst. "Risk Allocation in Large-Scale Resource Ventures." *Kyklos* 40, 4 (1987): 476–95.

Spalding, Mark J. "Is a Threat to Lloyd's of London Also a Threat to the Environment?" *Journal of Environment and Development* 2 (Summer 1993): 111–28.

Spooner, Frank. *Risks at Sea: Amsterdam Insurance and Maritime Europe, 1766–1780*. Cambridge: Cambridge University Press, 1983.

Stefani, Giuseppe. *Insurance in Venice: From the Origins to the End of the Serenissima*. 2 vols. Trans. Arturo Dawoson Amoruso. Trieste: Assicurazioni Generali, 1958.

Supple, Barry. *The Royal Exchange Assurance*. Cambridge: Cambridge University Press, 1970.

Svensk, Robert. "The Role of Private Sector Insurance." In Fariborz Ghadar, Stephen Kobrin, and Theodore Moran, eds., *Managing International Political Risk: Strategies and Techniques*, pp. 114–17. Washington, D.C.: Ghadar and Associates, 1983.

Vernon, Raymond. "Organizational and Institutional Responses to International Risk." In Richard J. Herring, ed., *Managing International Risk*, pp. 191–222. Cambridge: Cambridge University Press, 1983.

Westall, Oliver, ed. *The Historian and the Business of Insurance*. Manchester: Manchester University Press, 1984.

Winter, William D. *Marine Insurance: Its Principles and Practice*. New York: McGraw-Hill, 1919.

Wright, Charles, and C. Ernest Fayle. *A History of Lloyd's: From the Founding of Lloyd's Coffee House to the Present Day*. London: Macmillan, 1928.

Wu, Chunchi, and Peter F. Colwell. "Moral Hazard and Moral Imperative." *Journal of Risk and Insurance* 40 (March 1988): 101–17.

Business: Organization Theory and Political Analysis

Alchian, Armen, and Susan Woodward. "The Firm Is Dead; Long Live the Firm: A Review of Oliver E. Williamson's *The Economic Institutions of Capitalism*." *Journal of Economic Literature* 26 (March 1988): 66–73.

Barnett, Richard, and Ronald Muller. *Global Reach: The Power of the Multinational Corporations*. New York: Simon and Schuster, 1974.

Bergsten, C. Fred, Thomas Horst, and Theodore H. Moran. *American Multinationals and American Interests*. Washington, D.C.: Brookings, 1978.

Chandler, Alfred D., Jr. *The Visible Hand: The Managerial Revolution in American Business*. Cambridge: Harvard University Press, Belknap Press, 1971.

Coase, Ronald. *The Firm, the Market, and the Law.* Chicago: University of Chicago Press, 1988.
Dunning, John H. "The Changing Domain of International Business Activity." In Lee Preston, ed., *Multinational Enterprises in the Global Economy,* pp. 75–88. College Park, Md.: CIBER Maryland, 1994.
——. *The Globalization of Business.* New York: Routledge, 1993.
Evans, Peter. *Dependent Development: The Alliance of Multinationals, State, and Local Capital in Brazil.* Princeton: Princeton University Press, 1979.
Gilpin, Robert. *U.S. Power and the Multinational Corporation.* New York: Basic Books, 1975.
Kobrin, Stephen J. "The Assessment and Evaluation of Non-economic Environments by American Firms." *Journal of International Business Studies* 11 (Spring/Summer 1980): 29–43.
Miller, Gary J. *Managerial Dilemmas: The Political Economy of Hierarchy.* Cambridge: Cambridge University Press, 1992.
Minor, Michael. "LDCs, TNCs, and Expropriations in the 1980s." *CTC Reporter,* Spring 1988, pp. 53–55.
Moran, Theodore H. *Multinational Corporations: The Political Economy of Foreign Direct Investment.* Lexington, Mass.: Lexington Books, 1985.
Rugman, Alan M. *International Diversification and the Multinational Enterprise.* Lexington, Mass.: Lexington Books, 1979.
Spar, Debora L. *The Cooperative Edge: The Internal Politics of International Cartels.* Ithaca: Cornell University Press, 1994.
Stopford, John, and Susan Strange. *Rival States, Rival Firms: Competition for World Market Shares.* New York: Cambridge University Press, 1991.
Vernon, Raymond. *Sovereignty at Bay.* New York: Basic Books, 1971.
Williamson, Oliver. *The Economic Institutions of Capitalism.* New York: Free Press, 1985.
——. *Markets and Hierarchies: Analysis and Anti-trust Implications.* New York: Free Press, 1975.
——. "The Modern Corporation: Origins, Evolution, Attributes." *Journal of Economic Literature* 19 (December 1981): 1537–68.

Politics and General History

Aldcroft, Derek. *From Versailles to Wall Street.* London: Penguin Books, 1987.
Aronson, Jonathan David. *Money and Power: Banks and the World Monetary System,* Sage Library of Social Research, 66. Beverly Hills, Calif.: Sage, 1977.
Auster, Richard D., and Morris Silver. *The State as a Firm: Economic Forces in Political Development.* Boston: Martinus Nijhoff, 1979.
Axelrod, Robert. *The Evolution of Cooperation.* New York: Basic Books, 1984.
Axelrod, Robert, and Robert Keohane. "Achieving Cooperation under Anarchy: Strategies and Institutions." *World Politics* 38 (October 1985): 226–54.
Baldwin, David A. *Economic Statecraft.* Princeton: Princeton University Press, 1985.

———. *Neorealism and Neoliberalism.* New York: Columbia University Press, 1995.

Blair, David. *Trade Negotiations in the OECD: Structures, Institutions, and States.* London: Kegan Paul International, 1993.

Boyce, Robert W. D. "British Leadership in the International Economic System, 1925–31." In Gustav Schmidt, ed., *Konstellationen Internationaler Politik, 1924–32*, pp. 317–29. Bochum: Studienverlag Brockmeyer, 1983.

Braudel, Fernand. *The Perspective of the World.* Vol. 3 of *Civilization and Capitalism, 15th–18th Century.* Trans. Siân Reynolds. New York: Harper and Row, 1984.

———. *The Wheels of Commerce.* Vol. 2 of *Civilization and Capitalism, 15th–18th Century.* Trans. Siân Reynolds. New York: Harper and Row, 1982.

Cain, P. J., and A. G. Hopkins. "Gentlemanly Capitalism and British Expansion Overseas I. The Old Colonial System, 1688–1850." *Economic History Review,* 2d ser., 39, 4 (1986): 501–25.

Cairncross, Alec, and Barry Eichengreen. *Sterling in Decline: The Devaluations of 1931, 1949, and 1967.* Oxford: Basil Blackwell, 1983.

Cerny, Philip G. *The Changing Architecture of Politics: Structure, Agency, and the Future of the State.* London: Sage 1990.

———, ed. *Finance and World Politics: Markets, Regimes, and States in the Post-hegemonic Era.* Aldershot, England: Edward Elgar, 1993.

Clarke, William M. *The City in the World Economy.* London: Pelican Books, 1967.

Cohen, Benjamin. "The Political Economy of International Trade." *International Organization* 44, 2 (1990): 261–81.

Cox, Robert. *Production, Power, and World Order.* New York: Columbia University Press, 1987.

Crowhurst, Patrick. *The Defence of British Trade, 1689–1815.* London: Dawson, 1977.

Cutler, Claire. "Global Capitalism and Liberal Myths." *Millennium* 24, 3 (1995): 377–97.

Darby, Phillip. *Three Faces of Imperialism: British and American Approaches to Asia and Africa, 1870–1970.* New Haven: Yale University Press, 1987.

Davis, Patricia. "Checkbook Diplomacy: The Normalization of German-Polish Relations." Manuscript. 1996.

Deane, Phyllis, and W. A. Cole. *British Economic Growth, 1688–1959.* London: Cambridge University Press, 1962.

Diaz Alejandro, Carlos. "Latin American Debt." *Brookings Papers on Economic Activity* 2 (1984): 335–89.

Eichengreen, Barry, and Peter Lindert, eds. *The International Debt Crisis in Historical Perspective.* Cambridge: MIT Press, 1989.

Feinberg, Richard. *Subsidizing Success: The Export-Import Bank in the U.S. Economy.* Cambridge: Cambridge University Press, 1982.

Feis, Herbert. *Europe, the World's Banker, 1870–1914: An Account of European Foreign Investment and the Connection of World Finance with Diplomacy before the War.* New Haven: Yale University Press, 1930.

Finnemore, Martha. "International Organizations as Teachers of Norms." *International Organization* 47 (Autumn 1993): 565–98.

Frieden, Jeffry. *Banking on the World: The Politics of International Finance.* New York: Basil Blackwell, 1989.

——. *Debt, Development, and Democracy: Modern Political Economy and Latin America, 1965–1985.* Princeton: Princeton University Press, 1991.

Gamble, Andrew. *Britain in Decline: Economic Policy, Political Strategy, and the British State.* Boston: Beacon Press, 1981.

Gilpin, Robert. *The Political Economy of International Relations.* Princeton: Princeton University Press, 1987.

Gourevitch, Peter Alexis. *Breaking with Orthodoxy: Comparative Responses to International Economic Crises.* Ithaca: Cornell University Press, 1986.

Gowa, Joanne. "Subsidizing American Corporate Expansion Abroad: Pitfalls in the Analysis of Public and Private Power." *World Politics* 37 (January 1985): 180–203.

Greif, Avner, Paul Milgrom, and Barry R. Weingast. "Coordination, Commitment, and Enforcement: The Case of the Merchant Guild." *Journal of Political Economy* 102, 4 (1994): 745–76.

Haas, Ernst. *When Knowledge Is Power.* Berkeley: University of California Press, 1990.

Haas, Peter. "Do Regimes Matter? Epistemic Communities and Mediterranean Pollution Control." *International Organization* 43, 4 (1989): 377–404.

Haas, Peter, Robert Keohane, and Marc Levy, eds. *Institutions for the Earth.* Cambridge: MIT Press, 1993.

Haggard, Stephan, Chung H. Lee, and Sylvia Maxfield, eds. *The Politics of Finance in Developing Countries.* Ithaca: Cornell University Press, 1993.

Haufler, Virginia. "Crossing the Boundary between Public and Private." In Volker Rittberger, ed., *Regime Theory and International Relations,* pp. 94–111. Oxford: Oxford University Press, Clarendon Press, 1993.

Helleiner, Eric. *States and the Reemergence of Global Finance: From Bretton Woods to the 1990s.* Ithaca: Cornell University Press, 1994.

Imlah, Albert. *Economic Elements of the Pax Britannica: Studies in British Foreign Trade in the Nineteenth Century.* Cambridge: Harvard University Press, 1958.

Jacobs, Jane. *Cities and the Wealth of Nations.* New York: Vintage, 1985.

Kennedy, Paul. *The Realities behind Diplomacy: Background Influences on British External Policy, 1865–1980.* London: George Allen and Unwin, 1981.

——. *The Rise and Fall of the Great Powers.* New York: Random House, 1987.

——. *Strategy and Diplomacy, 1870–1945.* London: George Allen and Unwin, 1983.

Keohane, Robert O. *After Hegemony: Cooperation and Discord in the World Political Economy.* Princeton: Princeton University Press, 1984.

——. "The Demand for International Regimes." In Stephen D. Krasner, ed., *International Regimes,* pp. 141–72. Ithaca: Cornell University Press, 1983.

——. *International Institutions and State Power.* Boulder: Westview Press, 1989.

——. "Realism, Neorealism and the Study of World Politics." In Robert O. Keohane, ed., *Neorealism and Its Critics*, pp. 1–26. New York: Columbia University Press, 1986.

Keohane, Robert, and Joseph Nye, Jr. *Power and Interdependence*. 2d ed. Glenview, Ill.: Scott, Foresman, 1989.

Keylor, William R. *The Twentieth Century World: An International History*. 2d ed. New York: Oxford University Press, 1992.

Kindleberger, Charles. "Dominance and Leadership in the International Economy: Exploitation, Public Goods, and Free Rides." *International Studies Quarterly* 25 (June 1981): 242–54.

——. "International Public Goods without International Government." *American Economic Review* 76 (March 1986): 1–13.

——. *The World in Depression*. Berkeley: University of California Press, 1973 and 1987.

Kobrin, Stephen J. "Testing the Bargaining Hypothesis in the Manufacturing Sector in Developing Countries." *International Organization* 41, 4 (1987): 609–38.

Krasner, Stephen D. "Power Politics, Institutions, and Transnational Relations." In Thomas Risse-Kappen, ed., *Bringing Transnational Relations Back In: Non-state Actors, Domestic Structures, and International Institutions*, pp. 257–79. Cambridge: Cambridge University Press, 1995.

——. *Structural Conflict: The Third World against Global Liberalism*. Berkeley: University of California Press, 1985.

——. "United States Commercial and Industrial Policy: External Strength and Internal Weakness." In Peter J. Katzenstein, ed., *Between Power and Plenty: Foreign Economic Policies of Advanced Industrial States*, pp. 51–88. Madison: University of Wisconsin Press, 1978.

——, ed. *International Regimes*. Ithaca: Cornell University Press, 1983.

Kroll, John. *Closure in International Politics: The Impact of Strategy, Blocs, and Empire*. Boulder: Westview Press, 1995.

Krueger, Anne O. "The Political Economy of the Rent-Seeking Society." *American Economic Review* 64, 3 (1974): 481–87.

Krugman, Paul. "Competitiveness: A Dangerous Obsession." *Foreign Affairs* 73 (March 1994): 28–44.

Lake, David A. "International Economic Structures and American Foreign Economic Policy, 1887–1934." *World Politics* 35 (July 1983): 517–43.

Lane, Frederic. *Profits from Power: Readings in Protection Rent and Violence-Controlling Enterprises*. Albany: State University of New York Press, 1979.

——. *Venice: A Maritime Republic*. Baltimore: Johns Hopkins University Press, 1973.

Leggett, Jeremy, ed. *Climate Change and the Financial Sector*. Munich: Gerlag Akademie Verlag, 1996.

Lewis, Arthur. *Growth and Fluctuations, 1870–1913*. Boston: George Allen and Unwin, 1978.

Lindblom, Charles. *Politics and Markets: The World's Political-Economic Systems*. New York: Basic Books, 1977.

Lipson, Charles. "Banker's Dilemmas: Private Cooperation in Rescheduling Sovereign Debts." In Kenneth Oye, ed., *Cooperation under Anarchy,* pp. 200–225. Princeton: Princeton University Press, 1986.

——. "The International Organization of Third World Debt." *International Organization* 35 (Autumn 1981): 603–31.

——. *Standing Guard: Protecting Foreign Capital in the Nineteenth and Twentieth Centuries.* Berkeley: University of California Press, 1985.

——. "The Transformation of Trade: The Sources and Effects of Regime Change." In Stephen D. Krasner, ed., *International Regimes,* pp. 233–72. Ithaca: Cornell University Press, 1983.

Lopez, Robert S., and Irving W. Raymond. *Medieval Trade in the Mediterranean World.* New York: Columbia University Press, 1955.

Loriaux, Michael. *France after Hegemony: International Change and Financial Reform.* Ithaca: Cornell University Press, 1991.

McCloskey, Donald N. *Enterprise and Trade in Victorian Britain: Essays in Historical Economics.* London: George Allen and Unwin, 1981.

McKeown, Timothy. "Hegemonic Stability Theory and Nineteenth-Century Tariff Levels in Europe." *International Organization* 37 (Winter 1982): 73–92.

Malkin, Jesse, and Aaron Wildavsky. "Why the Traditional Distinction between Public and Private Goods Should Be Abandoned." *Journal of Theoretical Politics* 3, 4 (1991): 355–78.

Mendez, Ruben P. *International Public Finance: A New Perspective on Global Relations.* New York: Oxford University Press, 1992.

Milgrom, Paul, Douglass North, and Barry Weingast. "The Role of Institutions in the Revival of Trade: The Law Merchant, Private Judges, and the Champagne Fairs." *Economics and Politics* 2 (March 1990): 1–23.

Milner, Helen. *Resisting Protectionism: Global Industries and the Politics of International Trade.* Princeton: Princeton University Press, 1988.

Mitchell, Brian R., and Phyllis Deane. *Abstract of British Historical Statistics.* Cambridge: Cambridge University Press, 1971.

Moran, Theodore H. "Transnational Strategies of Protection and Defense of Multinational Corporations." *International Organization* 27 (Spring 1973): 273–87.

Nadelman, Ethan. "Global Prohibition Regimes: The Evolution of Norms in International Society." *International Organization* 44 (Fall 1990): 479.

Nau, Henry. *The Myth of America's Decline: Leading the World Economy into the 1990s.* Oxford: Oxford University Press, 1990.

North, Douglass C. *Institutions, Institutional Change, and Economic Performance.* Cambridge: Cambridge University Press, 1990.

——. *Structure and Change in Economic History.* New York: W. W. Norton, 1981.

——. "Transactions Costs in History." *Journal of European Economic History* 14 (Winter 1985): 557–76.

North, Douglass C., and Robert Paul Thomas. *The Rise of the Western World: A New Economic History.* Cambridge: Cambridge University Press, 1973.

North, Douglass C., and Barry R. Weingast. "Constitutions and Commitment: The Evolution of Institutions Governing Public Choice in Seventeenth-Century England," Political Economy Working Paper. St. Louis: Washington University School of Business and the Center in Political Economy, January 1989.

Nye, Joseph. *Bound to Lead: The Changing Nature of American Power.* New York: Basic Books, 1990.

Odell, John S. "From London to Bretton Woods: Roots of Economic Diplomacy." Paper presented at the Conference on Blending Economic and Political Analysis of International Financial Relations, Claremont Colleges and University of Southern California, May 1988.

Ohmai, Kenichi. *The End of the Nation-State: The Rise of Regional Economics.* New York: Free Press, 1995.

Olson, Mancur. *The Rise and Decline of Nations: The Political Economy of Growth, Stagflation, and Social Rigidities.* New Haven: Yale University Press, 1982.

Oman, Charles. *New Forms of International Investment in Developing Countries.* Paris: OECD, 1984.

——. *New Forms of Investment in Developing Country Industries: Mining, Petrochemicals, Automobiles, Textiles, Food.* Paris: OECD, 1989.

Orren, Karen. *Belated Feudalism: Labor, the Law, and Liberal Development in the United States.* New York: Cambridge University Press, 1991.

Ostrom, Elinor. *Governing the Commons: The Evolution of Institutions for Collective Action.* Cambridge: Cambridge University Press, 1990.

Oye, Kenneth. *Economic Discrimination and Political Exchange: World Political Economy in the 1930s and the 1980s.* Princeton: Princeton University Press, 1992.

——. "The Sterling-Dollar-Franc Triangle: Monetary Diplomacy, 1929–1937." In Kenneth Oye, ed., *Cooperation under Anarchy,* pp. 173–99. Princeton: Princeton University Press, 1986.

Pfister, Ulrich, and Christian Suter. "International Financial Relations as Part of the World-System." *International Studies Quarterly* 31 (September 1987): 239–72.

Polanyi, Karl. *The Great Transformation: The Political and Economic Origins of Our Time.* Boston: Beacon Press, 1957.

Porter, Tony. *States, Markets, and Regimes in Global Finance.* New York: St. Martin's Press, 1993.

Postan, M. M. *Medieval Trade and Finance.* Cambridge: Cambridge University Press, 1973.

Quattrone, George, and Amos Tversky. "Contrasting Rational and Psychological Analyses of Political Choice." *American Political Science Review* 82 (September 1988): 719–36.

Ray, John E. "The OECD 'Consensus' on Export Credits." *World Economy* 9 (September 1986): 295–310.

Risse-Kappen, Thomas. *Bringing Transnational Relations Back In: Non-state Actors, Domestic Structures, and International Institutions.* Cambridge: Cambridge University Press, 1995.

Rittberger, Volker, ed. *Regime Theory and International Relations.* Oxford: Oxford University Press, Clarendon Press, 1993.

Rittberger, Volker, and Michael Zürn. *Towards Regulated Anarchy in East-West Relations—Causes and Consequences of East-West Regimes,* Tübingen Arbeitspapiere zur Internationalen Politik und Friedensforschung, 11. Tübingen: Arbeitsgruppe Friedensforschung, 1989.

Rosecrance, Richard. *America's Economic Resurgence: A Bold New Strategy.* New York: Harper and Row, 1990.

——. *The Rise of the Trading State: Commerce and Conquest in the Modern World.* New York: Basic Books, 1986.

Rosenau, James. *Turbulence in World Politics.* Princeton: Princeton University Press, 1995.

Rosenau, James, and Ernst-Otto Czempiel, eds. *Governance without Government: Order and Change in World Politics.* Cambridge: Cambridge University Press, 1992.

Ruggie, John Gerard. "International Regimes, Transactions, and Change: Embedded Liberalism in the Postwar Economic Order." In Stephen D. Krasner, ed., *International Regimes,* pp. 195–232. Ithaca: Cornell University Press, 1983.

——, ed. *Multilateralism Matters: The Theory and Praxis of an Institutional Form.* New York: Columbia University Press, 1993.

Russett, Bruce. "The Mysterious Case of Vanishing Hegemony; or, Is Mark Twain Really Dead?" *International Organization* 39 (Spring 1985): 207–31.

Sassen, Saskia. *The Global City: New York, London, Tokyo.* Princeton: Princeton University Press, 1991.

Schlote, Werner. *British Overseas Trade: From 1700 to the 1930s.* Trans. W. O. Henderson and W. H. Chaloner. Oxford: Basil Blackwell, 1952.

Schmidt, Gustav, ed. *Konstellationen Internationaler Politik, 1924–34.* Bochum: Studienverlag Brockmeyer, 1983.

Schuker, Stephen A. *American "Reparations" to Germany, 1919–33: Implications for the Third World Debt Crisis,* Princeton Studies in International Finance, 61. Princeton: Princeton Department of Economics, International Finance Section, July 1988.

Shihata, Ibrahim. "Towards Greater Depoliticization of Investment Disputes." *ICSID Review* 1 (Spring 1986): 1–25.

Skidelsky, Robert J. A. "Retreat from Leadership: The Evolution of British Economic Foreign Policy, 1870–1939." In Benjamin Rowland, ed., *Balance of Power or Hegemony: The Interwar Monetary System,* pp. 147–94. New York: New York University Press, 1976.

Slaughter, Anne-Marie. "International Law in a World of Liberal States." *European Journal of International Law* 6 (1995): 503–38.

Smith, Adam. *An Inquiry into the Nature and Causes of the Wealth of Nations.* 1776. Reprint. New York: Modern Library, 1937.

Snidal, Duncan. "The Limits of Hegemonic Stability Theory." *International Organization* 39 (Autumn 1985): 579–614.

——. "Public Goods, Property Rights, and Political Organizations." *International Studies Quarterly* 23 (December 1979): 532–66.

Stein, Arthur. "Coordination or Collaboration: Regimes in an Anarchic World." In Stephen D. Krasner, ed., *International Regimes.* Ithaca: Cornell University Press, 1983.

——. "The Hegemon's Dilemma: Great Britain, the United States, and the International Economic Order." *International Organization* 38 (Spring 1984): 355–86.

——. *Why Nations Cooperate: Circumstance and Choice in International Relations.* Ithaca: Cornell University Press, 1990.

Stevenson, Adlai E., and Alton Frye. "Trading with the Communists." *Foreign Affairs* 68 (Spring 1989): 53–71.

Strange, Susan. *Casino Capitalism.* Oxford: Basil Blackwell, 1986.

——. "Cave! hic dragones." In Stephen D. Krasner, ed., *International Regimes,* pp. 337–54. Ithaca: Cornell University Press, 1983.

——. *The Retreat of the State: The Diffusion of Power in the World Economy.* New York: Cambridge University Press, 1996.

——. "Protectionism and World Politics." *International Organization* 39 (Spring 1985): 233–59.

Thomson, Janice E. *Mercenaries, Pirates, and Sovereigns: State-Building and Extraterritorial Violence in Early Modern Europe.* Princeton: Princeton University Press, 1994.

Tollison, Robert D. "Rent-Seeking: A Survey." *Kyklos* 35, 4 (1982): 575–602.

Unger, Roberto Mangabeira. *Plasticity into Power: Comparative Historical Studies on the Institutional Conditions of Economic and Military Success.* Cambridge: Cambridge University Press, 1987.

Veljanovsky, Cento G. "The Coase Theorems and the Economic Theory of Markets and Law." *Kyklos* 35, 1 (1982): 53–74.

Waltz, Kenneth. *Theory of International Politics.* Reading, Mass.: Addison Wesley, 1979.

Wapner, Paul. "Politics beyond the State: Environmental Activism and World Civic Politics." *World Politics* 47 (April 1995): 311–40.

Weber, Steven. "Origins of the European Bank for Reconstruction and Development." *International Organization* 48 (Winter 1994): 1–38.

Yarbrough, Beth, and Robert Yarbrough. "International Institutions and the New Economics of Organization." *International Organization* 44 (Spring 1990): 255–56.

Young, Oran. *International Cooperation: Building Regimes for Natural Resources and the Environment.* Ithaca: Cornell University Press, 1989.

——. *International Governance: Protecting the Environment in a Stateless Society.* Ithaca: Cornell University Press, 1994.

——. "Regime Dynamics: The Rise and Fall of International Regimes." In Stephen D. Krasner, ed., *International Regimes,* pp. 93–114. Ithaca: Cornell University Press, 1983.

Zacher, Mark. "Toward a Theory of International Regimes." In Robert L. Rothstein, ed., *The Evolution of Theory in International Relations,* pp. 119–38. Columbia: University of South Carolina Press, 1991.

Index

Virginia Haufler is Assistant Professor in the Department of Government and Politics, University of Maryland at College Park.